From Kleptocracy
to Democracy

Bassim Hamadeh, CEO and Publisher
Mieka Portier, Acquisitions Editor
Tony Paese, Project Editor
Berenice Quirino, Associate Production Editor
Jess Estrella, Senior Graphic Designer
Danielle Gradisher, Licensing Associate
Natalie Piccotti, Director Marketing
Kassie Graves, Vice President of Editorial
Jamie Giganti, Director of Academic Publishing

2370009436826

From Kleptocracy to Democracy

HOW CITIZENS CAN
TAKE BACK LOCAL GOVERNMENT

First Edition

Fred Smoller

For Rod,

the best teacher and friend a guy could have.

Contents

Preface

*"A public servant is privileged to serve
and public service is its own reward."*

—*Plaque in Bell's City Hall*

AT THE START of each semester, I hold out a $10 bill and ask my students to name our mayor and council members.[1] After more than 35 years of college teaching, I haven't lost the sawbuck yet.

Someday, one of my students will return the favor and ask me to name the county assessor or auditor or clerk or director of the municipal water district.

I'd flunk that test.

The fact is, few people pay much attention to local government. In general, there's much less partisan rancor in local government than there is in Washington; as the saying goes, there is no Republican or Democratic way to pave a street. News stories about one of the 60,000 local governments rarely show up on the evening news programs: Marquee politicians, national politics, and the spectacle of war is their métier, not city hall.

Instead, most locally elected officials and staff labor in anonymity. They're seen as trustworthy and competent and are mostly ignored by the press, opinion leaders, and academics. So, it is not at all surprising that Gallup continually finds that the American people trust local government more than the federal government or the 50 state governments.[2]

That all changed—for a time, at least—on July 15, 2010, when the *Los Angeles Times* began running a series of stories that detailed eye-popping corruption in the City of Bell, CA, a small, poor, and working-class city in Los Angeles County, composed mainly of Latinos and immigrants. Over the next two years, the *L.A. Times* uncovered one of the worst municipal corruption scandals in U.S. history. Bell was investigated by the Department of Justice, the FBI, IRS, SEC, the California Attorney General, the State Controller's Office, CalPERS (the state retirement fund), the State Department of Corporations, the Los Angeles District Attorney, and agencies that assign city credit ratings.

The Bell scandal—like scandals in municipalities such as Flint, Michigan, where local officials pumped contaminated water into residents' homes and then lied about it, and Ferguson, Missouri, where a white police officer shot and killed an unarmed black teenager resulting in two weeks of rioting— underlines how much local government matters, how much local officials need to be watched, and how much local government relies on our participation to keep it honest.[3]

In addition to keeping our streets safe and our water fit to drink, local government determines "where we can live, how we can dress, what we can eat, and how we can act in both public and private spaces."[4] Local government is the only form of government that people can create. It is also the fastest growing level of government. It collects more revenue than the federal government does in taxes and, according to the Bureau of Labor Statistics, employs nearly seven times more people than the federal government and three and a half times more people than all 50 state governments combined.[5] Also, it is in local government that citizens and elected officials—many of whom will go on to higher office—first learn about democracy.

It's a cruel and extremely costly paradox that this level of government, the arena closest to home, with such powerful and immediate impact on our lives, finances, and the quickening of democracy, is the one that most citizens ignore.

The Bell story has an engrossing plot, compelling characters, and important lessons about democracy: A watchdog press alerts the public about corruption in city hall; government agencies investigate; angry residents, led by an unusual coalition of first generation Latinos and Muslims, rally the community to win back democracy[6] by mounting a successful recall campaign; the old guard is kicked out of office, replaced by a slate of reformers. The legal system tries and punishes the Bell defendants; experienced city managers and other professionals work tirelessly to put Bell on the path to recovery; Sacramento enacts reforms; the city becomes a model of good governance.

The Bell story touched a nerve. It was covered in the nation's newspapers and on the evening news programs but also in Europe, the former Soviet Union, Asia, and Africa. People were captivated by the astonishing level of greed—the city manager was making $1.5 million in total compensation in one of L.A.'s poorest cities—and by the citizen revolt that toppled him and the city council that were in on the scam. Trials and hefty prison sentences for the ringleaders followed, and a group of dedicated public servants set about rebuilding city hall.

This book closely examines the Bell scandal. It retells the story with an eye on the many obvious and subtle factors that let democracy wither and corruption take hold. The goal here is to help prevent future "Bells" by offering concrete suggestions about how to keep local democracy alive and corruption at bay.

My research includes interviews with more than 50 people connected with the Bell scandal, including current and former council members, activists, attorneys, journalists, current and former staff and Bell citizens. I also read press accounts and trial transcripts and attended the trials. Rizzo and Angela Spaccia, the former assistant city manager, Bell's second-in-command, and Rizzo's partner in crime, declined to speak to me. However, I spoke with their attorneys, with Rizzo's stepbrother, and with people who had worked with Rizzo in Bell and at the previous cities where he had worked and who knew him well.

My research benefited from white papers that were written for a conference about the scandal I put on at Chapman University in February of 2015. The conference speakers included attorneys, academics, state officials, current and former city council members, Bell staff, the leaders of BASTA, the group that overthrew Bell's corrupt administration, and everyday citizens. These papers are referred to throughout the book.[7]

This conference and additional Bell research was sponsored with a generous grant from Fieldstead and Company.

I am grateful to my wife, Lidija, for her passionate support, for her many hours spent on the project, and for her thoughtful criticism and suggestions. I am also thankful to Donna Frazier Glynn, Min Suk Gim, and Madasen McGrath, Julian Smoller and Stephanie Friedenrich for their assistance.

I owe a special debt to *Los Angeles Times* reporters Jeff Gottlieb and Ruben Vives for their Pulitzer Prize-winning coverage, and the other reporters who wrote about the scandal. Much of the narrative is based on their reporting.

I am also grateful to the city managers who followed Robert Rizzo—Pedro Carillo, Ken Hampian, Arne Croce—and especially Doug Willmore, who, along with attorneys David Aleshire and Anthony Taylor, rebuilt the city—outstanding public servants, all. Also helpful were ICMA West Coast Regional Director, Kevin Duggan, and Bell's current (2018) city manager, Howard Brown.

This book was also enriched by the insights provided by Bell employees Allan Perdomo, James Corcoran, Mike Trevis, and Angela Bustamante, and Bell residents Roger Ramirez, Alfred Aryan, and Trina and Bob Mackin, and local business owners Eldon Neesan, Willie Salazar, and Gerardo Quiroz.

I also benefitted from the support and encouragement of my colleagues at Chapman University—Arthur Blaser, Mike Moodian, and Robert Slayton. A one-semester sabbatical from Chapman University allowed me to complete the manuscript.

The Bell story reaffirms the American dream. This dream stresses hard work, determination, education and upward mobility. Poor, non-English-speaking immigrants came to Bell seeking a better life, from south of the border and as far away as southern Lebanon.

Most entered the country without proper documentation. They took menial jobs, worked hard, purchased homes, learned English, and sent their children to public schools, where they learned about democracy and acquired critical thinking skills. All but one of these children went to college; some earned master's and law degrees. As adults, they were fluent in Spanish and English, confident and well spoken. They demanded information from city hall, and asked tough questions of and demanded answers from the city leaders who once ignored and demeaned their parents. When they found out that Bell was being run by thieves, they ran a successful recall campaign and demanded justice. Several of them went on to serve on Bell's city council and in the state legislature, or continue to serve democracy as members of the press. Ali Saleh, Cristina Garcia, Nestor Valencia, Denise Rodarte, Violeta Alvarez, Dale Walker, Ana Maria Quintana, Catalina Martinez, and Ruben Vives are all first-generation Americans, members of the "dreamers" cohort. As passionately loyal and patriotic Americans, they fought for and won back democracy in Bell from the kleptocracy[8] it had become. They are this saga's true heroes.

ENDNOTES

1   I've taught at Chapman University in Orange, California since 1983.

2   Justin McCarthy, "Americans Still Trust Local Government More Than State." Retrieved from: http://www.gallup.com/poll/176846/americans-trust-local-government-state.aspx.

3   See John Counts "How government poisoned the people of Flint." *MLive.com*. n.p., 21 Jan. 2016. Web. 02 June 2017. Retrieved from: http://www.mlive.com/news/index.ssf/page/flint_water_crisis.html, and Bonnie Kristian, "The DOJ's Ferguson report reveals a pattern of government abuse, corruption and injustice." *Rare*. n.p., 05 Mar. 2015. Retrieved from <http://rare.us/rare-politics/rare-liberty/police-state/the-dojs-ferguson-report-reveals-a-pattern-of-government-abuse-corruption-and-injustice.

4   Eric Oliver, *Local Elections and the Politics of Small Scale Democracy*, Princeton University Press, 2012, pp. 1–2.

5   Tom Lindmark, "Is Government Employment Shrinking?" Wall Street Journal Real Time Economics Blog, November 7, 2014. Retrieved from http://butthenwhat.com/2014/11/07/is-government-employment-shrinking/.

6   Political science refers to this as disturbance theory to explain how a potential interest group becomes an active interest group.

7   The conference proceedings can be found at: http://digitalcommons.chapman.edu/
    localgovernmentreconsidered/bellscandal/.

8   A kleptocracy "is a government with corrupt leaders (kleptocrats) that use their
    power to exploit the people and natural resources of their own territory in order to
    extend their personal wealth and political powers. Typically, this system involves
    embezzlement of funds at the expense of the wider population." Examples of klep-
    tocracies and the amounts their leaders have stolen include, Former Indonesian
    President Suharto ($15 billion–$35 billion), Former Philippine President Ferdi-
    nand Marcos $21.6 billion in 2014 dollars; Former Zairian President Mobutu Sese
    Seko ($5 billion); Former Nigeria Head of State Sani Abacha ($2 billion–$5 billion);
    Former Yugoslav President Slobodan Milošević ($1 billion); and The Russian pres-
    ident Vladimir Putin, $200 billion. Source: Wikipedia: https://en.wikipedia.org/
    wiki/Kleptocracy

CHAPTER ONE

The Rise and Fall of Bell

"In a democracy, the most important office is the office of citizen."

—Justice Louis D. Brandeis[1]

"People are busy just trying to survive, raising their families. They assume everything is fine at city hall, until something goes wrong."

—State Senator Hector De La Torre[2]

BEFORE BELL BECAME shorthand for corruption, it was a bastion of local democracy.

A sense of community came easily there at the beginning. Longtime resident Bob Mackin remembers it as a quintessential 1950s suburb, a "small, quiet, happy-go-lucky town, where fathers went off to work in the morning, often at a neighboring factory, mothers stayed home in their small modest homes, and the kids walked to school." From its founding in 1927 until the late 1950s, Bell was filled with predominantly white transplants from the Midwest who were drawn to the temperate climate and the abundant union jobs provided by manufacturers such as General Motors, Bethlehem Steel, and Firestone, which were clustered in the "Gateway" area southeast of downtown Los

Angeles. By 1940, there were 900 such factories within a three-mile radius of the city.[3]

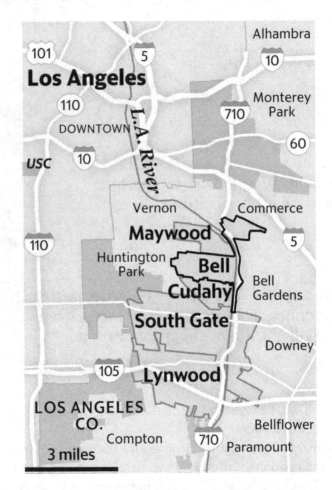

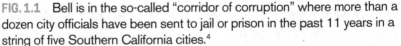
FIG. 1.1 Bell is in the so-called "corridor of corruption" where more than a dozen city officials have been sent to jail or prison in the past 11 years in a string of five Southern California cities.[4]

Bell and its neighboring communities served as "L.A.'s Detroit, an industrial belt for mass production of cars, tires, steel, and other durable goods," writes Becky M. Nicolaides in her study of the region, *My Blue Heaven*.[5] "Blue-collar workers built the suburb literally from the ground up, using sweat equity rather than cash to construct their own homes."

Safe, leafy, and prosperous, Bell was filled with mom-and-pop stores and luncheonettes and ringed by orange groves.

"Hardly anyone locked their back doors," remembers Mackin, who's now 83. "None of the schools had bars or fences around them. And there was absolutely no graffiti. People socialized around their churches. There were parades and holiday celebrations; family films were shown in one of the parks."

Bell was a desirable place to live in those early decades: People worked hard and paid down their mortgages. They sent their kids to well-regarded public schools. Streets were paved, and sewers, waterworks, and parks were built.

With a population of about 17,000 in the 1950s, the city was presided over by an "old guard" made up of middle-class white, male professionals and business owners who were committed to the city and knew how to get things done. They brought with them a culture of involvement that kept people engaged in the life of the city and a progressive council-manager system of government designed to thwart corruption by putting the daily decision-making into the hands of a professional, not a Tammany Hall-style pol doling out patronage. Average turnout of registered voters for municipal elections was a comparatively healthy 35%, and a host of civic groups including an active chamber of commerce, Kiwanis and Rotary clubs, Masonic and Moose lodges, a women's club, Boy Scouts and Girl Scouts, as well as local churches, provided venues for discussing what was going on in the community and comparing notes on how government officials were doing their jobs. Local politics was personal— and visible.

Looking back at that time, it's clear that the seemingly mundane elements like the civic clubs, parades and pancake breakfasts, and newspaper items on park plans or sewer boards were doing more than giving Bell a small-town Mayberry air. They were feeding and protecting Bell's civic integrity. City leaders could be vetted in candidate debates at clubs and schools, which provided an opportunity for those outside of city hall to get the exposure they needed to mount a successful campaign and gave voters a chance to take their measure. Service clubs served as farm teams where future leaders could prove they had what it takes to be on the council and offered forums where the city manager and council could float ideas and get feedback from a cross section of the community. Plans for the city were shared and dissected at state-of-the-city addresses, prayer breakfasts, and picnics, and when something seemed off about a city official, there were watchdogs throughout the community that would "bark," providing an important check on officials' power. Residents who wanted to dip a toe in the process of governing Bell could volunteer for the planning commission, parks and recreation commission, or a host of other boards and committees that gave them a close-up view.

Taken together, this array of organizations, events, and opportunities for residents to come together in the public square is known as a city's civic infrastructure, and Bell's was vibrant.

Roger Ramirez, a longtime Bell resident, recalls that his childhood in the 1960s was filled with city-sponsored picnics, parades, Easter egg hunts, and celebrations marking July 4th, Halloween, Thanksgiving, and Christmas. The city set up a stage in a local supermarket for concerts for young people, and large swaths of the community turned out. Those who didn't could read about them in the *Industrial Post*, a local paper that covered local events large and small, paying close attention to the doings in city hall. It was a "watchful eye and a voice to be reckoned with."[6]

But that era was coming to an end. The 60s delivered the first in a series of devastating blows that knocked the city off its foundations and swept away the leaders and civic culture that the city had so carefully cultivated. During that decade, many of Bell's homeowners—the white, middle-class base that shaped the city—left for newer and more spacious suburbs in communities that were popping up farther away from downtown L.A. More were driven off by the riots in Watts, six miles to the southwest, in 1965.[7]

Then, in the early 1970s, the jobs that had supported the city began to disappear. Manufacturers moved their operations to cheaper labor markets overseas, factories paying union wages began to close, and more families moved out. By 1990, stable, prosperous Bell had become one of the poorest communities in Southern California.[8] William Fulton, in *The Reluctant Metropolis,* includes a chapter called "The Suburbs of Extraction" that describes this new iteration of the city. As Fulton explains, "'suburbs of extraction' ... was a play on long-standing political science theory, which makes a distinction between 'suburbs of consumption' (where people live) and 'suburbs of production' (where factories are located)."[9] As cities like Bell and its neighbors declined, Fulton writes, "It seemed to me, the primary economic activity in these communities was not consuming things or producing things, but extracting what little wealth remained as a mining company might extract coal or copper. Apartment builders, casinos, scrap-metal recycling companies—all were in the extraction business. So too, I suspected, were some of the politicians, especially those with close relationships with these other businesses."[10]

Taking the place of factory workers and their families were immigrants, most of them from Mexico and other Central American countries, drawn to the cheap housing Bell's exodus left behind. They generally found non-union, low-paying jobs in manufacturing, transportation, sales and office work, or service-related professions. Bell went from 76% Anglo in 1970 to 11% in 1990. Eighty-six percent of Bell's population was Latino in 1990, about the time Robert Rizzo, the ringleader of the scandal, came to town (1993).

As of 2013, 48% of Bell's residents were foreign born, with 34% being identified as noncitizens and 89% self-reported as speaking a language other than English at home. Only 4% of Bell residents had a bachelor's degree or higher, and only 30% had a high school degree. Of adults 25 years and over, 35% reported less than a ninth-grade education.[11] Density more than quadrupled over time as garages were converted to apartments and add-ons were built in backyards to house the new immigrants.

TABLE 1.1   *Ethnic Change in Bell, 1970–2010[1]*

	1970	1980	1990	2000	2010
WHITE	76%	13%	11%	6%	5%
HISPANIC	21%	63%	86%	91%	93%
OTHER	3%	4%	3%	3%	2%
TOTAL POP	21,830	25,449	34,221	36,664	35,477

Adapted from Tom Hogen-Esch "Failed State: Political Corruption and the Collapse of Democracy in Bell, California." California Journal of Politics and Policy, 3 (1), pp. 1–28. 2011 *Source:* 1970, 1980, 1990, 2000, 2010 U.S. Census. The 1970 Census used the term "Spanish" to denote individuals from Latin America.

The city was on its way to becoming the Bell of today: a space-starved, working-class community of 36,000 packed like sardines into rental homes and apartments owned by absentee landlords who lived in much wealthier communities; its 2.8-square mile area packed with thrift shops, auto parts and repair stores, car washes, fast-food restaurants, banks, storefront churches, and a boxing club.

WELCOME TO THE CONCRETE JUNGLE

It can be hard to picture the original beauty of the nondescript city, which extends to the west of the I-710 Long Beach Freeway and the concrete channel of the Los Angeles River, eight miles southwest of downtown L.A. Except for the single exit signs on the I-710 and I-5 Freeways, you'd never know you were passing through. The city has the overall shape of a swan, with a body that encompasses the residential and commercial, and a long neck of land that stretches north along the I-710 connecting it to a "head" comprising an industrial area filled with large warehouses and loading docks that was annexed in the 1960s.[12]

Cars and trucks waiting to enter the freeways pack Gage and Atlantic, the major streets that intersect in the heart of downtown Bell. There is no relief from the congestion.

Most people reside along streets that run from Randolph Street, parallel to the Union Pacific train tracks along Bell's northern border, and Florence Avenue, the city's southern border. Homes are modest, the original 1,000-square-foot, one-story framed structures with stucco facades built in the 1930s and 1940s. Some now have bars on their windows and doors (as does Bell High School), and many have workmanlike rental units in converted space on the property. Less than a third of the city's housing is owner-occupied.[13]

The town's hard-working men, some with cuffed jeans, boots, and cowboy hats, gather by the convenience stores and mini-malls, which provide the necessities they can afford, and where many of the signs are in Spanish. The women, many employed in low-wage service jobs, often accompanied by children, are dressed modestly. Cars are everywhere: parked on both sides of the streets, on driveways, and, occasionally, on lawns because most garages have been turned into rentals. The once-lush suburb now has the least amount of green space per resident of any city in L.A. County. It's a "concrete jungle," said Alan Perdomo, Bell's community services director.[14]

Other than a newer community center adjacent to the city hall complex and a small, heavily-used urban park—Camp Little Bear Park—that was built behind a small grocery store,[15] there are few places for residents to come together.

AN OPENING FOR A KLEPTOCRAT

Along with the loss of physical space that carried Bell toward its current form came the disappearance of the less-tangible spaces where the community built its sense of itself, those layers of clubs, discussions, and community-defining activities that fed Bell's sense of itself as a city, not simply an anonymous collection of individuals. Bell's old guard had been good at nurturing democracy but failed to leave a blueprint for those who came next. The civic structures, voter participation, and news coverage that came in with Bell's founders largely left with them, and they gave little thought to creating continuity or mentoring new leadership among the city's incoming residents. Political culture eroded—and so did awareness of what was happening in city hall.

The costs of that erosion became apparent as early as the municipal elections of 1964, which brought into the city council an ambitious outsider named Pete Werrlein.

Werrlein, who owned an auto parts store in downtown Bell, not far from city hall, had a politician's gift of gab and knack for remembering names. "Pete was very charming, but also very ambitious. He was constantly working on ways to make money," said longtime resident Mackin.[16]

Werrlein was a new kind of public servant for Bell. In stark contrast to his predecessors, who had been well educated, economically secure, and focused on the needs of the community, he was a high school graduate from a poor home in the neighboring city of South Gate. He had no real record of service, no involvement in community groups. It was unclear how he'd gotten the money for his auto parts business. But with the old guard quickly vanishing from Bell and the ranks of engaged and discerning voters thinning, he breezed into office and served off and on for 16 years, including three terms as mayor. It was the beginning of a sea change. Werrlein, who was later found to be an associate of legendary Los Angeles mobster Mickey Cohen (Bugsy Siegel's sidekick), brought the city an "if it's good for business, it's good for Bell" ethos. But what he really meant, emerging in 1977, was: "If it's good for *me*, I'll sell it to Bell."

Nineteen seventy-seven was the year that Werrlein and then-city manager John Pitts sold the city council on the idea that, with revenues declining, Bell needed a sure source of tax money: a card club. Gambling, often seen as a financial life raft in struggling suburbs of extraction, would have rich rewards for master extractors Pitts and Werrlein. A group of local businessmen had agreed to put up the money for the California Bell Club if the two men would use their positions to ensure that the city council would give the backers an exclusive permit to operate it without seeking other bids. Werrlein and Pitts sold the idea to the council by insisting that the deal would generate badly needed revenue for the city. They sold the club to the community by promising to locate it in the city's industrial area (the swan head) rather than the city proper. For brokering the deal, they got 51% secret ownership in the club, a clear violation of the law, and the opportunity to let the cash profits of the casino pass through their hands.

The card club became one of the state's largest casinos, closed only on Christmas. People flocked there from all over, hundreds on weekdays and as many as a thousand on the weekend, generating up to $2 million per year, one-fifth of the city's budget.

It seemed like a win for the city until 1984, when federal investigators uncovered the illegal ownership scheme—and charged that Werrlein and Pitts had skimmed $1.5 million from the profits due the city.

There are always questionable characters in city government, but in the old Bell, where there were so many eyes on the city's business and so many experienced hands in office, darker impulses were kept in check. It's no coincidence that Werrlein's brand of corruption took root during the years of peak disruption in Bell when civic culture disintegrated and two-thirds of the city's white residents were replaced by immigrants from Mexico, South America, and Lebanon.

Kleptocracy is a crime of opportunity. And opportunity knocked.

There's nothing that says civic participation belongs only to the white and privileged, but survival, not government, was the priority of many of the newcomers. They kept to themselves, and the city made no effort to engage them. But they did have children in school, did receive city services, did pay local taxes—and they were as capable of gossiping or complaining about potholes or trash collection as anyone who ever lived in Bell. There were ways to pull the new citizens and potential citizens into community events, to make their traditions Bell's, and painlessly begin to involve them and their children in civic life. But even if that had occurred to the likes of Werrlein and Pitts, it wasn't in their interests to do so. It was far more advantageous for them to simply let participation slide, and slide it did.

Average turnout in city elections fell from 36% in the 1960s to 26% in the 1970s. A huge chunk of the city's new Latino majority was eligible to vote, but with no outreach or voter-registration efforts, few did.[17]

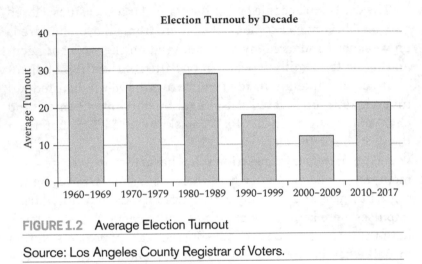

Election Turnout by Decade

FIGURE 1.2   Average Election Turnout

Source: Los Angeles County Registrar of Voters.

Journalist Sam Quinones, who has chronicled migrant culture, talks about the "Mexicanization" of places like Bell, describing the arrival of people who "came here to work in jobs they believed, even after decades, would be temporary. They focused their lives on returning home someday. They packed into cheap housing and spent their savings on building homes in Mexico."[18]

But he didn't take into account the children of the new arrivals for whom Bell *was* home. The immigrant tide seemed to wash away Bell's civic infrastructure along with what Matthew Desmond calls collective efficacy, "the stuff of loosely linked neighbors who trust one another and share expectations about how to make their community better."[19] Far less visibly, however, it also began to cultivate the talent that would, in the space of a generation, fight to reclaim the city.

CULTIVATING HIDDEN LEADERS

Even as Werrlein planted the seeds of corruption in Bell, Maximino Quintana was quietly nurturing its redemption. Part of an early wave of Mexican immigrants, Maximino came across the border in the 1940s as part of the Bracero guest worker program, which brought cheap labor to the United States to do manual labor. After traveling back and forth to Mexico, where he now owns several hundred acres of land, he and his family settled in Bell where he felt there were better schools and more opportunity.

He worked for 24 years at a Thrifty's coffee shop, lost that job when the shop closed, then found a job at a local manufacturing firm where he rose to supervisor.

His wife, Ursula, who didn't speak English, was a seamstress in a local sweatshop where she was paid by the piece, earning less than minimum wage. Their daughter Ana Maria, who was nine when the family put down roots in town, remembers "counting up the pieces of dresses she made and fighting for an extra 10 cents. We were literally fighting for peanuts," she says, "but those peanuts represent your livelihood. As an eighth grader, I was working at a family-owned video store and I started working at $3.35 an hour and I was earning more than she did."[20]

Maximino spoke limited English with a heavy accent and didn't have any formal education, but he was an avid reader who passed that love to Ana Maria, putting her in his lap as he read Spanish-language newspapers and talking politics with her as though she were an adult, piquing an interest she still carries with her.

Like the wave of immigrants who followed him, Maximino had little time to pay attention to local politics; his job, as he saw it, was to see that his children got a good education, which they did. Ana Maria, born in 1977—the year Werrlein's card club scam began—grew up whip smart and well spoken, became an honor student at Bell High School in the 1990s, as well as its student body president, homecoming queen, and, at 16, founder of its Rotary-sponsored community service club. While political participation among adults like her parents was low, what remained of the civic infrastructure—school programs and the Rotary, which stayed in Bell when so many other clubs left—fed the interest in government she'd picked up from her father. She and a group of students toured Washington, D.C. with their government teacher. She won a Rotary scholarship and studied for a summer at Cornell University, then got a B.A. in American studies from Yale and a law degree from Columbia University. After Yale, Ana Maria taught economics and statistics at the University of Navarra in Pamplona, Spain, where she received her M.A. degree. Later, she would be elected to the post-Rizzo city council.[21]

The arrival of immigrants was widely thought to have wiped out the talent for politics that Bell's founders had brought, but people like Maximo and Ana Maria are part of a counternarrative that would surface after the long, ignominious fall of the city that Werrlein set in motion.

THE YAROUNIANS OF LEBANON

Ali Saleh, whose story begins in Lebanon, is part of that narrative as well.[22] He, with Cristina Garcia, founded BASTA—the citizen's group that led the recall (Chapter 6) and would be elected to the post-Rizzo council, rising to Mayor.

Even as Latinos poured into Bell in the 1970s, Lebanese-Americans began arriving "from Yaroun, a village in southern Lebanon, near Israel's northern border."[23] Pushed out of their country by war—the village was frequently shelled by Israel—and pulled to the United States by the promise of a better life, they chose Bell because of its proximity to downtown Los Angeles and the temperate southern California climate, which is much like Lebanon's.

Ali's father was one of the first to come to Bell early in the decade, and Ali recalls the system that helped others from Yaroun follow. His father would get called to "pick them up at the airport, bring them to Bell, they would live a few weeks in the apartment, and they would start working and get their own apartment."[24] The community started with 10 or 20 people, he says, and slowly grew. "Little by little, as people came, they would move into Bell and get apartments, and later people would start buying homes."[25]

They became the core of the city's small but vibrant Lebanese-American community of about 2,000, an enclave the "Yarounians" established on the streets surrounding city hall. They built a mosque and community center, started businesses, and saw to it that Bell Senior High School would offer Arabic courses, one of the few secondary schools in the nation to do so.

Like the Quintanas, Saleh's family came to the United States with nothing but determination and faith in the American dream.

"[My father] would go buy stuff from downtown L.A. from the market, either stereos or so on, and go sell door to door, until he moved on from there and started selling at swap meets and created his own business."[26] The elder Saleh didn't have time or the desire to get involved in politics but insisted that his kids get a good education.

Ali was in Quintana's graduating class at Bell High, though the two did not know each other then. As Werrlein's abuses were coming to light, this son of the new Bell, fluent in Spanish, Arabic, and English, was coming of age, weaving himself into the fabric of the city by entering the expanding clothing business his father had built.

Bell's civic life and governance devolved for another decade and a half before Saleh, Quintana, and others like them, progeny of Bell's new immigrant majority, made themselves visible in civic affairs. But the picture of Bell's decline that is about to unfold is incomplete without an awareness of their presence in the background, their potential waiting to emerge.

TRYING TO GET RID OF A BAD PENNY

The casino corruption case wound its way through the courts, and in 1985, Pete Werrlein was fined $421,000 and sentenced to three years in federal prison.[27] He ended up serving about 10 months.

But there was no happy ending for Bell. Despite being indicted for bribery, fraud, and racketeering, City Manager John Pitts, who had collected his cut of the casino profits weekly from an intermediary in $5,000 packets of $100 bills, refused to resign—and the city council declined to fire or suspend him. Instead, he took a paid sick leave for "chest pains and hypertension." He was later sentenced to six months in federal prison for accepting a bribe in the form of hidden ownership in the poker club.

The card club investigation revealed a disturbingly dark side of Werrlein and Bell. It disclosed not only his connection with mobster Mickey Cohen but also that he and the former police chief of nearby Huntington Park had participated "in sex parties in nearby Cudahy where teenage prostitutes were supplied by Kenneth Bianchi, who was later convicted in the Hillside Strangler murders."[28] The scandal would lead to Werrlein's defeat in the 1980 election.

In 1984, two incumbent council members who had supported Pitts were replaced by two reformers, George Cole and Ray Johnson, who pledged to restore confidence in city government. Johnson, a community college administrator who had lived in Bell for more than 40 years, said he decided to run because he "wanted to clean up the corruption. I was surprised by how deep it went." Cole, a burly 34-year-old former steelworker and union activist, said he was similarly motivated. The son of a minister and medical social worker, he was one of the last leaders produced by the Bell's vanishing political culture. He'd created a foundation to provide meals and services to laid-off and retired steelworkers and was an advocate for Bell's schools, immigrant community, and the elderly.

They were joined by Bryon Woosley, who had been appointed city manager earlier that year as the case against Pitts unfolded, who said, "It's going to be a tough battle to restore public confidence in city hall." Woolsey, who had started working for the city in 1972 as a civil engineer, added,

"We realize that we've got kind of an uphill road, but we are going to do it."[29]

But incredibly, when a new collection of owners proposed reopening the card club nine years later, in 1993, the city council brought back Werrlein, now a convicted felon, to run it, ignoring objections from the public and the California Department of Justice, paying him a handsome salary. George Cole voted for the hiring, saying that he didn't see anything wrong with it. "Sure it sounds crazy," he told the *L.A. Times*. "But is it any crazier than hiring a convicted burglar to teach people how to secure their houses against break-ins? He knows how to spot loan-sharking, he knows how to spot skimming. He knows how to spot rip-offs … We want to put in place the toughest monitoring system in California."[30]

There was little pushback from the community when the next city council elections rolled around and scant monitoring of casino monitor Werrlein, who, among other activities, was also building a gun-sales department in Western Auto, the auto parts store he owned in downtown Bell. He added the gun division while on the council. (In 2010, Western Firearms, which sold semiautomatic weapons that were the favorite of drug cartels, placed 10th in a *Washington Post* list of U.S. gun shops that sold the most guns in Mexico.)[31] Red flags seemed to abound in a scenario that put a felon with known mob connections and a lucrative new sideline in guns into a city-funded position overseeing a casino.

But the city, like other California local governments, was squeezed for cash. Voters in 1978 had passed Proposition 13, which capped property taxes, cutting local revenues by 60% and forcing them to scramble for funds. At the same time, cities faced the pressures of covering bloated pension benefits for their police unions and other employees. The casino generated 20% of Bell's general fund, and Werrlein knew how it ran. In strapped, postindustrial Bell, that made him an attractive, if unsavory, resource. Moral compromise was expedient, and it was becoming the new normal.

Werrlein's return as a city hall insider came as both transparency and citizen involvement in government were falling to new lows. The *Industrial Post*, established in 1924, had kept its eye on local government, but as the 1980s rolled into the 90s, the community newspaper was bought out by a succession of newspaper chains, with fewer and fewer resources devoted to covering Bell. The rising cohort of Bell natives like Ali Saleh and Ana Maria Quintana was in its 20s, establishing itself, often in locales that offered more opportunity than Bell while the ranks of white leaders who remained in town thinned. It was difficult to fill the city council with capable leaders, and with little in the way of interest or oversight from voters, community organizations, or the press, city hall was left to run itself, often under the influence of old hands like Werrlein.

The stage was set for Robert Rizzo, who became Bell's city manager in 1993.

DEMOCRACY, KLEPTOCRACY, AND "GOOD DEMOCRATIC PRACTICE"

We can use political scientist Bruce Buchanan's notion of "good democratic practice" to understand what happened.[32] According to Buchanan, three main groups animate presidential electoral politics—citizens, candidates, and the press (Figure 1.4). Buchanan's focus is national politics. His model, with some modification, helps explain the scandal.

Citizens are the most important group. Citizens are sovereign, the source of government power. They loan power to elected officials who serve at their behest. Their job is to be engaged: They need to learn about the major problems affecting the community and keep tabs on local officials. They also have to vote.

The city council and top city administrators are supplicants. In exchange for public support and acceptance of their authority, they're expected to be honest and trustworthy and to promote the public interest. They're supposed to explain major issues and to respond to queries from citizens and the press in a respectful, forthright, and timely manner.

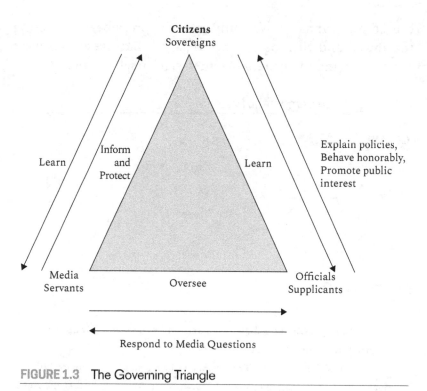

FIGURE 1.3 The Governing Triangle

Source: Adapted from Bruce Buchanan, *Presidential Campaign Quality: Incentives and Reform.* Pearson-Prentice Hall. New Jersey, 2004.

Several groups oversee local government. These include auditors, the city attorney, various state agencies, and, of course, the press. These groups are the public's servants, especially the press—which is why the Framers of the Constitution gave it its own Constitutional amendment. It is the press' job to provide citizens the information they need to make informed assessments of public officials and their policies. As the public's watchdog, it closely monitors performance and "barks" when it senses wrongdoing.

Each pillar of the system—citizens, officials, press—needs to work for democracy to succeed and for kleptocracy to be kept at bay.

Unfortunately, in Bell, all three failed: Citizens weren't engaged, top officials had poor character, and there was no oversight. This simultaneous failure on all three fronts is what caused the scandal. It was only after the press began covering the abuses and citizens became engaged that the crooks were thrown out and the system began to right itself. (Table 1.2).

TABLE 1.2 *Good Democratic Practice*

GROUP	ROLE
Citizens	Engagement
Officials	Character
Press	Oversight

ENDNOTES

1   Louis D. Brandeis Quotes, AZQuotes: Retrieved from: http://www.azquotes.com/author/1818-Louis_D_Brandeis.

2   As quoted in, Alexei Koseff, "'California politicians stole their money. Will that make them care about democracy?" Sacramento Bee. May 7, 2017. Retrieved from: http://www.sacbee.com/news/politics-government/capitol-alert/article148912624.html#storylink=cpy

3   Becky M. Nicolaides, My Blue Heaven: Life and Politics in the Working-Class Suburbs of Los Angeles, 1920–1965 (University of Chicago Press, 2002) p. 25.

4   See Alexei Koseff, "California politicians stole their money. Will that make them care about democracy?" Sacramento Bee. May 8, 2017. Retrieved from: http://www.sacbee.com/news/politics-government/capitol-alert/article148912624.html

5   Ibid, p. 3.

6   The local weekly, the *Bell-Maywood-Cudahy Industrial Post*, provided the community "diligent news coverage by veteran newspaper reporters ... with experience watching small-town politics." It went out of business prior to Rizzo coming to town. See, Terry Francke, "Why The Bell Scandal Happened And What Can Be Done," *Voice Of OC*, July 28, 2010. Retrieved from https://voiceofoc.org/2010/07/why-the-bell-scandal-happened-and-what-can-be-done.

7   Tammy Audi, "In One City, An Islamic Center Unifies," *Wall Street Journal*, September 20, 2010. Retrieved from https://www.wsj.com/articles/SB100014240527 487046444404575482001778588866.

8   Census 2010, American Community Survey 2010. Retrieved from https://www.census.gov/programs-surveys/acs/.

9   William Fulton, Bell: The Latest 'Suburb of Extraction, California Planning and Development Report. July 27, 2010. Retrieved from: http://www.cp-dr.com/articles/node-2740

10 William Fulton, *The Reluctant Metropolis: The Politics of Urban Growth in Los Angeles* (Solano Press Books, 1997).

11 Thom Reilly, The Failure of Governance in Bell, California. (Lexington Books, 2016). See also, Michele Fuetsch and Tina Griego, T. "Census Shows Asian, Hispanic Surge." *L.A. Times*, February 28, 1991. Retrieved from: http://articles.latimes.com/1991-02-28/news/hl-3079_1_long-beach.

12 Tom Hogen-Esch used the image of a swan to describe Bell in his paper, "Failed State," which he delivered at the City of Bell Scandal Revisited conference at Chapman University February 19, 2015.

13 In 2010, only 28% of the city's housing was classified as owner-occupied, according to the American Community Survey, 2013. Retrieved from: https://factfinder.census.gov/faces/tableservices/jsf/pages/productview.xhtml?src=CF.

14 Bell has only 13.7 park acres for its 36,000 residents or about .4 park acres per 1,000 residents. The county average is 3.3 park acres per 1,000. So, if Bell had the county average of 3.3 park acres per one 1,000, it would have more than 118 park acres, rather than only 13.7. Source: Los Angeles Countywide Comprehensive Park & Recreation Needs Assessment. Retrieved from: http://lacountyparkneeds.org/wp-content/uploads/2016/06/ParksNeedsAssessmentSummary_English.pdf

15 The grocery store is owned by Mayor Oscar Hernandez. The city purchased the adjoining land for the park. The residential property at 6708 Orchard, Bell, CA 90201 was just one (1) of several purchases in the area that when combined eventually make up the Camp Little Bear Park acreage. Community Housing Authority purchased the property known as 6708 Orchard, Bell, CA 90201 for $260,000 in January 2004 and was conveyed to the City of Bell on June 27, 2005.

16 Personal interview with Bob Mackin.

17   Meaning that they were 18 years of age or older. Adapted from Tom Hogen-Esch, "Failed State: Political Corruption and the Collapse of Democracy in Bell, California," *California Journal of Politics and Policy*, 2011, 3 (1), pp. 1–28.

18   Sam Quinones, "How Mexicans Became Americans," *New York Times*, Jan. 18. 2015 SR7. Retrieved from: https://www.nytimes.com/2015/01/18/opinion/sunday/how-mexicans-became-americans.html.

19   Matthew Desmond, *Evicted: Poverty and Profit in The American City* (New York: Crown Publishers, 2016), p.70.

20   Personal interview with Ana Maria Quintana.

21   Ana Maria Quintana was not involved in the BASTA or the recall campaign.

22   As quoted in Mike Moodian, "Unity Through Crisis: How a Latino and Lebanese Coalition Helped Save Democracy in the City of Bell," paper delivered at the City of Bell Scandal Revisited conference held at Chapman University, February 19, 2015. The section on Yarounians draw heavily from this paper.

23   Ibid.

24   Ibid.

25   Ibid.

26   Ibid.

27   See, Bill Farr, "Ex-Mayor of Bell Gets 3 Years in Prison for Secret Casino Interest," *L.A. Times*, May 14, 1985. Retrieved from http://articles.latimes.com/1985-05-14/local/me-19039_1_california-bell-club.

28   Jill Gottesman, "Bell's Hiring of Felon Threatens Reopening of Card Club, State Says," *Los Angeles Times*, Dec 15, 1993, p. B1.

29   Melinda Burns, "Bell Reforms Aimed at Poker Club Corruption," *L.A. Times*, January 3, 1985. Retrieved from http://articles.latimes.com/1985-01-03/news/hl-11350_1_california-bell-club.

30   Ibid.

31   Simone Wilson, "Weapons Dealer From City Of Bell Ranks 10th For Most Guns Found In Mexico," *LA Weekly*, December 13, 2010. Retrieved from http://www.laweekly.com/news/weapons-dealer-from-city-of-bell-ranks-10th-for-most-guns-found-in-mexico-2397797.

32   Bruce Buchanan, *Presidential Campaign Quality: Incentives and Reform.* (Pearson-Prentice Hall, 2004) p. 2.

CHAPTER TWO

Training: How Rizzo Perfected the Art of Graft

"I seen my opportunities and I took 'em"

—*George W. Plunkitt*[1]

THE PHOTOGRAPH OF a short, corpulent man with bowed head being led away in handcuffs is how the world remembers Robert Rizzo. Armed investigators from the district attorney's office arrested him at his $1 million home. They put him in the back seat of their unmarked car and took him to jail. The wheeler-dealer city manager, who made $1.5 million a year in total compensation and was slated to get $880,000 dollars a year in retirement pay, making him the highest paid pensioner in California, finally got caught.[2] And while there is much more to the Bell scandal than Robert Rizzo, any exploration of what took place must begin with him.

TWO RIZZOS

Two portraits of Rizzo emerge from conversations with people who knew him well at different stages of his life. One (the "good" Rizzo) was that of a highly competent, industrious, innovative, knowledgeable, well-connected, hard-working, and driven city manager. This Rizzo was good with numbers, was results-oriented, and knew how to get things done. He was often kind to his subordinates, "inquiring after their families, granting them leaves to tend to sick relatives, and extending them city reimbursements for tuition."[3]

The other portrait (the "bad" Rizzo) was of a man who was secretive, cunning, greedy, paranoid, and unethical, a man who was prone to taking the "low road" for what he thought was a higher purpose. Rizzo was not extraordinarily bright or exceptional in any way other than, perhaps, in his level of greed.

Rizzo's two sides were present throughout his early career. However, somewhere in the first decade of the new century, the dark side overtook the good.

Rizzo had an insatiable appetite for money and power and an uncanny ability to manipulate others to do his bidding. "He liked to play the Godfather, the guy who manipulated things and pulled the strings that got other people to do what he wanted them to do. He was never the center of attention. He had this undertow about him ... 'speak softly and carry a big stick' well describes him," his half-brother Gene said.[4] Bell city clerk Rebecca Valdez said Rizzo was a micromanager and a "control freak." "It was pretty well-known to the employees that important events that happened in your life, like going to school, having a baby, or buying a house—he had to be the first one to find out," Valdez said. "If he found out through a second person or third person, the employee would kind of be in the doghouse. He was the first one to know before any of my peers knew that I was getting married."[5]

CHILDHOOD

No one really knows for sure what motivated Rizzo to plunder the city of Bell—and why he thought he could get away with it—especially since he and all but one of his close family members have declined to talk to researchers, but it is reasonable to assume that his childhood holds some of the answers.

Robert Rizzo grew up in a working-class family in San Leandro, California, in the San Francisco Bay Area. His father, Joe, owned a jewelry store and, for a time, was a cook in a local restaurant. When Joe was in the Air Force and stationed in Texas, he met Rizzo's mother, Nadine, a waitress, who already had a child, Gene, from a previous relationship. After he left the service, Joe and Nadine moved to Oakland, California, where they had Rizzo. In 1957, they moved to San Leandro where they purchased a modest three-bedroom house, the home where Rizzo grew up.[6] Rizzo was their only child together.

According to Gene, Rizzo was a typical kid who played little-league baseball and became an Eagle Scout, the highest rank one can attain in scouting. Making Eagle Scout requires a substantial amount of community service and may have sparked Rizzo's interest in local government. Rizzo was proud of this accomplishment and included it on the resume he submitted to Bell.

When Rizzo was three and Gene was thirteen, Nadine left Joe and her two sons for another man, with whom she had a third son, Mike, with whom neither Gene nor, presumably, Rizzo have had any contact.

Joe and Nadine divorced in 1967. Rizzo, then a teenager, chose to stay with his father. Gene said their mother was an "ally-cat" who had three sons with three different husbands. She was also an alcoholic who was so abusive toward Gene that he ran away from home many times and eventually became a ward of the state, living in foster homes before joining the military. Rizzo rarely talked about his mother except to say that she left the family when he was young. He'd then quickly change the subject.

Children who grow up in alcoholic homes share similar character traits, including: low self-esteem due to a sense of shame and embarrassment, a compulsive need to impress others, a fear of losing control, and a need to suppress emotions. Also, adult children of alcoholics tend to lead isolated lives, are more comfortable living in chaos or drama than in peace, are paranoid about potential threats to their power, and often engage in compulsive behavior, including eating and drinking disorders.[7] Although he was only three when his mother left and 13 when his parents divorced, Rizzo exhibited many of these traits throughout his life.

Rizzo's life, however, wasn't always in the shadows of his unfortunate circumstances. He went to Pacific High School in San Leandro where, according to Gene, he was an average student. He then went to Chabot Community College in Hayward, which was inexpensive and close to home. After spending two years there, he made the Dean's List and was accepted to the prestigious University of California at Berkeley as a transfer student. Throughout his college years, Rizzo worked as a fry cook at a hamburger restaurant in Hayward. He was a talented cook who loved to eat and battled a weight problem later in life.[8]

While his peers were hanging out, going to rock concerts, or playing sports, Rizzo exhibited a love for the racetrack. Unlike games of chance, like craps or slot machines, successful horse race betting—also known as handicapping—requires the ability to assess each horse's strengths and weaknesses based on information and statistics provided by the *Daily Racing Form*. "He was a good handicapper," says Gene who often accompanied Rizzo to the track. Rizzo never became emotional even when one of the horses he bet on was racing to victory. Betting on horses appealed to his quiet personality and desire for anonymity, facility with numbers, and love of strategic thinking. Rizzo's mastery of horseracing undoubtedly gave him a sense of power and control. It also allowed him to make a quick buck and feel good about himself.

The skills Rizzo honed at the racetrack jibed well with his choice of academic major, political science at UC Berkeley, where he graduated in 1976. Political science teaches people how to think politically—how to analyze people and situations from a political point of view to develop strategies to advance one's goals. When combined with "personnel management"—the focus of his studies in his Master's in Public Administration (MPA) program at Cal State East Bay—Rizzo became highly skilled at office politics, a handicapper of people and organizations, and rose quickly. His master's thesis, "An Investigation of a Local Government Endeavor in Designing and Implementing a Public Awareness Program" to reduce littering is competently done, but not especially imaginative.[9]

RANCHO CUCAMONGA

In 1980, following internships with the Housing Authority of Alameda County and the City of San Leandro, Rizzo left the East Bay and journeyed 400 miles south to take a job in the city of Rancho Cucamonga, an upscale and trendy community in San Bernardino County, which had recently incorporated in 1977.

At the time he was hired, Rancho Cucamonga had about a dozen employees. Rizzo was hired as an administrative aide, an entry level position, to work in the community services department. Rizzo did basic research and performed routine chores, such as preparing staff reports, analyzing fees, evaluating recreation programs, and coordinating the use of public facilities, such as parks and community buildings. Within two years, Lauren Wasserman, Rancho Cucamonga's first city manager, promoted Rizzo to administrative analyst.[10]

After a few years, Rizzo was promoted again to assistant city manager, a post he would hold for four years. While at Rancho Cucamonga, Rizzo was involved in development, redevelopment, and planning issues—but Rizzo wanted to climb higher. "What he wanted more than anything else was to become a city manager, the person in charge, in the worst way," according to Liz Stoddard, the finance director.[11] She added that Rizzo frequently applied for positions that required far more experience. After eight years, he left for a new assignment.

HESPERIA

Rizzo's desire was finally satisfied when he was hired as the city manager of Hesperia, California, where he stayed for four years.

It's not just the poor and recent immigrants whose city governments are vulnerable to the manipulations of kleptocrats. Local government offers easy pickings for opportunists in wealthier communities, as well, especially those with council-manager systems. In stark contrast to federal and state government, which emphasize *separation* of powers and checks and balances, the council-manager system *fuses* power in the city manager, who runs the city daily and who generally has quiet contempt for those elected, part-time, generalists who are supposed to oversee him or her. Nevertheless, the council is taking a huge risk if it decides to simply hand the keys of the city to their city manager and keep their own involvement at a minimum.

That was the case in the town of Hesperia, where Robert Rizzo broke into the graft business at an uncommonly young age of 34.

Hesperia is a community in the High Desert of the Mojave in San Bernardino County, 80 miles northeast of Los Angeles. Hesperia possessed cheap land, which meant housing dollars went much further there than they did in Los Angeles or Orange County, and by the time Rizzo arrived in the mid-1980s, it had grown into a semirural, white (85%), middle-class suburb with large lots and a variety of amenities. Most of its 25,000 residents owned their own homes (81%), held steady jobs, and commuted to work. Local elites wanted Hesperia, which was unincorporated and governed by San Bernardino County, to become a city, hoping to give the community greater control over land-use planning and other issues. They set out looking for someone who could lead them through the incorporation process and become its first city manager.

Managing a city isn't for beginners, but the Hesperia founders were drawn to one, a candidate who had taken his first paid municipal job as an administrative aide in the upscale community of Rancho Cucamonga just seven years before. Rizzo had a Master's in Public Administration (MPA) from Cal State East Bay and had been an administrative analyst involved with development and planning issues; but when he applied for the Hesperia job, he'd never headed a department, much less run a city, and he had no background in finance. His co-workers in Rancho Cucamonga were stunned Hesperia would hire him.[12]

Still, the members of Hesperia's city council *liked* him. He struck them as young, energetic, resourceful, and knowledgeable about local and state government and connected to a host of influential people. To the older, part-time, civic leaders, he seemed like just the person to turn their town into the next Rancho Cucamonga. "None of us had ever started a city before, and he seemed to know what he was talking about," remembers Howard Roth, a Hesperia councilmember who participated in the hiring.[13]

"Seemed to know what he was talking about" was enough for them. Roth and his peers believed they could trust their guts and forego such basics as background and reference checks and "meet the community" sessions. That was a serious mistake.

At first, Hesperia's city council admired Rizzo's aggressive style. To get the legislature's final approval for incorporation, Rizzo even led a contingent of city leaders up to Sacramento, charging the flights to his personal credit card.[14]

Hesperia's inexperienced founding council was pleased to allow its new city manager to lead the way, even though it is the council—not the city manager—that is supposed to set policy. (The same situation would happen in Bell.) Rizzo established core services for the new city, including police and fire, animal control, city clerk, planning, public works, finance, and community relations—filling many key positions with talent poached from Rancho Cucamonga, much to the chagrin of his former employer.

Once he had a foot in the door, Rizzo bowled the council over with his flair for showmanship. The day Hesperia took over road maintenance from the county, he rolled out a fleet of street sweepers at a minute past midnight to show that the new city was on the job.[15]

Rizzo loved his new job, and the city council loved him back. A glowing article in the *San Bernardino Sun* that appeared on the one-year anniversary of his appointment described Rizzo as "a legend who dazzled the city council with a youthful exuberance and wisdom beyond his 35 years."[16] Councilman Howard Roth said, "We got the best city manager we could get. He is innovative, aggressive, and still cares about people. He's got the right combination for the job."[17]

Rizzo "scored points quickly by finding revenue opportunities for the High Desert city, former co-workers say. They recall that

Rizzo had visions of turning the dusty, working-class town into a thriving center of commerce; sometimes, they said, he would court developers with rides in a sheriff's helicopter to survey building sites."[18]

Rizzo's first-year city budget was $6.9 million; by his second year, it was more than double: $17.5 million. He put $4 million in the bank as a reserve, developed a General Plan, entered joint projects with neighboring special districts to save money, and even proposed that the city build a sports stadium.[19]

Confident that they had made a sound choice, council members fell into the trap of thinking they could cede all governing responsibilities to an "expert" like Rizzo, not realizing that their ongoing oversight was essential—and the only thing that would keep him in check.

Rizzo, however, was willing to bend and sometimes break the law to get what he wanted. Robert Zuel, then in his early 30s, was a planner for Hesperia and was one of the first people hired by Rizzo. Rizzo put the young Zuel in charge of several important land projects, the biggest of which was the Rancho Las Flores Development.

The Rancho Las Flores Development was a 10,000-acre master-planned community on the city's southern end. Rizzo envisioned 15,000 houses, condos, and apartments for the community. The project required the council's approval, so Rizzo arranged for council members to take helicopter rides to pick out lots for their potential new homes in the gated golfing community. Zuel was shocked and troubled by this potential conflict of interest; however, the housing project was never built.[20]

To defeat the candidates who did not share—or at least wanted to discuss—his pro-growth agenda in the 1990 election, Rizzo sent Zuel to neighboring Orange County to meet with real estate developers. The developers gave Zuel a manila envelope stuffed with checks. Each check was signed and made out for $99, with the payee line left blank. By keeping the checks below the $100 threshold, Rizzo could skirt the state law which required the disclosure of the donor's identity. Rizzo filled in the payee line and gave the checks to three candidates who would maintain the pro-development ruling coalition and who went on to win the election.

Zuel said, "Rizzo led the council around like they were sheep. These guys were neophytes. They were brand new at the business of politics and Rizzo was not ... They didn't know what they were doing."[21] Rizzo wined and dined the council members and escorted them to fundraisers where they rubbed shoulders with Republican headliners, such as Vice President Dan Quayle and Bay Buchanan, former United States Treasurer, and to conferences in different parts of the country—trips that were paid for by the city. "I left local government because of Rizzo. He was a steamroller—a real Napoleon," Zuel added.

Rizzo built a lavish house for himself and his family in Hesperia where he occasionally entertained department heads. But such flaunting was frowned upon, according to Lauren Wasserman, the now retired city manager of Rancho Cucamonga: City managers should maintain a low profile lest they generate envy among staff, city council, and the public. Rizzo would remember the importance of appearances when he became Bell's city manager.

Over time, it became clear that behind the pomp and bluster of Rizzo's office was a deeply dysfunctional government. Serious budget problems emerged, along with allegations that Rizzo defrauded the city by misusing credit cards, misappropriating funds, and attempting to intimidate reporters.

Liz Studdard, Hesperia's finance director, said she wrote Rizzo a long memo outlining the budget problems. Rizzo walked the memo to her office, gave it back, and said he didn't want it in his office. Later, he would tell the city council that Studdard didn't tell him there were revenue shortfalls. "Rizzo threw me under the bus. I left for another job before he brought me down with him ... Rizzo was always analyzing what he could get away with. He was always trying to figure out an angle. He had a lust for power," she said.

Soon, other improprieties came to light, and the city council pressured Rizzo to step down. In April of 1992, Rizzo resigned as city manager of Hesperia. He received a $108,414 severance package.

After he left, an audit of the city's books revealed a multimillion dollar deficit and evidence of the misappropriation of funds as well as the transference of money into the city's general fund that was supposed to be kept in sequestered accounts for specific restricted purposes, according to several newspaper reports.[22] However, no charges were filed even though there were other allegations of fraud by Rizzo regarding the abuse of credit cards, misappropriation of funds, and the attempted intimidation of reporters.[23]

Mark Gutglueck ran the *San Bernardino Sentinel*, a weekly newspaper. He covered Rizzo closely when he was city manager of Hesperia. He said, "I think Bob was an intelligent and capable fellow. But he was also very greedy and an opportunist. In Bell, he saw a city that could be easily exploited due to the shortcomings of the elected leadership and the lack of a sophisticated citizenry and press. As George W. Plunkitt (that old-time political boss from Tammany Hall) said, "I seen my opportunities and I took 'em."[24]

LESSONS

Hesperia's excuse for its laxity in hiring and supervising Rizzo was that it was setting up a city government for the first time and didn't know where to begin. But no community has to start from scratch in vetting its officials or learning the basics. A professional group called the International City/County Management Association (ICMA) has protocols for the hiring process and resources for communities, including the advice of retired city managers.[25] Myriad organizations offer orientation materials and suggestions for best practices for newly elected local officials.[26] First, though, citizens must know to ask. If Hesperia had conducted a background check before hiring Rizzo, it would have revealed a telling trait: Rizzo was a gambler who played the horses. Former colleagues found him to be highly skilled at office politics, a handicapper of people and organizations. Concerns about his abilities might've surfaced if anyone asked—but no one did. This scenario played out again in Bell, where Rizzo, who'd become a "consultant" after being fired from Hesperia, would be hired without anyone questioning or investigating his past.

ENDNOTES

1   George W. Plunkitt, as quoted in William L. Riordan, *Plunkitt of Tammany Hall*. Penguin, 1995.

2   Russell Goldman, "Bell City Manager Paid Twice President Obama's Salary Resigns," abcnews.go.com, July 23, 2010. Retrieved from http://abcnews.go.com/ US/bell-city-fires-manager-paid-president-obamas-salary/story?id=11236299. The pension consisted of $650,000 per year from the state retirement system (CalPERS) and an additional $200,000 per year from a supplemental retirement plan.

3   Paul Pringle, Corina Knoll, and Kim Murphy, "Rizzo's horse had come in," *Los Angeles Times*, August 22, 2012. Retrieved from: http://www.latimes.com/local/ la-me-rizzos-horse-had-come-in-08222010-m-story.html

4   Personal interview with Gene Pasqual.

5   Corina Knoll and Ruben Vives, "Bell city clerk testifies signatures on documents were forged," *Los Angeles Times*, January 30, 2013. Retrieved from:http://articles. latimes.com/2013/jan/30/local/la-me-0131-bell-trial-20130131.

6   Personal interview with Gene Pasqual.

7   Searidge Foundation. Retrieved from http://www.searidgealcoholrehab.com/article-adult-children-of-alcoholics.php. See, Dr. Janet Woititz, Adult Children of Alcoholics. Health Communications Incorporated, 1983 Rizzo also had a problem with alcohol throughout his life according to his half-brother Gene and others.

8   Throughout his college years, Rizzo, whose father taught him how to cook, worked as a fry cook at a hamburger restaurant in Hayward. Rizzo, who was an excellent cook, loved to eat and battled a weight problem his entire life.

9   After a protracted battle, I secured Rizzo's master's thesis, which he wrote for his Master's in Public Administration (MPA) program at California State University Hayward (now East Bay).

10   Personal interview with Lauren Wasserman.

11   Personal interview with Liz Studdard.

12   Personal interview with Jack Lam, who was Rizzo's supervisor at Rancho Cucamonga and would later become its city manager. July 2015.

13   Priscalla Nordyke, "Hesperia's City Manager Uses Pomp, Practicality to Set Pace for New Town," *The San Bernardino County Sun*, July 1, 1989, p. A1.

14   Ibid.

15   Ibid.

16   Ibid.

17   Ibid.

18   Paul Pringle, Corina Knoll, and Kim Murphy, "Rizzo's horse had come in," *Los Angeles Times*, August 22, 2012.

19   Ibid.

20   Mark Gutglueck, "Penrod Protected Rizzo as He Plundered Hesperia," *The San Bernardino County Sentinel*, July 30, 2010, p. 1 and following.

21   Personal interview with Robert Zuel.

22   Paul Pringle, Corina Knoll, and Kim Murphy, "Rizzo's horse had come in, *Los Angeles Times*, August 22, 2012. Also see, "Former Hesperia manager quits lucrative post in Bell", *The Daily Press*, July 23, 2010. Retrieved from http://www.vvdailypress.com/article/20100723/NEWS/307239979. The Daily Press is part of the High Desert Media group which covers Hesperia.

23   Interview with Gutglueck.

24   Personal correspondence from Mark Gutglueck, who wrote for the *San Bernardino Sentinel*, a weekly which covers Hesperia and other High Desert communities. Gutglueck wrote several articles about Rizzo when he was city manager of Hesperia.

25   See, the International City Managers website: https://icma.org/.

26   See, for example a "Primer for New City Council Members." Retrieved from https://www.commerce.alaska.gov/web/Portals/4/pub/A_Primer_For_City_Council_Members.pdf.

CHAPTER THREE

The Fox Moves Into the Hen House: Rizzo in Bell

"L'État, c'est moi." ("I am the State")

—*Louis the XIV*

IN THE SPRING of 1993, Bell was a wreck. City revenues from sales taxes and other user fees were down due to a prolonged economic recession. To make things worse, Bell, like other cities across California, especially poor ones, was sandwiched between revenue cuts due to Proposition #13, which capped local governments' property tax revenues and escalating costs for public safety pensions and health care.

There was a real threat that the city would have to declare bankruptcy, said former councilman George Mirabal.[1]

Amid the slowly unfolding crisis, the city manager, John Bramble, left for another job, and Mayor Jay Price, 78, who had been on the Bell city council since the 1950s, suddenly died.

Pete Werrlein, the civic wheeler-dealer and former councilman, knew the council was in a jam, so he reached out to Bob Rizzo, whom he may have met at the track or at a casino—since both were gamblers—and urged him to apply for the city manager job. Rizzo said he'd take the job for $78,000 a year—$7,000 less than Bramble had been making. The Bell City Council hired him on the spot.

"He was willing to work for the least amount of money," said Councilman Rolf Janssen. "That was what attracted me and several other council members."[2] "My guess is they were happy to have anybody," Bramble said.[3]

No one took a closer look at Rizzo's troubling past.[4]

Rizzo saw real opportunity in Bell for power and money. After his hasty retreat from Hesperia, the once flamboyant city manager knew he needed to be more cautious now and operate below the radar. Janice Bass, the widow of former Bell council veteran George Bass, who hired Rizzo, said, "Bob could come into a room, and other than his portly size, you'd never know he was there; he was so quiet."[5]

When Rizzo first moved to Bell, he rented an apartment from Pete Werrlein.[6] Mike Trevis, who worked in Bell's police department for 22 years—nine as chief—helped move him in. The two frequently had coffee.

"Bob was attracted to the city because it had a commonplace name—there's a Bell Gardens, Belmont, Bellflower, and the famous Hollywood neighborhood, Bel Air—and because there was no local media covering city hall. I always thought he was hiding something," Trevis added. "He was absolutely paranoid of being photographed. If he felt he was being photographed or videotaped, he'd dart away."[7]

At first, just as in Hesperia, Bell's city council members and residents were pleased with Rizzo's performance. He "won praise from his elected bosses for righting the cash-starved city's financial course by restructuring bonds that teetered on default and taking other measures to firm up the bottom line," the *Los Angeles Times* noted.[8] This included cutting staff, outsourcing, and pinching pennies. Police patrol cars are usually retired after they hit 100,000 miles; Rizzo wouldn't replace them until they reached 200,000. The carpets in city hall weren't cleaned. Computers, software, and the phone system didn't get necessary upgrades. Rizzo even gave a bridge that was costly to maintain to a neighboring city.[9]

Rizzo improved the city's trash collection, made sure graffiti was cleaned up before sunrise, built a new skate park and spruced up existing parks, purchased and demolished abandoned buildings, increased street lighting, introduced employee flex time, and supported youth soccer.

Council members appreciated Rizzo's facility with finances. The fiscal squeeze was especially hard on poor cities like Bell and several others—Stockton, Vallejo, Desert Hot Springs—had already declared bankruptcy while Oakland and Richmond had come close.[10] But Rizzo kept Bell in the black.

He also sought out new sources of revenue and, given the Werrlein connection, it wasn't surprising that high on the list was the possible reopening of the infamous poker club.

Gambling had once brought $2 million a year into Bell's coffers, 20% of the general fund. In other nearby cities, it provided as much as 60% of the general fund. Given the history of scandal, proposing to give the club another go was a test of the community resolve to stay clean. The council showed its colors when it not only reopened the club but put Werrlein, whose ties to organized crime were widely known, in charge of security.

It didn't escape Rizzo's attention that there was little outcry from the community. Bell was perfect for a power grab. When Rizzo took over as city manager, turnout in elections was between 30 and 35% among registered adults but in single digits among all voting-age adults because so many eligible voters, many of them Latino newcomers, didn't register.[11]

It was in Rizzo's best interests to keep it that way. There was no outreach by city hall to Spanish-language media or community ESL programs and no effort to translate the workings of government into Spanish—though the state mandates that cities do so. Council meetings were purposely held in the early evening, which made attendance nearly impossible for working people. Civic boards, advisory committees, and other avenues for weighing in on city business disappeared—all red flags in any community.

Rizzo's city government walled itself off from citizen participation and found mentors who could guide it to more sophisticated crimes. A political science concept called "contagion theory" suggests that corrupt cities and city officials spread questionable practices to each other, introduce each other to those who can aid and abet them, and create an atmosphere in which corruption and complicity become the new norms. Indeed, Bell was part of a cluster of small cities in southeast Los Angeles County known as the "corridor of corruption."[12]

In Bell, Werrlein was the corruption epidemic's Patient Zero, seeming to infect city hall and weaken its defenses even after he left. Along with Rizzo, he recruited a string of dubious council members, including George Bass, a former fire chief from the neighboring city of Vernon, which was already so corrupt the California State Legislature considered disbanding it.[13]

Rizzo further weakened the city council's integrity by stacking it with his own picks, using a clever system that involved pushing departing council members to leave midterm so he could appoint interim replacements. He hand-selected weak, unqualified people who would rubber stamp his decisions—and gave them the advantage of running as incumbents when elections rolled around. If no one challenged them, the city election would be cancelled, which happened three times in the first decade of the new century (2001, 2003, and 2005).

With city council under his control, eventually other aspects of his personality began to emerge.

"Bob was the greediest person I have ever met," Mike Trevis said. "We [the cops] used to joke that he must not have had shoes when he was a kid because he was so preoccupied with making more money. There just was never enough money to satisfy him," he said. "He was always thinking of ways to increase his paycheck and retirement benefits, and even had a small TV on his desk that was on all the time so he could monitor the stock market."[14]

One of Rizzo's idols, as well as his confidant and golfing partner, was Bruce Malkenhorst, the former city manager of Vernon, who was then the highest paid city manager ($911,000) in all of California and the highest paid retiree in the public employee retirement system ($551,000, yearly). To get yet another salary boost, Rizzo wanted to succeed Malkenhorst as Vernon's city manager, according to Trevis and Bass. Malkenhorst was later convicted of embezzling public funds and had his yearly pension reduced from more than $500,000 a year to $115,000.[15]

Sure, Rizzo wanted the money. But he also enjoyed gaming the system, in the same way he loved handicapping horses.

Rizzo's paranoia and desire for control surfaced at city council meetings, Trevis recalled. When he spotted someone he didn't know in the audience of the sparsely attended meetings, Rizzo would pass around a Post-it Note to department heads that asked, "Who is that?" "Bob's idea of a great city council meeting was when no residents showed up," said George Cole.[16]

Rizzo flew into a rage when challenged or when he didn't get his way. One time, when he received a 4–1 instead of a 5–0 vote on an agenda item, he stormed outside and kicked a fence, breaking one of his toes.[17] On another occasion, when one of his department heads disagreed with him in front of the council, Rizzo's face turned beet red, and he violently hurled his briefcase across the room.[18]

THE MAGICIAN

Rizzo had several nicknames, including "Penguin" a character from the *Batman* television series because of his short stature and wide girth, but the one that stuck was "The Magician" because, according to Trevis, "He was great at getting people to see what he wanted them to see." For example, Rizzo wanted people to think Bell had absolutely no money. So, he purposely refused to fix badly worn and broken seats in the 1960s era city council chambers. Also, instead of replacing an attractive mosaic on the floor of the lobby of city hall that was removed to fix broken water pipes, Rizzo had an inexpensive mat thrown over the floor. Another example of his preoccupation with appearances occurred when he moved into his new office; he got rid of the previous city manager's furniture and replaced it with a cheap desk and chairs purchased from a thrift store. He never put any personal items, such as family photographs, on his desk because he wanted the council to know that there was nothing keeping him in Bell; he could pack up and leave on a moment's notice.

On the surface it looked like things were going well, but sometime after 2000, Rizzo started to unravel. He put on 150 pounds, a weight gain which he attributed to his divorce from his first wife, Sheila, with whom he had two daughters.[19]

He also drank a lot. Pete Werrlein, in an interview with the *Los Angeles Times*, said that he once confronted Rizzo at an election night party at city hall. "You're drunker than a hoot owl," Werrlein recalled telling Rizzo. "You're going home." When Rizzo tried to argue, Werrlein said, he got the city administrator's attention by striking him across the face with a half-open hand. "I whacked him and said, 'Let's go.' I think he knew I'd reached the end of my patience."[20]

Years later he was arrested after driving his car into a neighbor's mailbox and received a DUI—with a blood alcohol level three times the legal limit. He then entered an alcohol abuse program paid for by the city.

Publicly, Rizzo gave the appearance of a strapped-for-cash city manager. But privately he led a lavish lifestyle. In addition to his $900,000 home in an upscale beachside community 20 miles from Bell, he purchased a horse ranch in Auburn, Washington, that "included a stable full of thoroughbreds, among them a gelding named "Dépenser de l'Argent"—French for spend money."[21] His high-rolling lifestyle also included expensive cars, cigars, and alcohol. "I always thought he was living beyond his means," said Bell Chamber of Commerce President Ricardo Gonzalez.[22] Rizzo, who frequently quoted TV mob boss Tony Soprano,[23] had already started robbing, deceiving, and cheating to pay for his lifestyle.

Unchallenged by the council, Rizzo saw himself *as* city hall and believed that he should be compensated like a private sector CEO.

THE PUBLIC CEO

From its inception in the early 1900s, the council-manager system merged business and political values in an elected city council that represented the people's voice with a professional city manager who ran the city daily according to business values. The hiring of professional city managers by city councils was one of the Progressive Era (1890s-1920s) reforms designed to curb the power of corrupt political bosses who ran many of the nation's big cities. The council-manager system, which was the centerpiece of its reform efforts, fused and balanced political and professional needs.

Since the 1980s, in jurisdictions that use the council-manager form, there has been a shift in power and responsibility from the council to the city manager.[25] The council-manager form is now a de facto city manager government. There are several reasons for this shift.

First, the issues that local government has had to deal with have become more numerous and complex. These include issues regarding litigation, human relations, public employee unions, state and federal regulations, and especially finance, to name just a few. Most council members (being part-time generalists) simply do not have the expertise to make informed decisions in these areas. Instead, councils look to the city manager and staff for direction. These professionals are subject-matter experts who must meet minimum qualifications and requirements to get hired.

Second, as revenues have fallen and budgets have grown tighter, councils have looked to the city manager to drum up new revenue streams. Such a task requires the authority to nego-tiate contracts, make deals, and pursue other entrepreneurial activities.

A third factor that was responsible for the shift in power from the council to the city manager was the widespread notion that local government was a service-providing business like Bank of America or AT&T. The only difference was that the city provided public services such as police and fire protection and street sweeping.

City managers, then, are "public" chief executive officers with budgets, employees, and responsibilities commensurate with those in the private sector.[26]

The city manager's rising power is reflected in his or her market power. Rizzo's total compensation ($1.5 million) may have been excessive, especially for a poor city, but city managers are receiving increasingly lucrative total compensation packages and have little difficulty finding employment.

The public is largely unaware of who its city manager is and how powerful he or she has become. Most city managers keep a low profile. They do not flaunt their power (e.g., by, say, openly challenging council members or the council's decisions or getting visibly involved in politics), and they do not flaunt their compensation by living an ostentatious lifestyle. They are trustworthy and competent public servant professionals who obey the law. At the same time, most council members are unwilling to concede that their role is increasingly symbolic and that the city manager runs the city. Doing so would undermine the prestige of being on the council. They know, however, that they don't have the goods needed to be hired for even the lowest position in city hall.

Rizzo saw himself as the CEO of a "firm" that provided services to the public. To Rizzo, Bell's citizens were customers whose interest in city hall went no further than the quality of the services they received and the amount of taxes they paid.[27] Given this thinking, it follows that elections were trivialized, elected officials were marginalized, and that power was centralized. This thinking is reflected in Rizzo's decision to change his title from city manager to the more private-sector-sounding Chief Administrative Officer (CAO). Rizzo administered the delivery of public services to 35,000 residents.

Like a good businessman, Rizzo's policy decisions were driven by the profit motive with little regard for other values (e.g., equity, fairness, justice, transparency).[28] City departments, such as law enforcement, were evaluated based on return on investment (ROI)—how much money they generate given their slice of the city budget.

Rizzo saw himself as Bell's chief executive officer; the city council was the board of directors, and citizens were customers. He felt his job was to maximize return on investment, which he did by cutting costs, shaking down local businesses, instituting a for-profit police department, and squeezing Bell's residents with unnecessary tax assessments. Rizzo could point to the heads of similarly sized firms and university presidents who made more than he did.

Rizzo often went to extremes to keep expenses down and revenue high. He refused to spend money on needed office infrastructure (e.g., furniture, staff training, technology, even cleaning the carpets.) To boost revenue, he pushed the police to illegally tow cars from poor people, code enforcement officers to extort hefty fees from local businesses, and Bell's residents to pay unfairly high taxes. Just as businesses look for new markets, Rizzo pursued merger opportunities with the neighboring cities of Maywood and Cudahy. Of course, as in the private sector, there was no democracy or transparency.

To him, citizens were primarily consumers, who wanted good public services (e.g., police, fire, parks, garbage collection) and low taxes and had little interest in participating in politics.[29]

It is certainly true that Rizzo and his friends were greedy and that they milked the system as best they could. But it is also true that Rizzo believed cities should be run as businesses, which is why, when confronted about his salary, Rizzo was unapologetic, "If that's a number people choke on, maybe I'm in the wrong business," he said. "I could go into private business and make that money. This council has compensated me for the job I've done."[30]

The New Bossism

Scholars, such as George Frederickson and Jack Meek, see Rizzo as a modern day political boss, and the Bell scandal fitting "squarely in the traditions of the municipal reform movement .... and echoes of corruption in city government across the United States in the early twentieth century."[31] This characterization is unfair to machines and political bosses.

Political bosses emerged after the civil war in nearly every big city in the nation. Bosses headed a local political party which selected and elected candidates for office. The indebted office holder would then provide the boss the "spoils" of victory—government jobs, revenues, and lucrative contracts— to enrich themselves and reward party loyalists, with no regard for the public interest. Bosses were intimidating individuals who lusted after power and money.

The local political party organization which the boss headed was referred to as a "machine" due to its efficiency in get- ting votes and winning elections. The machine consisted of a small army of campaign workers who solicited people's vote in exchange for political favors. The job of a precinct captain was to deliver the vote for his party's slate of candidates. Precinct cap- tains moved up the ranks of the machine based on their ability to deliver the votes of their neighborhood. They worked for ward leaders who supervised dozens of precincts. Precinct captains and ward leaders often held bogus city "jobs" which required little or no work, and would sometimes seek public office them- selves. Machine workers were loyal to and worked hard for their constituents.

Machines were popular in areas of the city with highest con- centrations of poor, non-English speaking immigrants, who were pleased to exchange their vote for the proverbial lump of coal in the winter and help navigating the city bureaucracy.

Indeed, Rizzo had a lot in common with big city political bosses: He was greedy and corrupt, and saw public service as a way to get rich. He manipulated elections, controlled elected offi- cials, centralized power, and engaged in waste, fraud, and abuse. He gamed the system to boost his pay and pension to outrageous levels. He shook down Bell's small businesses and preyed upon its vulnerable citizens by instituting a for-profit police depart- ment, abusive code enforcement, and by forcing them to pay the highest taxes in the region. He plundered the city's treasury to pay lavish salaries and dole out interest-free loans for himself and to fellow employees—in exchange for their loyalty. He nearly bankrupted the city by getting the council and the community to approve bonds which the community didn't need and couldn't afford, for facilities that were never built. These funds were put into bank accounts that drew no interest, thus depriving the city of much needed revenue. National chains—whose jobs and tax dollars the city desperately needed—wouldn't locate in Bell because of him.

There are, of course, important differences. Unlike machine-run cities such as New York or Boston, Bell is a very small city. Also, Rizzo was a city employee, not a party leader. He headed the city bureaucracy whereas the old-school bosses headed political machines. The first job could be done in quiet, the second required a very public presence, so unlike flamboyant city bosses who loved getting their picture in the paper and interacting with constituents, Rizzo was an extremely quiet introvert who abhorred any sort of publicity or citizen interaction.

The bosses derived their power from their ability to "deliver the vote." Rizzo's power derived from his expertise in knowing how to run a city. Cities have become vastly more complex entities since the turn of the last century. Bell's city council abdicated nearly all the legislative power to Rizzo because many of them weren't up to the task of running a city, and were intimidated by him.

However, the biggest difference between the old-time bosses and Rizzo is that he gave nothing back to the community. The machines took plenty, but they also gave back to the community, providing a wide variety of social services functions for their people. As Robert Slayton writes in his biography of Al Smith,

> These people were poor, adjusting to the rules of America, but also the rules of unrestrained urban capitalism. They had few friends outside their fellow immigrants. If you got in trouble, if you were just simply hungry, there was no [one to help]. In steps the machine. If your son got picked up by the cops, they sent a lawyer to court. If you were cold, a load of coal arrived. If your house burned down ... the first person on the scene was the ward leader. The list was endless, and included even such simple acts of status and recognition, as attending a wedding or a funeral. And the most amazing thing was that all the ward leaders wanted in return was one little, tiny act; once a year you

were expected to go to the polls and vote for these people who had done so much for you. It seemed like the smallest of gestures, and the least you could do. Who cared if in the meantime they looted the city treasury and built structures like the Tweed Courthouse, originally budgeted at $250,000 but after graft and corruption took hold, costing taxpayers more than $13 million?[32]

Machine workers were loyal to and worked hard for their constituents. Those who didn't have these virtues were shown the door. This ensured some measure of accountability by civic leaders to ordinary people. There was no such commitment to the people of Bell. There was no equivalent of the proverbial "lump of coal" in the winter or food, or a place to sleep for those in need. There were no special favors or special attention paid to Bell's many poor, or the newly arrived who desperately needed someone to help them navigate a strange new world. Rizzo saw himself as CEO. He was "duty bound" to ignore such pleas. He gladly did.

LESSONS

As in Hesperia, there was no vetting, no community involvement, and no questions asked—not even of Rizzo's most recent employers—when Rizzo was hired. A lesson that resonates loudly through the Rizzo story is that "I know a guy who'd do it" is no basis for hiring someone to help manage a city. Yet when city hall becomes a kleptocrats' clubhouse, that reasoning will often suffice to put someone with an iffy history into a position of power.

Reviewing a city's personnel procedures may seem like an unlikely step in gauging how vulnerable the city is to manipulation, but cities embed values and safeguards in their hiring and personnel requirements. City government can't play by the rules if it hasn't bothered to make any. The Bell experience reaffirms that cities must establish and follow rules and procedures based on International City Manager (ICMA) guidelines for hiring city managers.

Rizzo's tenure as Bell's city manager also illustrates the tremendous shift in power that has taken place from council to city managers. City managers are exposed to the same level of temptation—including the temptation to abuse power—as elected officials, but they answer to the council, not to the people.[33] The council must vigorously oversee the city manager, and the public must elect council members who are willing and able to do so. This criterion needs to be part of council campaigns, but it never is. How often, for example, do candidates for city council say they will be a "check" on the city manager? Bell taught us that the public must be vigilant in monitoring the city manager and that there needs to be a public component in decisions regarding city manager compensation and performance evaluation. The city manager position must be forced out of the shadows.

ENDNOTES

1 Personal interview with George Mirabal.

2 Councilman Rolf Janssen, as quoted in Christopher Goffard, "How Bell hit bottom," *L.A. Times*, December 28, 2010. Retrieved from http://articles.latimes.com/2010/dec/28/local/la-me-bell-origins-20101228.

3 Ibid.

4 "Former Councilman George Bass said that he regretted that he and fellow council members did not diligently investigate Rizzo's background before hiring him," as quoted in Paul Pringle, Corina Knoll, and Kim Murphy, "Rizzo's horse had come in," *L.A. Times*, August 22, 2012. Retrieved from http://www.latimes.com/local/la-me-rizzos-horse-had-come-in-08222010-m-story.html.

5 Personal interview with Janice Bass.

6 Werrlein would later be a witness at Rizzo's marriage ceremony to his second wife, Eugenia Chiang.

7 Personal interview with Mike Trevis.

8 Paul Pringle, Corina Knoll, and Kim Murphy, "Rizzo's horse had come in," *L.A. Times*, August 22, 2012. Retrieved from: http://www.latimes.com/local/la-me-rizzos-horse-had-come-in-08222010-m-story.html.

9   Christopher Goffard, How Bell hit bottom," *L.A. Times*, December 28, 2010. Retrieved from http://articles.latimes.com/2010/dec/28/local/la-me-bell-origins-20101228.

10   Andrew DePietro, "Cities that went bankrupt or came close," MSN.com, April 12, 2017. Retrieved from https://www.msn.com/en-ca/money/topstories/10-us-cities-that-have-gone-bankrupt-and-5-that-came-close/ss-BBzLvMc. That spiraling cost started with Public Safety Unions convincing city councils that they had to have 3% at 50 to be competitive and recruit. That means that police and fire can retire at age 50 with 3% of their final year's pay for each year that they worked. For example, someone who started with the city at age 25 and retired at 55 would get 90% of his or her final year's pay until he or she dies. In practice, this is 100% due to pay increases during the final years that "spike" pensions up to 100% of the pay. The result is that cities have two work forces—one that is working and one that is retired. See Steven Greenhut, *Plunder*. (The Forum Press, 2009.)

11   Tom Hogen-Esch "Failed State: Political Corruption and the Collapse of Democracy in Bell, California." California Journal of Politics and Policy, 3 (1), pp. 1-28. 2011

12   The aptly named "corridor of corruption" is a region to the southeast of Los Angles bordered by four freeways: the 110 Freeway to the west, the 710 Freeway to the east, the 10 and 105 to the south. It includes the cities of Maywood, Bell, Cudahy, South Gate, and Lynwood. More than a dozen city officials from these cities have been convicted in the past 11 years of fleecing residents. Six other cities in the area—Vernon, Commerce, Huntington Park, Bell Gardens, and Compton—have also had notable corruption scandals. Contagion theory is one of the four theories presented by Thom Riley to explain the Bell scandal. See, Thom Riley, *Failure of Governance in Bell, CA* (Lexington Books, 2016).

13   Rick Cole, "The Corruption in Vernon" L.A. Times. December 12, 2010. Retrieved from: http://articles.latimes.com/2010/dec/27/opinion/la-oe-cole-vernon-20101227

14   Personal interview with Mike Trevis.

15   John Healey, "Bruce Malkenhorst: Poster boy for public employee pensions?" *L.A. Times*, July 23, 2013. Retrieved from http://www.latimes.com/opinion/opinion-la/la-ol-bruce-malkenhorst-vernon-pensions-fight-20130723-story.html.

16   Personal interview with George Cole.

17   Personal interview with Mike Trevis.

18   Ibid.

19 Paul Pringle, Corina Knoll, and Kim Murphy, "Rizzo's horse had come in," *L.A. Times*, August 22, 2012. Retrieved from: http://www.latimes.com/local/la-me-rizzos-horse-had-come-in-08222010-m-story.html

20 As quoted in Christopher Goffard, "How Bell hit bottom," *L.A. Times*, December 28, 2010. Retrieved August 3, 2015, from http://articles.latimes.com/2010/dec/28/local/la-me-bell-origins-20101228.

21 Paul Pringle, Corina Knoll, and Kim Murphy, "Rizzo's horse had come in," *L.A. Times*, August 22, 2012. Retrieved from:http://www.latimes.com/local/la-me-rizzos-horse-had-come-in-08222010-m-story.html

22 Ibid.

23 From the American crime drama television show *The Sopranos*, which ran on HBO from 1999–2007. According to former Bell police officers Mike Trevis and James Corcoran. Goffard also mentions Rizzo's penchant for quoting Tony Soprano. See Christopher Goffard, "How Bell hit bottom," *L.A. Times*, December 28, 2010. Retrieved August 3, 2015, from http://articles.latimes.com/2010/dec/28/local/la-me-bell-origins-20101228

24 Jeff Gottlieb, "Bell council used little-noticed ballot measure to skirt state salary limits," *L.A. Times*, July 23, 2010. Retrieved fromhttp://articles.latimes.com/2010/jul/23/local/la-me-0723-bell-charter-20100723.

25 See, Richard J. Stillman, *The Rise of the City Manager*. (University of New Mexico Press, 1974).

26 The website PublicCEO.com suggests the popularity of this conception of the role of city manager.

27 This is in stark contrast to how he perceived the public's role in San Leandro's antilitter campaign, which was the subject of the thesis he completed for his Master in Public Administration (MPA) degree: "The campaign lacked an array of public involvement activities such as pick up drives, clean-up days, or events of this sort. Except for a poster contest, there was nothing else to generate public involvement. If there had been any other type of activity, the city council or a local group might have become more involved." See, Robert Adrian Rizzo, "Case Study: an Investigation of a Local Government's Endeavor in Designing and Implementing a Public Awareness Program." Spring Quarter, 1980, California State University, Hayward. Department of Public Administration.

28 See, Eugene Bardach, *A Practical Guide for Policy Analysis: The Eightfold Path to More Effective Problem Solving*. (Sage, 2000).

29 Rick Cole, city manager of Santa Monica, in a presentation at the City of Bell Scandal Revisited conference, Chapman University, February 19, 2015, describes

this as a "vending machine" view of government. "Citizens put their money in a coin slot and get their services out the bottom. When something gets stuck or they didn't get what they wanted, they hit and kicked the machine."

30 Gottlieb and Vives, "Is A City Manager Worth $800,000?" *L.A. Times*, July 15, 2010. Retrieved from http://articles.latimes.com/2010/jul/15/local/la-me-bell-salary-20100715.

31 George Frederickson and Jack Meek, "Searching for Virtue in the City: Bell and her Sisters." Paper delivered at The City of Bell Scandal Revisited held at Chapman University, February 19, 2015. Retrieved from: https://digitalcommons.chapman.edu/localgovernmentreconsidered/bellscandal/papers/3/

32 Robert A. Slayton. *Empire Statesman: The Rise and Redemption of Al Smith*. (Free Press, 2001), p.52.

33 Here are examples of city managers who have succumbed to the temptations of office: Opa-locka, Florida City Manager David Chiverton, who pleaded guilty to shaking down local businesses in exchange for water and other permits. Opa-locka was teetering on bankruptcy. See, Jay Weaver and Michael Sallah, "Former Opa-locka city manager pleads guilty in corruption probe," *Miami Herald*, September 12, 2016. Retrieved from http://www.miamiherald.com/news/local/community/miami-dade/miami-gardens/article101404632.html. In Eagle Pass City, Texas, City Manager Hector Chavez Sr. pleaded guilty to making false statements to a federal agent. He had bribed a Maverick County Commissioner, lied to federal agents, forged contracts to hide bribes, and falsified documents to "obstruct justice." See, Idenfonso Ortiz, "Former Texas Border City Manager Pleads Guilty in Corruption Probe," *Brietbart Texas*, September 12, 2017. In Crystal City, Texas, City Manager James Jonas was found guilty by a federal jury of on multiple counts of corruption including bribery, wire fraud, and conspiracy. See, John MacCormack, "Former Crystal City officials found guilty of corruption," MySA.com, June 26, 2017. Retrieved from http://www.mysanantonio.com/news/local/article/Former-Crystal-City-officials-found-guilty-of-11247509.php. George Perez of Cudahy, California, was arrested by the FBI arrested and charged with using drugs at city hall, tossing out election ballots to sway elections, and being chauffeured to a Denny's to pick up bribes. See, Ruben Vives, "Was this ex-city manager of a town riddled with corruption a 'man of the people' or an old school political boss?" *L.A. Times*, December 26, 2016. Retrieved from http://www.latimes.com/local/lanow/la-me-george-perez-cudahy-20160930-snap-story.html.

CHAPTER FOUR

The Election that Changes Everything

"'What can I do against them?' he said of the city, 'Nothing.'"

—*Alfred Moreno, Bell resident*

RIZZO'S GOLDEN TICKET was a seemingly innocuous ballot measure. But Measure A's passage changed everything.

California cities are classified into general law cities and charter cities. There are presently 370 general law cities and 108 charter cities. "General law cities are bound by the state's general law, even with respect to municipal affairs."[1] Charter or "home rule" cities can adopt their own charters, which serve as their constitutions. Charter cities have greater autonomy over municipal affairs, including employee relations and the conducting of elections. But the move to charter status requires voter approval.

In November 2005, the legislature passed a law that limited the pay of council members in general law cities. The law was written by Assemblyman Hector De La Torre, who was stunned at the pay raises he had seen city leaders vote themselves in South Gate, when he was on the city council. South Gate is one town over from Bell. But the new law applied just to general law cities, not to the more independent charter cities. The salary cap did not apply to staff. But Rizzo very likely felt that if he could boost councilmember salaries, they would return the favor.

Rizzo thought that Bell could skirt these state-ordered salary caps by becoming a charter city. If it won voter approval, Measure A would convert Bell to a charter city. The measure was Rizzo's idea, but the charter was drafted by city attorney Ed Lee, who lifted language from other cities' charters. The fact is, the charter *didn't* permit Bell to raise council salaries, but Rizzo *thought* it did, and that is what he privately told each councilmember. They were an easy sell.[2]

"Ed Lee probably goofed when he wrote the charter, and neither Rizzo nor the council members read it closely enough, if at all, to understand that it actually kept their pay at the state limits. Had the charter been worded differently, council members might not have faced criminal charges," said Jeff Gottlieb, the *L.A. Times* reporter who, with Ruben Vives, broke the Bell story.[3]

Becoming a charter city sounded vaguely positive. What could be wrong with giving a city more autonomy? What implications did that have for Bell? Voters had every right to ask and keep asking until they understood. But Rizzo knew he'd never have to explain. There was no public discussion or debate since the forums—newspapers, social groups, higher education panels, union meetings—where such discussions typically take place were long gone. But had he been pressed, it might have come out that becoming a charter city meant, as he understood it, that Bell was no longer subject to a 2005 law passed by the state legislature that put limits on the salaries of officials in general law cities. There was no mention of this in the ballot language or the ballot argument and no hint of the effect it might have on how much the city could pay Rizzo and the council. All five council members signed the "For" argument. There was no "Against" argument.[4]

So, on November 29, 2005, the city held a special election, which cost between $40,000 and $60,000 of taxpayer funds. The question put to the voters was: "Shall the voters of the City of Bell approve a City Charter, which allows the People of Bell to manage the business of the City of Bell?"

The charter measure passed 336 to54, with 2% of eligible adults voting.[5] The election was held the Tuesday after Thanksgiving weekend, a workday, when no other elections were being held, and there were no other issues or big-ticket contests (such as the presidency or governor) to draw voters to the polls, which suppressed turnout. In fact, this was the only item on the ballot.

At the time, on November 29, 2005, no one in Bell took note of the change that occurred or had a clue of the significance of this election. Shortly after becoming a charter city, council salaries rose from around $60,000 to $96,000 and, over time, launched Rizzo's salary into the stratosphere. It wasn't until five years later, when the L.A. Times began publishing its Bell stories, that people began to understand the impact this election had had on council salaries and their city.

Some people, however, did smell a rat and made formal charges of election fraud. James Corcoran was a 19-year veteran police sergeant who said that elections were frequently thrown in Bell. Corcoran filed a police report that "listed the names of 19 voters who allegedly were either living in Lebanon, or were deceased at the time that their votes were cast."[6] He also said that Mayor Oscar Hernandez, who owned a small market in Bell, kept a pile of absentee ballots in his store and paid young boys to distribute them. When they returned, he'd pull the ones supporting his side and deliver only those to city hall where they were kept in a closet accessible to Rizzo and staff. Councilman Victor Bello and other Bell residents confirmed these and other allegations of election fraud.[7] Others alleged that off-duty police officers and other officials went door to door and gave out absentee ballots and urged people—many of whom were Spanish speakers and couldn't read the ballot—how to vote. They later came back and picked up the filled-in ballots, which is illegal: Only voters can request that a ballot be mailed to them, and only they personally can return their completed ballot to a polling station or mail it in. Others were concerned that the 2005 special election was run by the City of Bell, not Los Angeles County, which meant that city staff ran an election that would materially benefit their supervisors. Both the district attorney and the U.S. Department of Justice opened investigations regarding voter fraud but no charges were ever filed. Corcoran later successfully sued the city after he said he was forced out of his job for being a whistle-blower.

INCREASED SPENDING

The charter vote further emboldened Rizzo. He and the council were convinced they could do whatever they wanted. The turnout numbers told them definitively that no one was paying attention. Once the ballot measure passed, Rizzo thought the conversion to a charter city cleared him to raise salaries for himself, other administrators, and the council.

Rizzo's starting salary in 1993 was $72,000. By September of 2004, he was making $300,000. By July 2005, his salary rocketed up more than almost 50% to $442,000.[8] And by 2010, Rizzo's base salary—$787,000—was twice that of the President of the United States.

A series of complex machinations, including the use of extravagant employment contracts, benefits, deals, and secret ledgers, allowed Rizzo to vacuum money from the city's coffers and to inflate his total compensation to $1.5 million per year in 2010, making him the highest paid city manager in California and, likely, the United States.

In 2008, Rizzo hired a full-time deputy, Angela Spaccia, who had held a series of finance positions in different municipalities, ultimately paying her $376,288 a year in salary and benefits. He later recruited a former Simi Valley and Ventura police chief, a friend of Spaccia, to oversee Bell's 46-member police squad, paying him $457,000—approximately 50% more than the city of Los Angeles paid its chief of police.

According to the L.A. Times, Rizzo had written contracts for himself and other administrative staff which included 28 weeks or seven months of paid sick and vacation days.[9] These could be turned into cash at Rizzo's discretion. Thus, Spaccia was entitled to 26 weeks of vacation and sick time each year, worth $188,640. For Adams, the figure was $76,428. This meant that Spaccia's total compensation came to $850,000 when her benefits are included. Adams could collect a total of $700,000. In addition, both Rizzo's and Spaccia's contracts included automatic annual increases of 12%. For 2011, Rizzo's salary was slated to go up an additional $94,516, with no performance review.

Had he not gotten caught, Rizzo would have retired as the highest paid public servant in the California Public Employees Retirement System (CalPERS), with payments around $650,000 annually.[10]

SUPPLEMENTAL RETIREMENT PLAN

But apparently, roughly $650,000 yearly for life wasn't enough for Rizzo.[11]

Back in 1944, the residents of Bell put an assessment—or "retirement tax"—on property to cover the cost of public employee retirements. The cost wasn't very much because there were only a handful of full-time city workers at the time, and pensions were very modest compared with what some public-sector employees get today. For example, more than 60,000 California goverment retirees receive pensions above $100,000.[12] Moreover, unlike most other public-sector pension plans, Bell did not require any employee contributions. The pensions were fully paid for by taxpayers.

In 2007, Rizzo and Spaccia designed an illegal Supplemental Retirement Plan for themselves and 40 other city officials, including the council, that boosted their pensions above the maximum permitted under California law and which would be fully funded by taxpayers. The city council readily approved increases in the retirement pay that raised pensions by 85%. It also doubled the retirement tax—though the state controller said this increase was illegal—to cover the rising costs of those sweetened pensions. The new deal meant that Rizzo could retire at age 62 and receive $1 million dollars a year, and Spaccia would receive $375,000 a year, according to estimates made by the *L.A. Times*.[13]

Rizzo cut the council in on the action, and they willingly went along. After Bell became a charter city, councilmember salaries skyrocketed to $100,000 per year, grossly more than what most city people make. Bell council salaries consisted of $673 per month for sitting on the council plus stipends for sitting on faux commissions "such as the Public Financing, Surplus Property, and Solid Waste and Recycling Authorities. City records indicate that those boards performed little work,"[14] and rarely met.

Following the publication of Jeff Gottlieb and Ruben Vives' eye-popping story—"Is a city manager worth $800,000?"—the outrageous compensation Rizzo and his cronies received became the focal point of news coverage of the Bell scandal. However, the headline-grabbing salary was just one part of a much larger problem: Rizzo had absolute and complete control over how the city's money was spent, according to the state controller, John Chiang.[15] The city council rubber-stamped everything Rizzo put in front of them, with little or no debate.

In the fall of 2010, the State Controller's Office (SCO) released a series of reports that found widespread corruption.[16] The scams were numerous, pervasive, and shocking. For example, "Rizzo authorized the purchase of a plot of land owned by the former mayor (Oscar Hernandez) of Bell, for $4.8 million, with no documentation"[17] regarding the property's true worth or how the purchase would benefit the city. Hernandez had purchased the property for $480,000 in 1981. Rizzo also arranged for a $100,000-a-year job for a former councilmember, Victor Bello, at a city-owned food bank staffed by volunteers. Bello was its only paid employee.

Rizzo also personally distributed at least $1.5 million in no-interest loans ranging from $1,000 to $130,000 to more than 50 Bell staffers, without the knowledge or consent of the city council. Loans were given to a local businessman and friend of Rizzo for $300,000. Also, three council members received

$20,000 each, and four top administrators—the assistant chief administrative officer (Spaccia), the director of administrative services, the director of community services, and a deputy chief of police—received together $69,000. The state controller deemed this an illegal gift of public funds.[18]

The state controller also criticized the city for contracting with an engineering firm which was owned by the city's director of planning services. The monthly retainer payments continued long after the contract expired.[19]

REVENUE SCAMS

To help pay for the outrageous salaries and favors to friends and colleagues, Rizzo concocted a series of scams which turned the city against its residents. One of the most disgraceful was the requirement that police officers spend most of their time earning money for the city by impounding cars and charging exorbitant fees to get them back rather than fighting crime.

To understand what was going on requires some context. The court has tried to strike a balance between public safety and civil rights when it comes to impounding a person's car. The term used here is the "community caretaker function." Under the community caretaker function, police can have a car towed when, for example, it is blocking traffic or is unsafe to drive or if an officer thinks it was stolen or used in the commission of a crime.[20] The police *can* also seize a vehicle if the driver doesn't have a license. But the police *cannot* pull someone over because he or she fits a racial or ethnic "profile" of people who often don't have licenses, such as undocumented workers who make up half of Bell's residents.

As "caretakers of the community," police are responsible for public safety, but it is not their job to enforce the Federal government's immigration laws and certainly not to use the law to harass people to generate profit.

Nevertheless, impounding cars and finding other revenue generating infractions was Bell's cops' major job. Cars were seized from Spanish-speaking drivers who were terrified that they could be ripped from their families and immediately deported. This was done on a routine basis—during day shifts and at checkpoints at night. "If we saw a little pickup truck with garden tools in the back or if it had a bumper sticker of a well-known Spanish-language Mexican radio disc jockey, *Piolin*, we'd pull it over because we knew the driver was likely to be unlicensed," said James Corcoran, a 19-year veteran of Bell's police force.

Thus, the city servants were victimizing the very residents they were supposed to serve and protect. To finance Rizzo's and the city council's outrageous and illegal salaries, they exploited the poorest and least vocal members of their city. So, were they angry, did they fight back? "No," said Corcoran, "they would just be shaking because they were afraid of being deported."[21]

A driver would have to pay $400—a week's pay for many—to get his or her vehicle back. Officers were expected to impound three cars per 8-hour shift. Some impounded as many as eight. "It was out of control," said Bell Officer Art Jimenez of the operation which generated nearly a million dollars during the 2008–2009 fiscal year.[22]

BUSINESS LICENSE FEES

The city also generated revenue by aggressively enforcing business license fees.[23] Those targeted included plumbers, carpet cleaners, a husband-and-wife team passing out handbills, a taxi driver dropping off a customer, a woman selling mangoes, and a homeless man picking up bottles. There was no rhyme or reason to the fines, which ranged from $25 to $1,000, depending on a negotiated settlement which was usually approved by Rizzo. The program was overseen by Eric Eggena, who, as the head of the department of code enforcement, earned $421,402 annually.

The settlements were supposed to be reviewed by a judge but this very rarely happened.

One of the stories reported in the *L.A. Times* was of plumber Frank Santiago. Santiago received a call one day to check out a leaking kitchen pipe. He went to a home but found nothing wrong. As he was backing his van out of the driveway, a code enforcement officer pulled up and blocked his way, the plumber recalled. The officer wanted to know if Santiago had a license to do plumbing in Bell. Santiago said he told the officer he hadn't even pulled out any tools, but the officer cited him anyway and towed his van.[24]

Another story reported by the *L.A. Times* was that of Alfredo Moreno.[25] Moreno, 73, who had been laid off from his job as a bagger at a local grocery store, collected bottles and cans and made about $10 to $15 when he turned them in to be recycled. One day, a code enforcement officer cited him for not having a business license for *handling recyclable material*. His 1999 Ford van was impounded as evidence, and he was fined $50. After borrowing money from his children, he paid the fine and $500 to retrieve his van. The *L.A. Times* reported that Moreno said he didn't understand the document and did not challenge it. "Moreno expressed the helplessness that many in Bell felt over the city's aggressive efforts to raise money —and the difficulty they faced in getting anyone to work on their behalf. 'What can I do against them?' he said of the city, 'Nothing.'"[26]

Another story is told by Officer James Corcoran. It involves a person he calls the "Avon Lady" because she sold women's beauty products door-to-door. One day, she pulled her 1970s Toyota Corolla hatchback to the side of a residential street. She walked up to a house and delivered a small pink bag. As she did, a code enforcement officer came up to her and cited her for operating a business without a license. Then he impounded her car for transporting "contraband"—the dozen or so pink bags filled with women's products underneath the glass hatch-back—enforcing a law typically used to seize a drug dealer's cache.[27]

CODE ENFORCEMENT

Rizzo also collected revenue through the aggressive enforcement of city codes. Code enforcement officers enforce city ordinances regarding public health, safety, comfort, morals, and welfare. Rizzo's code enforcement officers were notorious for fining local businesses for code violations. In one case, Rizzo used code enforcement to target and harass a local business whose property the city wanted to redevelop.

Jack Ellwood started Jack's Car Wash in the early 1950s. In 1986, Ellwood sold the business—but not the property—to Albert Neesan and his son Eldon, who agreed to lease the property for 20 years. The Nessan's also had a "right of first refusal" should Ellwood ever want to sell the property. The property was assessed at $612,000. Eldon Neesan said he offered Ellwood between $650,000 and $700,000 to purchase the property on several occasions but Ellwood declined.

The property was on a prime commercial stretch that Rizzo was intent on developing. The car wash was surrounded by fast-food restaurants which generated far more tax revenue for the city than the car wash. Unbeknownst to the Nessans, Rizzo purchased the property for the city from Ellwood for $1.35 million dollars, nearly twice its assessed value. As part of the agreement, the owner had a highly unusual deal which required him to send a check to the city for $425,000, which he did. Neither Bell city officials nor the seller could account for what happened to the donation.

Yet, the city could not move forward with its redevelopment plans while the car wash was still operating. So, the city began harassing him to get him to close. Nessan says that a city code enforcement officer came by two or three times a week and cited his business for such things as having a car's front tire on the sidewalk and electrical issues. "He'd park behind the building and would wait around to cite us. It was incredibly stressful. I had two jobs: operating a car wash and dealing with code enforcement." The citations accumulated, and eventually Neesan had to shut the car wash down for 13 months to address them. He kept afloat by refinancing his house, which he eventually lost to the bank.[28]

Another car wash owner, Gerardo Quiroz, said the city arbitrarily required him to make payments because of his "special location."[29] He was so outraged at paying his $300-a-month fee that he wrote "Mordida" ("bribe" in Spanish) on the memo line of some of his checks to the city. "I put that because I knew it was a bribe," said Gerardo Quiroz, who paid a total of $10,000 to the city.[30]

Businessman Willie Salazar, who owned All Day Tire, said he met with Rizzo at City Hall and negotiated the amount he'd pay for a permit to do business in the city. Some businesses paid tens of thousands of dollars; others paid nothing at all. It was all up to Rizzo.[31]

BONDS

Two years prior to the infamous 2005 Measure A (charter city conversion) election, a special election was held in which voters were asked to authorize the sale of up to $70 million dollars in general obligation bonds to finance the construction of a sports complex, a new library, and a community theater.[32]

Rizzo wrote the measure, and the city council approved it unanimously with little discussion or debate. There was no agreed upon timetable about which projects would be built or how much they would cost. It was all at Rizzo's discretion. Only 933 ballots were cast for this untethered slush fund. There was a "For" argument, which was signed by all the members of the city council. No "Against" argument was filed.

The city eventually issued $50 million in bonds under Measure A, which put taxpayers on the hook for the borrowed funds plus the accrued interest which would total well over $100 million by the time the bonds were scheduled to be paid off in 2040.[33] This is an unsustainable amount of indebtedness for a city with a $13.5 million-dollar annual general fund budget.

Neither the sports complex nor any of the promised facilities were ever built. Moreover, to add injury to injury, the proceeds from the bond sales, State Controller John Chiang said, "inexplicably were deposited in a *non-interest* bearing checking account" at a [local] Wells Fargo Bank. This cost the city $1.7 million in lost interest.[34]

The revenues from the various scams were placed in the city's general fund, not in separate accounts as the law requires. This placement had several benefits for Rizzo: First, it masked the true impact on the general fund of the increased compensation agreements, which the new revenues helped offset. Second, it made Rizzo look "good" (or less bad) because "under [his] employment agreement with the city, his salary increases were contingent on a positive cash position in the general fund,"[35] which the new and highly unusual extorted revenue streams made possible. Finally, the increased revenue provided greater flexibility to increase compensation even further.

Chiang challenged the legal authority of the city to jack up fees for things like sanitation, refuse, recycling, and lighting without voter approval.[36] Also, state law requires "that charges against assessment districts must be directly related to services provided to the districts,"[37] but the controller could not find any such justification for the higher rates. However, he did conclude that 24% of the rate increases were used to fund Rizzo's and Spaccia's over-the-top salaries.

The controller also found that Rizzo had used low income housing funds to boost his and other administrators' pay and for perks such as city cell phones, car washes and for vacation, retirement contributions, and holiday time. A separate audit of a fund to improve streets funded by state gas tax revenue showed that the city had paid an engineering consulting firm, whose director was serving as the city's director of public planning services, $301,810 although there was no contract for services. "Public money dedicated to increasing affordable housing and maintaining local roads was instead used as a self-indulgent slush fund to pay for excessive salaries, perks, and other unlawful expenses," the state controller concluded.[38]

IMPACT ON BELL'S ECONOMY

According to Doug Willmore, Bell's first permanent city manager after Rizzo, Rizzo's most damaging legacy was the harm he did to Bell's economy. Under Rizzo, Bell became a horrible place to do business. Businesses closed. Others left town. National "big box" chains and auto dealerships—which are crucial sales tax providers—wouldn't locate in Bell because of the city's notorious reputation for corruption. "While Rizzo and his cronies gave great time and effort to schemes designed to enhance their paychecks, the City of Bell's commercial infrastructure was ignored, and surrounding communities advanced as retail providers. Due to the dwindling commercial tax base that Rizzo allowed to crumble over his almost 20-year reign, most of the city's largest taxpayers were now gas stations."[39]

TAX REVENUES

With no sales tax to fund its operations, Bell's tax burden became the second highest in Los Angeles County. Its residents, among the poorest in Los Angeles County, paid higher tax rates than people in such tony enclaves as Beverly Hills or Huntington Beach—30 miles and a world away from Bell—where Rizzo owned a 1.2 million dollar home with an ocean view.

LESSONS

Bell's city attorney, Anthony Taylor, who helped unravel the scandal, points to a variety of tools and allies available to anyone trying to unearth financial conflicts and self-dealing in a city. Here, too, there's no need to go it alone or start from scratch.[40]

Taylor offers simple starting points in California law, as well as tactical advice for people who suspect all is not right in city hall. For instance: Instead of simply grumbling, make a public records request for all policies related to nepotism and conflict of interest. Then, collect examples of the city not following its own rules. Alert the city attorney and the city council to concerns first, Taylor says, and, if needed, the state auditor, the grand jury, and the ethics commission if one exists. Citizens can also look to Ballotopedia (ballotopedia.org) for information on government initiatives and other related matters. Finally, they can contact the media to sound alarms about kleptocrats' behavior. That's what the activists did in Bell.

ENDNOTES

1 League of California Cities. "Charter Cities vs. General Law Cities—The Basics." Retrieved from: http://www. cacities.org/Resources-Documents/Resources-Section/Charter-Cities/ Charter-Cities-A-Quick-Summary-for-the-Press-and-Researchers.

2 Defense attorneys argued that "In addition, members shall receive such reasonable and adequate *amounts as may be established by ordinance*" permitted the council to pay themselves stipends above their council salaries for sitting on the four authorities that never met or did any real work, but the jury didn't buy this argument.

3 Jeff Gottlieb, "Bell: A Total Breakdown." Paper presented at the City of Bell Scandal Revisited, Chapman University. February 19, 2015. Retrieved from: https:// digitalcommons.chapman.edu/cgi/viewcontent.cgi?referer=https://www.google. com/&httpsredir=1&article=1200&context=localgovernmentreconsidered.

4 Section 502. Compensation. Of the Bell City charter passed by voters on November 29, 2005. See http://www.cityofbell.org/home/showdocument?id=682. The Charter says, "The members of the City Council shall receive compensation for their services as may be prescribed by ordinance or resolution, but with respect to service as a Councilmember not to exceed the amount which Council members of general law cities of similar population would receive under State law ..."

5 Tom Hogen-Esch. "Predator State: Corruption in a Council Manager System: The Case of Bell, California." Paper presented at the City of Bell Scandal Revisited Conference Chapman University. February 19, 2015. Retrieved from: https:// www.chapman.edu/wilkinson/_files/pdf%20white%20papers/tom-hogen-esch.

pdf. Also see, Jeff Gottlieb, "Bell used little-noticed ballot measure to skirt salary limits. July 23, 2010. Retrieved from: http://articles.latimes.com/2010/jul/23/local/la-me-0723-bell-charter-20100723

6   Richard Winton, Jeff Gottlieb, Andrew Blankstein, L.A. County D.A. expands probe into Bell government. Los Angeles Times. July 28, 2010. Retrieved from: http://articles.latimes.com/2010/jul/28/local/la-me-bell-elections-20100728

7   Paloma Esquivel and Jeff Gottlieb, "Voters in Bell tell of possible fraud," *L.A. Times*, August 5, 2010. Retrieved from http://articles.latimes.com/2010/aug/05/local/la-me-election-fraud-bell-20100806. Also see, Chase Davis, "Tipster in Bell scandal waited months for D.A., then was arrested," *California Watch*, October 11, 2010, Retrieved from: http://californiawatch.org/dailyreport/tipster-bell-scandal-waited-months-da-then-was-arrested-5508.

8   Jeff Gottlieb and Ruben Vives, "Is A City Manager Worth $800,000?" *L.A. Times*, July 15, 2010. Retrieved August 3, 2015, from http://articles.latimes.com/2010/jul/15/local/la-me-bell-salary-20100715.

9   Ibid.

10   Catherine Saillant and Jeff Gottlieb, "Huge checks won't end with Bell officials' ouster," July 22, 2010. Retrieved from http://articles.latimes.com/2010/jul/22/local/la-me-0722-bell-pension-20100722.

11   Jeff Gottlieb, "Pensions for Rizzo, 40 other Bell employees will be larger than estimated." September 30, 2010. Retrieved from: http://articles.latimes.com/2010/sep/30/local/la-me-rizzo-pensions-20100930.

12   Eric Boehm, "California's six-figure pension club." Reason Magazine. https://reason.com/blog/2017/10/23/californias-six-figure-pension-club-2016. October 23, 2017.

13   Op. cit

14   Richard Winton, Jeff Gottlieb, Andrew Blankstein, L.A. County D.A. expands probe into Bell government. *L.A. Times* July 28, 2010. Retrieved from: http://articles.latimes.com/2010/jul/28/local/la-me-bell-elections-20100728

15   John Chiang, City of Bell, Audit Report, Administrative and Internal Accounting Controls, July 1, 2008, through June 30, 2010. Letter to Pedro Carrillo, Interim City Administrator. Retrieved from: https://sco.ca.gov/Press-Releases/2010/sco_bell_audit_2010.pdf

16   Also see, John Chiang, City of Bell, Audit Report, Special Gas Tax Street Improvement Fund, July 1, 2006, through June 30, 2007, and Traffic Congestion Relief Fund Allocations, July 1, 2000, through June 30, 2007. Also see, John Chiang,

City of Bell, Audit Report, State and Federal Expenditures, July 1, 2008, through August 31, 2010, and City of Bell, Audit Report, Special Gas Tax Street Improvement Fund, July 1, 2006, through June 30, 2007, and Traffic Congestion Relief Fund Allocations, July 1, 2000, through June 30, 2007. Retrieved from: https://sco.ca.gov/Press-Releases/2010/sco_bell_audit_2010.pdf

17   John Chiang, City of Bell, Audit Report, Administrative and Internal Accounting Controls, July1, 2008, through June 30, 2010, p .8. Retrieved from: https://sco.ca.gov/Press-Releases/2010/sco_bell_audit_2010.pdf

18   Ibid. p. 6

19   Ibid. p. 7.

20   In *Miranda v. Cornelius*, Oregon, the Ninth District Appellate Court ruled that an officer must have a compelling reason related to the care of the community to impound someone's car. Retrieved from: http://caselaw.findlaw.com/us-9th-circuit/1075130.html.

21   Interview with James Corcoran. See Paloma Esquivel, "Impounded cars boost Bell's coffers" *L.A. Times.* September 05, 2010. Retrieved from: http://articles.latimes.com/2010/sep/05/local/la-me-bell-impounds-20100906.

22   Ibid,

23   Robert J. Lopez and Paloma Esquivel, Bell Collected Hefty Fines in Numerous Code-Enforcement Cases. December 16, 2010, *L.A. Times.* Retrieved from: http://articles.latimes.com/2010/dec/16/local/la-me-bell-code-enforcement-20101216.

24   Ibid.

25   Ibid.

26   Ibid.

27   Interview with James Corcoran.

28   Paloma Esquivel and Robert J. Lopez, "Money missing after suspect redevelopment deal in Bell," *L.A.Times*, March 24, 2011. Retrieved August 3, 2015, from http://articles.latimes.com/2011/mar/24/local/la-me-03-24-bell-car-wash-20110324.

29   Robert J. Lopez and Paloma Esquivel, "D.A. investigates Bell's business fees," *L.A. Times*, November 6, 2010. Retrieved August 3, 2015, from http://articles.latimes.com/2010/nov/06/local/la-me-bell-fees-20101106.

30   Ibid.

31   Ibid.

32   The ballot measure read: "Shall the City of Bell develop the Bell Sports Complex to include a gymnasium for indoor soccer, basketball, cheerleading and a baseball facility; expand the Bell Community Center and other parks, recreational and

cultural facilities; construct a full service Bell Community Library, Performing Arts Theatre, public safety and civic facilities; and issue general obligation bonds not to exceed $70,000, to fund costs, to acquire, construct and improve these community service facilities?" John Chiang, City of Bell, Audit Report, Administrative and Internal Accounting Controls, July1, 2008, through June 30, 2010. Retrieved from: https://sco.ca.gov/Press-Releases/2010/sco_bell_audit_2010.pdf

33 John Chiang, City of Bell, Audit Report, Administrative and Internal Accounting Controls, July 1, 2008, through June 30, 2010. Retrieved from: https://sco.ca.gov/Press-Releases/2010/sco_bell_audit_2010.pdf

34 Ibid.

35 Ibid.

36 Proposition 218 (1996) requires that "no local government may impose, extend, or increase any general tax unless and until that tax is submitted to the electorate and approved by a majority vote." Article XIII, California Constitution.

37 John Chiang, City of Bell, Audit Report, Administrative and Internal Accounting Controls, July 1, 2008, through June 30, 2010. Retrieved from: https://sco.ca.gov/Press-Releases/2010/sco_bell_audit_2010.pdf

38 Ibid.

39 Doug Willmore, "City of Bell—Reformed and Reborn," paper presented at "The City of Bell Scandal Revisited," Chapman University, February 19, 2015.

40 Interview with Anthony Taylor, Esq. of Aleshire and Wynder, Bell's city attorney.

CHAPTER FIVE

We're Being Robbed: The Press Takes Notice

"A popular government without popular information or the means of acquiring it, is but a prologue to a farce or a tragedy or perhaps both."[1]

—James Madison

"Things got so bizarre that if someone had told me they had proof that Rizzo was sent to Earth by Martians to loot Bell, we would have had to investigate."[2]

—Jeff Gottlieb

RIZZO AND COMPANY might have bilked Bell for another decade or longer if it weren't for *L.A. Times* reporters Jeff Gottlieb and Ruben Vives. Their first story appeared on July 15, 2010, on the front page, above the fold, with a stunning headline—"Is A City Manager Worth $800,000?"—and an eye-popping graph showing Robert Rizzo's salary rising from $72,000 when he was hired in 1993 to an astonishing $800,000 in 2010. The *L.A. Times* later reported his total compensation—salary and benefits—was nearly $1.5 million a year. Over the next year, the *L.A. Times* published more than 100 Bell scandal stories, winning a Pulitzer Prize for public service.

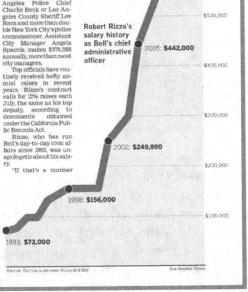

IS A CITY MANAGER WORTH $800,000?

Bell isn't a big town, or a wealthy one. But some of its top officials are paid two or three times as much as their counterparts elsewhere

JEFF GOTTLIEB
AND RUBEN VIVES

Bell, one of the poorest cities in Los Angeles County, pays its top officials some of the highest salaries in the nation, including nearly $800,000 annually for its city manager, according to documents reviewed by The Times.

In addition to the $787,637 salary of Chief Administrative Officer Robert Rizzo, Bell pays Police Chief Randy Adams $457,000 a year, about 50% more than Los Angeles Police Chief Charlie Beck or Los Angeles County Sheriff Lee Baca and more than double New York City's police commissioner. Assistant City Manager Angela Spaccia makes $376,288 annually, more than most city managers.

Top officials have routinely received hefty annual raises in recent years. Rizzo's contract calls for 12% raises each July, the same as his top deputy, according to documents obtained under the California Public Records Act.

Rizzo, who has run Bell's day-to-day civic affairs since 1993, was unapologetic about his salary.

"If that's a number people choke on, maybe I'm in the wrong business," he said. "I could go into private business and make that money. This council has compensated me for the job I've done."

Spaccia agreed, adding: "I would have to argue you get what you pay for."

Bell Mayor Oscar Hernandez defended the salaries. "Our city is one of the best in the area. That is the result of the city manager. It's not because I say it. It's because my community says it."

[See Bell, A23]

Robert Rizzo's salary history as Bell's chief administrative officer

2010: $787,637

2005: $442,000

2002: $249,990

1998: $156,000

1993: $72,000

$700,000
$600,000
$500,000
$400,000
$300,000
$200,000
$100,000

Source: Contracts between Rizzo and Bell

Los Angeles Times

FIGURE 5.1 Jeff Gottlieb and Ruben Vives, "Is a City Manager Worth $800,000?" Los Angeles Times. July 15, 2010. Retrieved from: http://articles.latimes.com/2010/jul/15/local/la-me-bell-salary-20100715

The framers of the Constitution anticipated a man like Robert Rizzo and fashioned the document accordingly. As James Madison famously wrote in Federalist No. 51, "But what is government itself, but the greatest of all reflections on human nature? If men were angels, no government would be necessary. If angels were to govern men, neither external nor internal controls on government would be necessary. In framing a government which is to be administered by men over men, the great difficulty lies in this: you must first enable the government to control the governed; and in the next place oblige it to control itself. A dependence on the people is, no doubt, the primary control on the government; *but experience has taught mankind the necessity of auxiliary precautions.*" [italics by author][3]

Paramount among those "auxiliary precautions" was a free press—the only industry with its own Constitutional amendment. The press was established to protect citizens from corrupt leaders and wayward policies. Acting as the people's representatives, a "watchdog" press is supposed to monitor government officials and their policies and "bark" when something is wrong. Citizens, in this view, would read the newspaper regularly and raise hell when they felt that government officials were serving themselves rather than the public good. They'd use the information they gathered from the press to question political leaders and make informed choices on election day.

Thomas Jefferson also understood the importance of the press to safeguarding democracy. In a letter to Edward Carrington, a fellow Virginia statesman, Jefferson wrote, "The basis or our governments being the opinion of the people, the very first object should be to keep that right; and were it left to me to decide whether we should have a government without newspapers or newspapers without a government, I should not hesitate a moment to prefer the latter. But I should mean that every man should receive those papers and be capable of reading them."[4]

Unfortunately, while the First Amendment safeguarded the press from government, no provision was made in the Constitution to ensure newspapers' financial survival. The 20th century solution was advertising. The press would be commercial enterprises that would connect consumers with businesses.

That solution worked until the Internet came on the scene in the 1990s, gutting advertising revenue. This caused newspapers to fold, merge, and drastically cut back staff. Even the illustrious *L.A. Times*, one of the nation's largest papers, was forced to lay off half its staff over the years following the decision by its new owner, the Tribune Company, to declare bankruptcy in 2008. The layoffs have continued. The *L.A. Times'* newsroom has shrunk from more than 1,000 in the late 1990s to fewer than 400 employees.[5]

"When I arrived at this newspaper 10 years ago, I was assigned to cover the city of Anaheim, and I went to every single city council meeting—I mean, that was part of my job," said Kimi Yoshino, the assistant city editor who helped to guide coverage of the Bell scandal. "[W]e don't have any reporters, with the exception of those covering Los Angeles city council, who go to every single council meeting anymore."[6]

In the early days of Bell, the *Industrial Post* (then the *Bell-Maywood-Cudahy Industrial Post*) covered the doings of the city government and organizations like the Chamber of Commerce and the Women's Club, and it was common to send a reporter to every meeting of the city council. But by the time Rizzo arrived on the scene, the press ranks had thinned considerably, and no outlet, large or small, was regularly covering Bell. Rizzo and company were able to rip off the people of Bell because the press wasn't watching. That changed, of course, in the summer of 2010 when Vives and Gottlieb started asking questions and demanding documents.[7]

The press can sound the "hue and cry," but it requires an informed and engaged public to bring about change. Such an attentive public was not present in Bell prior to the scandal becoming front page news.

JEFF GOTTLIEB

Jeff Gottlieb had been a reporter or editor for nearly 30 years when he was asked to help Ruben Vives cover Bell. He grew up in a middle-class Jewish home in North Hollywood. He had a stay-at-home mother who died of cancer when he was 15. His father graduated from UCLA and was a deputy probation officer. It was a bookish home; Gottlieb took cello lessons as a kid, and magazines like *Time* and *The Nation* adorned the coffee table.

TABLE 5.1 *US Newspaper Revenue, Circulation and Jobs*

YEAR	ADVERTISING REVENUE IN BILLIONS	CIRCULATION IN MILLIONS	NEWSROOM EMPLOYEES IN THOUSANDS
1990	32	62	—
2000	48	59	65 (2004)
2010	25	44	51
2016	18	34	41

Source: http://www.journalism.org/fact-sheet/newspapers.

Gottlieb went to Francis Polytechnic High School, a public school, and then to Pitzer college, a small, selective, liberal arts school in Claremont, California. He majored in sociology, was a disc-jockey for the college radio station, and played basketball during his freshman and sophomore years.

"At Pitzer I had my first exposure to kids who grew up in Big-Time money. I had a friend who lived in Beverly Hills and I remember going to his house for the weekend, and they had a tennis house that was bigger than our house. It had an original Picasso painting on the wall—of the tennis house!"

At Pitzer, he became obsessed with the Kennedy assassination. "It was clear the government was lying about the Kennedy assassination, just as they would later lie about the war in Vietnam and Watergate. The government lies. That is what I learned from these things," he said.

After graduation, he moved to Cambridge, Massachusetts to join a band of assassination buffs called the Assassination Information Bureau (AIB). He spent hours holed up in a small apartment discussing the CIA, assassinations, and conspiracy theories. The group paid the bills by giving lectures about the assassinations of JFK, RFK, and MLK on college campuses and by selling assassination paraphernalia. During this time he wrote several columns for magazines which appeared under AIB's byline. He realized that he liked writing and that he liked sticking it to the bad guys.

"I liked being able to tell stories, to do investigations, and to unravel and explain complex things." Gottlieb freelanced for several years, contributing articles to *The Nation*, *New West Magazine*, and *LA Weekly* before going to the Columbia Journalism School to get his master's degree. He co-authored articles about the civil suit against the Chicago Police Department for the wrongful death of Fred Hampton, the Black Panther leader. Another story focused on a ring of Los Angeles cops who spied on an anti-police-brutality group. He won the prestigious George Polk award for exposing overcharging by Stanford University for federal grants. His story led to congressional hearings and the resignation of Stanford's president.

"The Bell council salaries reminded me of a story I had written for the East Palo Alto Sanitary District when I worked for the *San Jose Mercury News*. East Palo Alto is one of the poorest cities in the Bay Area. It had the highest murder rate in the country. My story showed that the sanitary district spent more money on parties than it did repairing sewer lines, and its part-time directors traveled around the country at district expense, staying at fancy hotels and eating expensive meals. On top of that, the district had spent $1.8 million to build a new headquarters, the nicest building in the city, driving up its customer charges to the highest in the Bay Area. After my story appeared, one of its directors, a Harvard grad who had spent time at Stanford law school, was charged with theft," Gottlieb said.

RUBEN VIVES

Ruben Vives shared Gottlieb's commitment to justice and was equally fearless but came from a completely different world.

Vives was born in a small town in Guatemala. His parents migrated to Los Angeles when he was a year old, leaving him with his grandmother. When he was five, she and other relatives drove to the U.S. border where Vives crossed illegally, posing as his aunt's son. He was reunited with his parents, traumatizing the little boy who thought his grandparents were his parents.

During elementary and middle school, Vives lived in a small apartment in a gang-infested part of Los Angeles. His father was a machinist; his mother cleaned houses. When he was eight, his mother became pregnant with his little sister, and his parents divorced.

His mother told him, "You are the man now. You have to help out where you can."

His childhood was over.

Gangs tried to recruit him, but Vives refused. Rebuffed, they used him as a guinea pig to train kids how to rob people. At least a half-dozen times he was attacked—sometimes at gunpoint—on his way to public school. "I never carried any money or anything of value, just my books and my backpack," he said. "Soon, you learn the ropes around the neighborhood. You know where to go and who to hang out with, who to walk home with," he said.

After the Northridge earthquake (1994), he and his mother and little sister moved to Whittier where his mother cleaned the home of *L.A. Times* columnist and reporter Shawn Hubler.

Unlike Los Angeles Unified School District, where people of color are in the majority, his high school in Whittier was dominated by whites from middle-class and wealthy families.

"I didn't fit in with the whites who saw me as a dark-skinned Latino, and I didn't fit in with the Latinos who saw me hanging out with the gringos," he said.

Vives discovered his passion for writing in high school. "I remember that one of my teachers read my fiction essay to the class. I loved hearing her say the words I had written while people were listening. She said I had a future as a writer."

Hubler helped Vives get a summer job in the *L.A Times* newsroom as a copy boy who ran errands, fixed copy machines and delivered mail. The teenager worked hard and eventually landed a full-time job at the paper.

Things were tough at home. His mother, who suffered from schizophrenia, was in and out of hospitals and, as a result, the family was deeply in debt. "There were times when I'd get calls from the police or fire department saying we found your mom wandering around the street screaming," he said. Vives had to drop out of college in his junior year to take care of her and never finished his degree. "It was very hard. It was quite a struggle for me. I just kept telling myself that things would get better. Some days I believed that, and some days I didn't."

Meanwhile, Vives was moving up the ranks at the *Times*. His big break came in 2004 when the paper ran an investigation of the Martin Luther King, Jr. Drew Medical Center. Incompetent doctors and nurses, rather than saving lives, were killing poor people of color, most of whom only spoke Spanish, at an alarming rate. However, none of the reporters or editors assigned to the story spoke Spanish fluently. So, Vives was asked to translate. The series won a Pulitzer Prize for public service.

Vives' colleagues at the *L.A. Times* took note of this talented and hardworking young reporter who was now hooked on journalism. "We were sitting there and listening to these people tell their stories, and they were crying and showing us pictures of their loved ones who died. I loved the fact that reporters could expose wrongdoing and stand up for the little guy."

In 2008, the editors at the *L.A. Times* turned over a homicide blog—which chronicled stories about Los Angeles murder victims and their families—to Vives, who put his heart and soul into it.

In 2010, he was sent to the so-called "corridor of corruption" in southeast Los Angeles County. With his reporter's notebook and BlackBerry alongside him, Vives drove his blue Scion hatchback to Maywood, a 1.2 square mile city on Bell's north, and started talking to people and attending council meetings.

"Everyone started telling me that Maywood was corrupt, going broke, and falling apart. One of the rumors I heard was that the city was going to take the unprecedented step of disbanding its police department," he said.

Vives wrote a story about how the city's insurance carrier declined to renew its coverage due to excessive claims filed against the department, which forced city leaders to lay off all city employees, dismantle the police department, and to contract with the city of Bell to handle core administrative services.[8] Bell's Assistant City Manager Angela Spaccia had been serving as Maywood's interim city manager for several months before it decided to lay off every employee and dismantle the police department. She had been sent over by Rizzo. Maywood's city hall is less than a mile away from Bell's. Vives' editor, Shelby Grad, sent Gottlieb to help. This was the first time they had met. "This was a story about Maywood laying off nearly all its employees. This was not supposed to be some investigative saga, but a one-day story," Gottlieb said.

As Vives and Gottlieb wrote stories about Maywood, they started hearing rumors about excessive salaries earned by Bell City Council members and about investigations into public corruption being conducted by the Los Angeles County District Attorney's Public Integrity Division (PID). Gottlieb called Dave Demerjian, the head of the PID.

The PID was established by L.A. District Attorney Steve Cooley in 2001 in response to the rampant corruption in local government. The PID was charged with investigating misconduct by elected or appointed officials or public entities. The PID has prosecuted public officials from Vernon, Lynwood, Bell Gardens, South Gate, and other public entities throughout Los Angeles County. The office had a staff of eight attorneys, including Max Huntsman, Ed Miller, and Sean Hassett—the attorneys who would go on to prosecute the Bell case.

Gottlieb first asked Demerjian about Maywood. Demerjian said the PID had backed off Maywood because other agencies were already investigating. Gottlieb then asked, "What about Bell?" Demerjian said his office had received a complaint that council members were being paid nearly $100,000 a year for their part-time jobs.[9] According to state law, he said, the council members should be making $4,800 a year.[10] The complaint letter, dated May 6, 2009, was sent by then Councilman Victor

Bello, a phone jack installer, who left the council but continued to receive his $100,000 salary for working at a city-run food bank, a job which was arranged by Rizzo. Bello had made at least two other complaints about Bell council members, one of them as far back as October 2006.

The PID also heard from James Corcoran, a 19-year police veteran. In 2009, Corcoran alleged that Bell elected "officials might have engaged in voter fraud, unlawful vehicle seizures and illegal selling of building permits."[11] He first took his corruptions allegations to his boss, Bell Police Chief Randy Adams. But Adams became furious and forced him to retire. Corcoran later sued the city. He won $400,000 was reinstated into the department. [12]

The PID wrote Bell asking for a justification for the over-the-top councilmember salaries. The city responded that as a charter city they could pay themselves whatever they wished. Gottlieb and Vives wrote a story about the over-the-top council salaries and the city's response.

A few days after the story appeared, the two reporters went to city hall—a modest, one-story brick building built in the late 1950s—to ask for contracts and minutes to see what types of work the council members were doing to justify these high salaries.

The first thing they did was ask to speak to Rizzo. Instead, Rizzo sent Rebecca Valdez, the city clerk, to speak to them. Valdez, who stood behind a laminate counter, was a Bell High School graduate and a former intern who owed her $75,000 job—a very good salary in Bell—to Rizzo, who hired, groomed, and promoted her.

Valdez said she was too busy to make copies of the requested documents and asked Gottlieb to fill out a form. She told him he'd have to wait 10 days. Gottlieb filled out the forms and asked for a copy. Valdez charged him a buck for each. In the meantime, the reporters asked if they could simply *view* the documents, but Valdez said she was too busy.

These were red flags for the two reporters. They threw each other a knowing glance: "She's hiding something," they said to themselves.

"Valdez was being very bureaucratic. She should have walked to the files, pulled out the records we had requested, handed them to us, and said, 'Knock yourselves out.' It might have taken her 10 minutes," Gottlieb said.

Gottlieb and Vives then asked to talk with Rizzo, but Rizzo—whose office was a mere 15 feet from where they were standing—refused to meet with them. More red flags went up. "It's not every day that two reporters from the *L.A. Times* show up in Bell's city hall," said Gottlieb.

Valdez's stonewalling angered Gottlieb. He stared at her from across the counter and barked, "We want the city manager's contract; we want the city attorney's contract; we want everyone's contract."

In a subsequent phone conversation Gottlieb had with Valdez, he said he wanted to see Valdez's contract. "We want to know how much you make," he said.

Up until this point no one was asking questions about administrative salaries, which would now become the focal point of their coverage.

CALIFORNIA PUBLIC RECORDS REQUEST ACT

Gottlieb knew that reporters, who represent the public, had a right to these documents. The legislature passed the California Public Records Request Act (CPRA) in 1968 to ensure transparency and accountability in government. He also told Valdez if she didn't turn over the documents, the *L.A. Times* would sue, and the city would have to pay all court costs and legal fees when it lost, another proviso of the CPRA. "We walked out of city hall thinking something was wrong here," Gottlieb said, "They were making it too difficult to get simple records."

The reporters spoke with several residents, among them city hall watchers Nestor Valencia, Cristina Garcia, and Ali Saleh.

Garcia and Saleh would later found BASTA, the group that forced Rizzo and Spaccia to resign and lead the recall against the city council.

"No one could provide evidence or put his or her arms around it, but it was clear something was wrong. People kept telling me Rizzo made a lot of money. How much? I'd ask. The highest I heard was $300,000 to $400,000, close to double what you'd expect he would be paid," Gottlieb said.

Nine days after they made their public records request, Gottlieb got a phone call from Valdez saying that Rizzo wanted to meet with him and Vives. To his surprise, Rizzo wanted the meeting to take place at a local children's park, not city hall.

LITTLE BEAR PARK MEETING

Little Bear Park is a popular children's park in the middle of Bell, across from an elementary school and adjacent to a grocery store owned by then-Mayor Oscar Hernandez. Hernandez was the original owner of the Little Bear Park property—until he sold the property to the city for an inflated price determined by Rizzo.

Gottlieb and Vives arrived at the park in separate cars. The streetwise Vives, who dodged gangs as a kid, felt something was wrong. "Why were we meeting him in a park rather than city hall?" he asked. "I had heard stories about people being threatened and followed if you messed with the wrong people. For instance, in Cudahy, I was told gang members would threaten people if they supported candidates that weren't incumbents. There were Molotov cocktails thrown at one of the candidates. In Huntington Park, I was told of a candidate who was approached by two men and told not to run for office, or else. In South Gate, Henry Gonzalez, a councilman, had been shot in the head. It was unclear if it was related to politics, but he wasn't well liked by the political machine that was being accused of corruption. At the park, I wasn't worried about it. I was a reporter and didn't think anyone could harm me. But my imagination ran wild when

I got to the parking lot. I started thinking of the what ifs. One of them being what if a white van pulls up and someone forces me into it and takes me somewhere else."

Vives wrote down the make and models of the cars and their license plates of the cars next to his. He ripped out the piece of paper from his notebook and placed it under the passenger's seat. "I hadn't told anyone in the office where I was going, and I presumed if anything happened to us, those license plate numbers would be found by those who searched my car and this would lead them to my kidnappers."

The meeting took place in the park's high-ceilinged, hunting lodge themed community center which had a large stone fireplace surrounded by American and Cub Scout flags. The reporters thought they were just going to meet with Rizzo, but there were nine people there. They'd been summoned by Rizzo to appear. "Rizzo was obviously trying to intimidate us," Gottlieb said.

They took seats at a 10-foot rectangular-shaped table. Gottlieb sat in the middle. To his right were City Clerk Rebecca Valdez, Police Chief Randy Adams, Tom Brown, a consulting attorney, Rizzo; Angela Spaccia, the assistant city manager, Mayor Oscar Hernandez, councilmember Luis Artiga; Pedro Carrillo, a consultant who would become interim city manager following Rizzo's resignation; Ed Lee, who was the city's attorney, and, finally, Vives. Many of the requested documents were stacked neatly in the middle of the table.

Gottlieb, the seasoned veteran, took the lead and started asking questions. Both reporters furiously scribbled notes. Vives occasionally asked follow-up questions when something needed to be clarified.

Since they had already written about the council salaries, Gottlieb started off with softballs to loosen people up, asking Artiga and Hernandez if they made as much money in their day jobs as they did from their council salaries. Hernandez, who owned a small grocery store next to the park, smiled and said he did. Artiga, pastor of the Bell Community Church, said, "No way."

Rizzo jumped in, trying to justify the salaries, saying council members have no staff and pay their own travel to conferences and expenses. "Look at West Hollywood," he said, "each councilmember has a staff member, phone, car, discretionary fund. Add all these up, they're probably going to come to the same number [as Bell]," Rizzo said, according to Gottlieb.

Then Gottlieb, to Vives' surprise—since they were there to talk about council salaries—turned to Rizzo, who was seated about 10 feet from Gottlieb, and asked the pivotal question:

"So, Bob, how much do you make?"

"$700,000," Rizzo said sheepishly.

Gottlieb was taken back by the amount, so he leaned in and asked again to be sure he got it right.

"How much?"

"$700,000," Rizzo responded in a raised voice.

Vives quietly exclaimed, "Jesus Christ."

Both Vives and Gottlieb knew that this was an outrageous number and would be a major story. Others, such as Bell's Attorney Ed Lee, did too.

"I'll bet you're the highest paid city manager in L.A. County?" Gottlieb asked.

"I don't doubt it," Rizzo replied, looking down at the table. "If that's a number people choke on, maybe I'm in the wrong business. I could go into private business and make that money. This council has compensated me for the job I've done."

Mayor Oscar Hernandez jumped to Rizzo's defense. "Our city is one of the best in the area," he said. "That is the result of the city manager. It's not because I say it. It's because my community says it."

Gottlieb then turned to Police Chief Randy Adams, who had retired as chief in Glendale, with a population of nearly 200,000, and taken the job in Bell a week later. "How much do you make?"

"$457,000," Adams replied, which was 50% more than L.A.'s police chief, who oversaw a department of 10,000 officers.

"How much did you make in Glendale?"
"About $245,000, $250,000."

Then Gottlieb turned to Angela Spaccia, Rizzo's number two.

"How much do you make?"
"I don't know," she replied.

Vives felt this was an astonishing answer. "Everyone knows what they make," Vives said.

"What do you mean?" Vives asked. "How can you not know what you make?"
Spaccia hemmed and hawed. Rizzo stepped in. "She makes about $315,000," he said.

Nearly everyone around the table began justifying the salaries, including future defendants Hernandez, Artiga, and Spaccia.

Hernandez said that when Rizzo became city manager in 1993, Bell was nearly bankrupt, and Rizzo had brought financial security. The streets were clean, and the parks were the nicest in the area.

"This is a 24-hour-a-day job. I'm always going to people's houses at three in the morning," Artiga said.

"I would argue you get what you pay for," Spaccia said.

Adams said he used his own car and that he had paid for his office furniture. How much was the furniture?
"$6,000" Adams replied.

The two attorneys—Ed Lee and Tom Brown—stayed quiet for the entire meeting, which lasted four hours, ending at 5 p.m. "I really thought the attorneys would jump in and say, 'you don't have to answer this,' but they never did," Vives said. "We went over to Tom Brown and said we didn't have to have a meeting if they had just given us the documents. Brown said he told Rizzo he had to turn them over but also said, "I told Bob and the others this will all blow over in a few days."

"We nodded, but I am thinking, you are so wrong," Vives said.

Gottlieb and Vives left with the pile of documents they had requested from Valdez. They went back to city hall the following Monday to get more.[13]

Over the next few days, they reviewed contracts and minutes and calculated that Rizzo was making $787,637, which included an astonishing 12% guaranteed minimum annual raise, which was far more than the $700,000 he had told them. Gottlieb called Rizzo and told him what they had discovered.

"Bob, tell me where I'm wrong?" Gottlieb asked.

"You're a little high," he said, "but that's OK."

Then Rizzo told Gottlieb that he was going to Washington for a wedding that weekend. In fact, according to Gottlieb, he was going to his horse farm outside Seattle along with Brown, Hernandez, Artiga, and others for what the prosecutors would later call "The Jig is Up" meeting.

The story hit the *Times'* web edition July 14 during the evening and was in the print edition on Thursday, July 15, which is when all hell broke loose. "Is a city manager worth $800,000?" the front-page headline asked. This is when the world first heard of the Bell scandal.

Vives was then living with a roommate in a house in La Mirada, about 40 minutes from the *Times'* headquarters in downtown L.A. "It was around 5 a.m. and I was in my bed. My phone was on vibrate, and it keeps buzzing and buzzing and buzzing. And I am saying, what the hell is going on. I could see all these emails that were coming from across the country. People were furious," Vives said. "I knew it was a good story, but I never thought it was going to get this type of reaction. I got at least 100 emails."

"We were both flooded with emails and phone calls that ranged from congratulations to people wanting us to investigate their cities—in New Jersey, Connecticut and Kentucky. Editors across the country were sending their reporters to their city halls to find out how much local officials were earning," Gottlieb said.

Hernandez denounced the story and said the *Times* skewed the facts to advance the paper's own agenda.

Vives went back to Bell to cover the council meeting on Monday, July 19th. Bell's council chamber holds about 100 people. Only a handful of people attended most council meetings. Rizzo started council meetings at 6 p.m. rather than the more customary 7 p.m. This suppressed attendance since most people didn't get home from work until 6 p.m.

So, when Vives showed up at city hall that day, he was astonished to see dozens of television vans and all the parking spaces filled and hundreds of people gathered in front of city hall, many carrying signs and chanting in English and Spanish. Gottlieb came over after Vives asked his editor for help. Gottlieb and Vives got a hero's welcome.

"When I got there, I tried to make my way through the crowd and into the council chambers. By that time, Ruben and I had been in a video on the paper's website, and I was carrying a thin reporter's notebook in my hand, so people recognized me. It's not easy pushing through a group of angry people, but the crowd parted to let me through as if I was a celebrity. People were slapping me on the back, congratulating me, cheering, asking for autographs, and approaching me with tips," Gottlieb said.

The council chamber was packed. A long line of people waited for their chance to chew the council out. They yelled and screamed at them in English and Spanish, calling them scum and disgusting individuals. "I was surprised the mayor didn't break the gavel, he hit it so hard and so many times trying to restore order," Vives said. Rizzo, the focal point of the *L.A. Times'* story, didn't show up. The council retreated into closed-door session to negotiate the resignations of Rizzo, Spaccia and Adams, which would take place the following day.[14]

> "I was sitting at the front in the council chambers and Ali Saleh started chanting my name and the crowd joined in. 'Ruben, Ruben, Ruben' and they all started clapping.

I was uncomfortable, and I didn't really know what to do. I looked up, turned my body slightly to the crowd, smiled, and lifted my hand a little and waved slightly. It was awkward, but that to me was a moment in my career as a journalist I will never forget. It is a moment I cherish, deeply in my heart. Whenever I start to have doubts about journalism, I think about that moment, and I know what we are doing really matters," Vives said.

THE ROLE OF THE MEDIA IN DEMOCRACY

Democracy requires a stalwart media to provide citizens the information they need to make informed choices. The press also needs to be a "watchdog" that critically analyzes those in power and the policies they pursue and "barks" when something is amiss. Bell lacked such media coverage: Its last newspaper, the *Industrial Post*—a weekly which covered Bell, Maywood, and Cudahy—went out of business in 1985.[15] Many newspapers have been forced out of business due to steep declines in circulation and ad revenue. Newsroom budgets have been slashed, and reporters have been fired, with the result being there are not enough of them to cover the 88 cities in Los Angeles County, of which Bell is one.[16]

The city manager and council members were emboldened to take risks because when they looked out on the sparsely attended council meetings, they didn't see a single reporter. Had just one reporter been covering the meetings on a regular basis, many Bell watchers have suggested, the scandal could have been avoided.

LESSONS

The Bell scandal vividly demonstrates the vital role the press plays in democracy. The lesson here is that citizens must subscribe to local newspapers, and local newspapers must cover city hall.

Unfortunately, the legacy press (i.e., radio, television, and especially newspapers) has gone missing in many communities, and there's no certainty that an investigative team will swoop in and dig into a scandal or spread the word about community resistance to kleptocrats. But local websites, blogs, podcasts, newsletters, and even low-tech flyers can step in to fill the gap, publicizing meetings, sharing information, and providing vehicles for discussion.

ENDNOTES

1   James Madison, letter to W.T. Barry, August 4, 1822. Founding Father Quotes, #298: Retrieved from: http://www.foundingfatherquotes.com/quote/298.

2   Personal communication with Jeff Gottlieb.

3   "The Federalist Papers #51." Retrieved from http //fd.valenciacollege.edu/file/jhelligso/federalist.pdf.

4   Thomas Jefferson to Edward Carrington, 1787. Retrieved from https://famguardian.org/subjects/politics/thomasjefferson/jeff1600.htm.

5   Meg James And James Rufus Koren, "Billionaire Patrick Soon-Shiong close to deal to buy the *L.A. Times* and *San Diego Union-Tribune*," *Los Angeles Times*, February 6, 2018. Retrieved from http://www.latimes.com/business/hollywood/la-fi-ct-los-angeles-times-patrick-soon-shiong-20180206-story.html.

6   David Folkenflick, "How the L.A. Times Broke The Bell Corruption Story". Retrieved from http://www.npr.org/templates/story/story.php?storyId=130108851.

7   This chapter is based on extensive interviews with Jeff Gottlieb and Ruben Vives.

8   Ruben Vives, "Insurance agency pulls Maywood's coverage," *L.A Times*, June 6, 2010. Retrieved from http://articles.latimes.com/2010/jun/06/local/la-me-maywood-insurance-20100606.

9   Dan Whitcomb, "Mayor, officials arrested in California pay scandal" Reuters. September 21, 2010. Retrieved from: https://www.reuters.com/article/us-california-payscandal-arrests/mayor-officials-arrested-in-california-pay-scandal-idUSTRE68K40N20100921

10 Bell council members received $150 a month for attending city council meetings and $60 per month for sitting on the Redevelopment agency. They paid $1,574.65 per month for sitting on each of the other five boards which rarely met and did little work. See Jeff Gottlieb, Richard Winton and Ruben Vives, "Bell Council was

paid for boards that seldom met" *L.A. Times* August 25, 2010. Retrieved from: http://www.latimes.com/local/la-me-bell-meetings-20100825-story.html

11 Paul Pringle, "Former Bell police chief accused of quashing an internal investigation." *L.A. Times.* October 26, 2010. Retrieved from: http://articles.latimes.com/2010/oct/26/local/la-me-randy-adams-20101026

12 Jeff Gottlieb, "Sergeant who reported Bell corruption wins whistle-blower settlement." Retrieved from http://articles.latimes.com/2012/aug/04/local/la-me-0804-bell-whistleblower-20120804.

13 Vives said in a note on this manuscript, "We went back because the documents—minutes and agendas—were the originals. We couldn't take those so we went back to look over those documents in regard to the salaries of the council members. Jeff and I wanted to know what kind of work they were doing at the board meetings."

14 Jeff Gottlieb and Ruben Vives, "Three Bell leaders to quit in pay scandal" L.A. Times. July 23, 2010. Retrieved from: http://articles.latimes.com/2010/jul/23/local/la-me-bell-council-20100723

15 L. Garavaglia, "Bell, California, city government," Bell, CA: City of Bell. 1966.

16 "Newspaper Newsroom Workforce Continues to Drop," Pew Research Center, March 20, 2014. Retrieved from http://www.journalism.org/2014/03/26/the-growth-in-digital-reporting/newspaper-newsroom-workforce-continues-to-drop/.

CHAPTER SIX

A Community Rediscovers its Power: BASTA (Enough!)

"We are BASTA (the Bell Association to Stop the Abuse) ... Please join us in protesting these abuses by our city officials at Monday's Bell City Council meeting ..."

"Please join us. Help Stop the abuse!"[1]

—*BASTA flyer*

DESPITE HIS BEST efforts, Rizzo hadn't stamped out every facet of civic concern. As news of corruption in city hall began to trickle out, people became outraged. There was a small group of council watchers who were galvanized by the council reports. Some had previously been in city politics and some were newcomers, but all were children of immigrants or had been groomed within the community to take the reins when the opportunity arose. Their deeper stories are layered with insights for future activists about how to find and nurture talented political outsiders and build a base from which to take on entrenched kleptocracy.

Cristina Garcia knew instantly that the article—"Is A City Manager Worth $800,000?"—was the spark needed to mobilize the community.[2] The recall effort she helped start got a further jolt when city council members Teresa Jacobo, George Cole, George Mirabal, Victor Bello, Luis Artiga, and Oscar Hernandez were arrested two months after the *L.A. Times* city manager story came out and a judge ordered them not to come within 100 yards of Bell's city hall and not to participate in any community or governmental functions. Still, with one exception, the council, intent on holding on to their elected positions, refused to step down. It became obvious that a recall was the only way to remove them.

CRISTINA GARCIA

Garcia grew up in Bell Gardens, which borders Bell on its eastern side. The Long Beach Freeway (710) separates the two cities which are virtually indistinguishable from one another. Her parents had migrated here from Mexico, without documentation. After graduating from Bell Gardens High School, she studied math and political science at Pomona College and became a math teacher. She taught math for 13 years in middle school, high school, and community colleges in Los Angeles. She'd later be elected to the California legislature.

Like so many of its young people, including her four siblings, Garcia never expected to return home, but when she was 30, she had to move back to care for her aging parents. Garcia had a political calling from a young age. She followed local politics since she was in her early teens and organized city council candidate debates and town hall meetings on city issues while in high school.

Back in Bell Gardens, Garcia started attending council meetings and became infuriated by how council members were treating residents: "They were so condescending and rude to anyone that was there with any questions, a challenge, or concern. They'd call community members who spoke during the public comment period ignorant, obstructionist, and would embarrass them by repeating gossip about their personal lives. I kept asking myself, 'How much are we paying them to belittle us at council meetings?' Their sense of entitlement was appalling."[3]

Well educated, self-confident, and outspoken, Garcia didn't put up with the belittling. She soon started asking for salaries and budgets and other information, but Bell Gardens' attorneys refused to comply. She successfully sued under the California Public Records Request Act (CPRA) to get access to the information. Word got around in the Southeast—Bell and its surrounding cities—that Garcia was the "go-to person" if you needed to wrest information from an opaque and uncooperative city council. People in other communities began asking Garcia how to pry loose information from their cities. One of these people was Bell's Nestor Valencia.

NESTOR VALENCIA

Valencia, a fireplug of a man, was the "old timer "of the anti-Rizzo core group, who had started the Bell Residents Club (BRC), the only politically minded group in town, which had been asking for several years why taxes were so high in Bell and how the city was spending its money.

Valencia also grew up in Bell and graduated from Bell High School. Like Garcia, his parents were from Mexico and undocumented. He ran for city council in 2007 and in 2009, losing both times, butting up against George Cole, who had been on the council for more than two decades. Big and burly, Cole was a former steelworker and political shot caller. He was well known throughout the Southeast. Neither Cole nor Rizzo wanted the very independent and reform-minded Valencia on the council.

Like other residents, Valencia was certain something was wrong in Bell and started asking questions: How does a councilmember from a working-class community, where the median income was $30,000 a year, afford to drive around in a $100,000 Mercedes Benz—when his main source of income was a small corner market? Or, why did property taxes continue to increase but services continued to decline? And, why did so many Latino teenagers get pulled over and have their cars impounded for the slightest infractions, such as expired license tags or a broken tail light and then have to pay nearly $1,000 in fines and impound fees to get their cars back? Why were the council members so enamored with a part-time job that paid little money? Why were requests for salaries and budget information repeatedly denied by the city's attorney? And why was it so hard to get a straight answer from Rizzo or council members about how taxpayer money was being spent?[4]

Valencia asked Garcia to speak to the Bell Residents Club. Garcia, the bilingual math teacher, had a knack for explaining property tax bills to Spanish speakers, many of whom had little formal education, but knew full well that they were being ripped off and mistreated by city hall. Residents had concerns about their taxes, how the council was spending money, and the lack of transparency. What could they do, they wanted to know.

This was Garcia's first introduction to Bell politics. "I was intrigued to find others who were organizing their community around the same issues I was."[5]

ALI SALEH

In March of 2009, Garcia read a newspaper article about a Lebanese-Muslim Bell city council candidate, Ali Saleh, 35, who was being smeared by his opponents who alleged he had terrorist ties.[6]

Saleh's parents had emigrated from Yaroun, a village in southern Lebanon.[7] They came in the 1970s, attracted by the city's cheap housing prices, good weather, and proximity to downtown Los Angeles. The Lebanese-American community of approximately 2,000, which they helped found, kept to themselves and rarely got involved in the civic life of the community, especially politics.[8]

Saleh grew up in Bell and graduated from Bell High School in 1993. When Saleh, who runs a family clothing business, filed candidacy papers for a council seat in 2009, his phone rang with what he described as a warning from then-city-manager Robert Rizzo. "You don't have a chance," he recalled Rizzo saying.[9]

This attempt to discourage the candidacy of a citizen exercising his right to run for office is outrageous, and a flagrant violation of the council-manager form.

Rizzo was right. Saleh didn't have a much of a chance, while Rizzo was city manager. During his long reign as city boss, Rizzo mastered a stratagem to keep his people in power year after year. Council members resigned midterm, and he handpicked replacements who enjoyed the momentum of incumbency when elections rolled around.

Also during the campaign, a flyer emerged featuring Saleh's head superimposed on a figure holding a sign reading "Islam will dominate the world." The flyer featured photos of people with black hoods standing above a hostage, a radical cleric Muqtada al-Sadr, and the burning World Trade Center towers. The bottom of the flyer read, "Vote NO Muslims for the City Bell Council 2009."[10] Saleh lost the election, receiving only 442 votes, about 800 votes fewer than the Rizzo-backed winning candidates, incumbent real estate agent Teresa Jacobo (1332 votes) and newcomer pastor Luis Artiga (1201 votes) out of the 2,285 votes cast.[11]

"Right when I lost, I decided that, I would never run again. All I did was hurt the Lebanese community here," Saleh said.[12]

In early 2010, a few months before the *L.A Times'* city manager story ran, Garcia called Saleh hoping to hit him up for a campaign contribution for a friend. They met and realized they could learn a lot from each other. Part of Rizzo's strategy for defusing challenges to his authority had been to keep the community divided, flaming suspicions that pit Bell's Latino community against its small but vibrant Lebanese community; Garcia knew that it would take a united front to bring Rizzo down. She saw Saleh not only as an ally but as a potentially formidable political athlete in a fair race. Tall and movie star handsome, he was fluent in Arabic, English, and Spanish and was serious about helping Bell thrive.

THE TIME IS RIGHT

Garcia was convinced the Bell City Council needed to be recalled but she was cautious and hard-headed about how to proceed. She knew that virtually all recalls failed. They were expensive and time consuming, and volunteers soon got worn out. Moreover, should a recall fail, reform efforts could be set back years as incumbents point to the election results as evidence of community support.

She passed on two previous opportunities to launch a recall. The first came when the city proposed disbanding the police department. The Rizzo-backed plan was for Bell to join a new consolidated police department that would service Bell, the city of Maywood, which is on Bell's northern border and about the same size (40,000), and the city of Cudahy (24,000), which borders Bell on the south and is somewhat smaller. The new arrangement would save the city millions of dollars due to increased economies of scale. However, Bell's cops hated the plan, especially since they'd have to reapply for jobs in the new department.

The proposal shocked Bell's residents. Even though Bell's "for profit" police department had preyed on the community, the police department was popular due to its involvement in community activities and because many officers lived in the city.

Also, losing the police department—which accounts for the biggest chunk of the city's budget—would be a huge blow to civic pride. Most importantly, many feared giving up local control over officers who carried guns (legally) and could pull you over and put you in jail.

Valencia wanted to channel public anger over the plan to close the police department into his effort to topple Rizzo and recall the council. With the police union's financial support, the Bell Residents Club launched a recall. Valencia asked Garcia to help but she declined. She didn't think the timing was right and the issue big enough. She also doubted Valencia and the Bell police knew how to run a successful recall. Her political instincts were validated: The recall effort failed to get enough valid signatures to qualify for the ballot.

Garcia also didn't act when a few weeks later the *L.A. Times* reported that the Bell council members earned $100,000 a year for a part-time job. Residents were furious, but, again, Garcia felt the issue and the timing wasn't right.[13]

However, when the "$800,000" city manager salary story broke, and the community erupted, Garcia pounced. "This is it. We can run with this. This is a big enough story that we can use to mobilize the community," Garcia said. Her job was made easier when the story was picked up by English and Spanish local TV news programs.

She immediately called Leo Briones, a local political consultant who had done work for the Latino Caucus in the state assembly and who was committed to reform. They met that afternoon to discuss strategy. To start, she needed a list of every person in Bell who might be able to lend a hand.

Garcia and Saleh had heard about a Facebook page about corruption in Bell started by two young Bell residents—Denise Rodarte and Dale Walker—that was befriended by 500 residents. She called them up immediately, and they met the next day at a Starbucks in nearby Bell Gardens.

DENISE RODARTE

Rodarte, 30, also grew up in Bell. Her parents were from Mexico and had come into the U.S. without documentation in the 1970s. Her mother was a housewife, and her father sold odds and ends he picked up at garage sales and swap meets until he cobbled enough money together to open his own small business.

Rodarte graduated from Bell High and the University of LaVerne, with a degree in broadcast communications. She, her three brothers, aunts, and uncles lived in Bell. Rodarte's younger brother graduated from Pepperdine and became a police officer in the Bell Police Department. She heard about the plan to disband Bell's Police Department on the radio while driving to the vintage clothing store she owns in Echo Park, a densely populated neighborhood near downtown Los Angeles. She was so shocked by the news that she turned around and drove home. She called her brother and other family members and friends to find out what was going on.

Rodarte had never been to a city council meeting or been involved in politics (other than voting), but she couldn't wait to go to the next council meeting. "I was appalled at how citizens were being treated. The council was extremely arrogant. They had such a smug look on their faces. They were so cocky and so enthralled in their own power that even if 100 residents showed up to a council meeting, they were just going to do what they wanted to do. Government was supposed to be for the people and by the people. There is something wrong here. I just started to do more digging for myself and talking to people, and the more I learned, the more I was convinced that we needed to do something."[14]

DALE WALKER

Dale Walker, 28, found out about the city's plan to disband the police department from a "robo call" put out by the Police Officers' Association. Up to this news, he says he disliked politics. Walker's parents divorced when he was five years old, and he was raised by his mother who had crossed the border from Mexico without documentation. Walker's mother worked sporadically but received some form of public assistance most of the time he was growing up. He graduated from Bell High and then attended Cerritos Community College where he majored in political science.

Shy by nature, Walker was also enraged by how Bell residents were being treated by the city council when they objected to Rizzo's plan to disband the police department. "These were simple people, and the council was being so disrespectful to them. These were the people who raised me, and I couldn't believe how the council was acting toward them," he said. Walker and Rodarte met and exchanged contact information.

BASTA IS BORN

Within 48 hours after the "$800,000" story broke, BASTA was born, with Garcia, Saleh, Rodarte, and Walker at the helm. They were all first-generation bilingual Americans from working-class homes. Walker and Rodarte were political novices. Saleh had run for office but was still new to the game. Garcia was the ace.

They made several big decisions in their initial meetings. First, they decided to start a new group rather than join Valencia's group, the Bell Residents Club. Garcia and Saleh didn't get along with Valencia. They thought he was behind the terrorist "hit" piece against Saleh, and they didn't think he would be a good team player. Valencia accused BASTA of being a tool of the Bell Police Department. He was also upset with Garcia and Saleh for taking over the movement *he* had founded. The bottom line was that Valencia and Garcia both wanted to be in charge of the recall movement and neither was going to budge.

Second, the media-savvy Garcia wanted the group to have a compelling name. "Right away, I decided the name of our group was a big part of convincing people to support us. BASTA means 'enough!' in Spanish, but the translation loses the emotion behind the word. BASTA captured how fed up people were. We then created the acronym, 'Bell Association to Stop the Abuse.' For its mission, BASTA stated on its website, 'We are committed to the empowerment of our residents and stakeholders through honesty, respect, and integrity. We demand good governance through transparency and accountability while respecting the community's diversity,'"[15]

Finally, BASTA decided to join forces with the Bell Police Officer Association (POA). The POA gave $10,000[16] to BASTA to support the recall. BASTA agreed to fight against the disbanding of the police department.[17]

The four discussed high-tech tools for community organizing such as the need for a website, use of social media, and setting up a database to recruit and organize volunteers. But they also agreed to use low-tech flyers to mobilize the community.

THE FLYER RUNS

One of those low-tech tools was 8 x 10 inch black and white flyers, which BASTA distributed to the entire city. The first flyer (below) was a reprint of the *L.A. Times* front page "$800,000" story. Garcia convinced a friend to open his print shop at night after the first BASTA meeting and print 15,000 black and white copies. It read:

> "We are BASTA (the Bell Association to Stop the Abuse). A collection of Bell residents and the Bell Police Officers Association. Please join us in protesting these abuses by our city officials at Monday's Bell City Council meeting. We demand action from council members including: The immediate suspension of salaries for Bell City Manager, Bell City Council members, Bell Chief of Police. The establishment of a resident's committee to review and reestablish salaries at reasonable rates. The immediate suspension of any plans to establish a regional police department or contract City of Bell policing responsibilities to any outside entity until reforms are established."

And then, at the bottom, in bold, centered text:

"Please join us. Help Stop the abuse!"

BASTA members awoke at 3 a.m. and walked Bell's streets, placing a flyer on the front porch or front door at every house and apartment in the city. They finished as the sun was coming up. "This was the cheapest, most direct way to reach people. We needed to cover every single household, and no one is going to bother you at 3 a.m. We could move fast because there was no traffic, especially on the side streets where we could easily park and get around fast. Everyone was asleep, so we didn't have to talk to people, which eats up time," Rodarte explained.

There were more than 20 such flyer runs. As many as 80 BASTA people would go out in pairs flyering the city. "I would have my alarm set for two or three in the morning and get dressed, and I'd look in the mirror and say to myself I was nuts. My wife and family thought I was crazy, especially that I had promised them no more politics after I'd run for city council and got harassed. I would walk until 6 a.m. and then go to work and, man, I was exhausted! We did this at least 20 times, likely more. I just wanted to get these bums out of office," Saleh said.

The Rizzo Regime Continues to Haunt Bell Residents
Property Taxes Will Increase Once Again

Please join us for our next BASTA Community Meeting
Learn how and why your property taxes will go up and how the new council is working to stop any future increases

Wednesday, Sep 7 at 6:30pm -8:00pm • EPOCA 6624 Atlantic Ave, Bell

BASTA • 323-560-4654• Basta4bell.com• info@basta4bell.com

BASTA and Bell residents must continue to work together to ensure that the abuses we suffered from these dishonest and under-qualified leaders can never happen again. All BASTA members are unpaid volunteers.

We won't stop until good government is restored

FIGURE 6.1 BASTA Flyer

BASTA volunteers also communicated with residents by putting up large yard signs announcing BASTA and council meetings and by writing messages on car windows with a soap bar. Volunteers' cars were parked in high traffic areas where advertising signs would have been cost prohibitive. The messages were later washed off, and the windows were readied for another missive.

The first flyer was circulated Sunday night, the day after the first BASTA leadership meeting at Starbucks. The council met Monday, five days after the "$800,000" story broke and two days after BASTA was born. The council chambers, which seat about 100, were packed, and a long line of furious people waited for their chance to chew out their representatives, yelling at the "scum" and "disgusting individuals" who sat before them on the council dais. Hundreds more surrounded city hall carrying signs and chanting in English and Spanish. The crowd didn't simply show up in a spontaneous display of outrage; it had been organized in less than 48 hours. BASTA collected everybody's contact information and realized they would have to find a space for several hundred people to meet. They had no money, and Bell didn't have many large meeting rooms. Also, no one wanted to be associated with a controversial group that was trying to bring down the entire city government that was such an intimidating presence in the community.

The only place big enough in Bell was the Islamic Community Center, which Garcia hoped they could get for free and use whenever they wanted. Garcia wondered if Saleh could ask the Lebanese elders if they could use it. It was a bold but necessary move.

"In the aftermath of 9/11, Muslims in Southern California have at times been victims of bigotry, discrimination, and xenophobia. Often times people in the communities in which they settled didn't want them to build mosques, were afraid of them as possible sleeper cells of terrorism, and often protested at events they attended," writes professor and author Mike Moodian.[18] "So it is no surprise Bell's Lebanese Muslim community didn't want to call attention to themselves by providing a gathering place for a great American activist movement that was receiving world-wide media attention."[19] However, community elders were won over by Saleh who stressed how important it was for the Lebanese community not to be passive bystanders to corruption.

The Latino community—which held many of the same prejudices regarding Islam as the larger community—was also giving Garcia a hard time about meeting in the Islamic Center. "The Latinos said to me that they didn't want to meet there. I said, 'If you can find me a place that is just as big, has all these chairs, that has a public address system, and will open up whenever we want, I will move the community meetings, but in the meantime, this is all I have," Garcia said.

Saleh explained, "We didn't know how people would take to meeting in the Islamic Center. To my surprise, they were very receptive. I remember that at our first meeting, people came in kind of wondering what to expect, but all they saw were some empty walls, photos, and a little library of religious books along one wall. We had all these stackable chairs. At first, the people would look to me to put the chairs out, one by one, perhaps because they were a little uncomfortable touching something that didn't belong to them. After a while, I (or someone else) would open the door to the El Hussein Center, and they would walk in by themselves and start organizing the chairs like it was their own house, which was neat because you could see that they felt comfortable being there, and we were all working together. We had at one point 600 to 700 people at the El Hussein Center, and it was packed to the last chair. This is where BASTA came together."[20]

Over the next nine months, up to the recall election in March of 2011, BASTA met about twice a week at the center. Usually 300 to 400 attended the meetings, which started at six and often went past nine.

Garcia ran the initial meetings, and then Saleh, Rodarte, and Walker took over. Each spoke in both English and Spanish. They took a break every so often and translated what had been said. BASTA's leaders presented information, answered questions, and talked about current business and next steps.

People wanted to know what was going on: "Do we have all the facts? How much money are they taking? Can you explain my tax bill to me?"

Garcia set the agenda and the topics. She had an easel with notepads and she would break down people's tax bills and explain why their taxes were so high. Garcia's ability to explain math to non-English speakers came in handy during BASTA meetings when she had to tell them why Bell's property tax bills were among the highest tax rates in Los Angeles County. To raise money, BASTA volunteers sold tamales at the twice-weekly meetings in the El Hussein center. In deference to their Muslim hosts, the tamales were made without pork.

In time, BASTA realized they needed a single spokesperson lest they be defined by the angry and shouting residents who were hammering the council every chance they got and were popping up in news programs and being quoted in articles about the revolt. They selected Garcia to better control their message when dealing with the media.

THE RECALL

BASTA supporters packed the city council chambers and protested in front of city hall twice a week. Even after Rizzo, Spaccia, and Adams resigned, the council members continued to defend their high salaries and refused to step down. Then, tired of the heckling, the city council refused to meet, which prompted BASTA to launch a recall. "We made two-sided yard signs. One side said 'Resign,' the other, 'Recall.' We first had people display the 'Resign' side with the councilmember's name. When the councilmember refused to step down, we flipped them over to 'Recall,'" said Rodarte.

BASTA set up a small office on Gage Avenue, one of Bell's main thoroughfares. They filled the small office with four desks and donated computers. Volunteers made phone calls, checked signatures, went over walking lists, and did all the other things the recall required.

"We took whatever people were willing to give us," Garcia said.

RECALL HISTORY

The recall was one of the reforms enacted by the Progressives in 1911 to combat the power of the Southern Pacific Railroad. Citizens could remove elected officials before their term was over. Article 2, Section 13 of California's Constitution has a lot to say about how recalls are conducted, but it is silent about the criteria for removing an elected official prior to the end of his or her term.

Recalls rarely succeed.[21] Incumbents can fend off most recall attempts, arguing that they were elected to make tough choices. Recalls require a special election, which is expensive. It is difficult to maintain voter and media interest. Also, collecting enough valid signatures is a time-consuming and exacting process that typically requires the hiring of a specialist. Garcia hired Susan Burnside, a signature gathering expert, to run the recall.

The number of signatures required to force a special election depends on the number of registered voters. The number of signatures required is 10% of the registered voters for populations over 10,000. The percentage jumps to 25% if the number of registered voters is less than 10,000.

In Bell, there were about 9,200 registered voters which meant that BASTA would have had to collect about 2,500 valid signatures. BASTA decided to launch a voter registration drive and a signature gathering drive simultaneously to qualify for the lower percentage. BASTA boosted the number of registered voters over the threshold to 10,453. This meant they only needed 1,000 valid signatures for each councilmember they were trying to recall. They circulated four recall petitions—one each for Mayor Hernandez, and council members Teresa Jacobo and George Mirabal, as well as Luis Artiga, who quit the council in 2010, but remained targeted for recall.[22] Burnside worried that Artiga could later claim that he resigned for reasons unrelated to the scandal and then run for council in the future. She wanted the community on record regarding his tenure in office.[23]

To get 1,000 *valid* signatures, BASTA needed to collect far more than 4,000 signatures because many of the people who signed the petition weren't registered voters who lived in the city of Bell. This would cause the Registrar of Voters (ROV) to disqualify the signatures and potentially the entire petition.

The ROV does a random check of 25% of the signatures; if the threshold of qualified signatures is high enough, they proceed without checking all of them; if it is too low, the ROV will reject the petition or check each signature. BASTA checked every signature against the voter rolls every night and rejected those that didn't qualify. On each petition, residents had to *legibly* print

their full legal name and address and then sign, and this information had to square with the voter rolls.

Over four weeks, BASTA collected three times as many signatures needed, according to Burnside. While many people signed
all four petitions, others declined. BASTA's 80 trained volunteers were a cross section of Bell's residents: Latinos, Anglos,
and some Lebanese, young and old, fanned out across the city
collecting signatures. They also registered people who weren't
registered to vote.

BASTA didn't trust city hall and petitioned the city council
to pay the Los Angeles County Registrar of Voters to run the
election. The city and the county split the cost of the recall which
was somewhere between $75,000 and $100,000.

In addition to the coverage by the *L.A. Times* and other local
English and Spanish print outlets, local TV news programs
through the region featured stories about the citizen uprising in
this poor Los Angeles city. Bell stories also appeared in the *New
York Times*, *Wall Street Journal*, and in the national evening news
programs. "Bell" was also covered by media in Europe, Asia, and
Africa. BASTA was getting emails and faxes from the Ukraine,
Slovak Republic, Japan and Ethiopia from groups who wanted
to know how they could overthrow their "corrupt" governments.

During this time, BASTA also fought skirmishes with rivals.
The local Republican Party wanted to use the Bell scandal to
increase its influence in the Southeast. Its message was that
Bell's Democratic council was stealing residents' money and that
Republicans would be better stewards of tax dollars. BASTA
feared that the effort to turn the conflict into a partisan fight
could confuse voters and undermine the recall.

Valencia was deeply committed to seeing justice in Bell. It
took enormous courage for him to publicly challenge an abusive
and powerful city manager and his council cronies. However,
Valencia saw BASTA as a front for Bell's police department and
felt his Bell Residents Club was the true voice of the people. So,
he became a persistent critic of BASTA and its leaders.

There were also a throng of elected officials, fly-by-night
attorneys, and political consultants who wanted to bask in the

publicity the scandal was getting. In doing so, they diverted the media's attention from the recall. BASTA needed to keep the recall story in the news if they were going to be successful.

"The press was intrigued by the unusual coalition of Latinos and Muslims. One of the reasons we had weekly meetings at the El Hussein Center was to keep BASTA and the recall in the news," said Garcia.

Garcia knew she needed professional help. For legal advice, she turned to Orange County Attorney David Aleshire, whose firm, Aleshire and Wynder, specialized in local government law. Aleshire had contacted Garcia after he had seen her on TV and offered to help BASTA, pro bono. His firm would later be hired as the city's attorney and would help win back millions of dollars for the city.

The other professional, Burnside, the recall specialist, hired Arianne Garcia (no relation to Cristina Garcia) who helped train and manage the volunteers and checked the signatures when the petitions were turned in.

Each day for about four weeks, two dozen people arrived at BASTA's headquarters at 9 a.m. and then went door to door gathering signatures. Signature gatherers usually get paid for each valid signature they collect. But in Bell, they worked for free. "The people were so outraged that it only took us about 25 days to collect all of the signatures," said Burnside. Some even came to the office to sign the petitions. The anger fueled interest in the race. By the end of 2010, there were seventeen candidates running for the five seats on the council that would be vacated if the recall was successful.

The election took place on March 8, 2011. It was run by the county—not the city—because residents didn't trust the city to count the votes, especially since it was the entire council that was being recalled. Turnout was 37%, more than nearly triple Bell's typical turnout. There were four polling sites, and the *L.A. Times* reported that they had lines with as many as a hundred people in them.

When the votes were counted, 90% of the voters voted to recall the entire city council. This included Mayor Oscar Hernandez and council members Teresa Jacobo, Luis Artiga, and George Mirabal. Also recalled was Pastor Luis Artiga, who had quit the council the previous year but remained targeted for recall. Lorenzo Velez, the only councilman not charged in the Bell corruption case, ran for reelection but was defeated. Jacobo's vacated seat was won by Danny Harber. Artiga's vacated seat was won by Ana Maria Quintana. Ali Saleh, Nestor Valencia, and Violeta Alvarez won the other three seats on the city council.[24]

Not long after, Garcia would announce that she was leaving BASTA. The following year, she was elected to the California State Assembly despite being outspent four to one. Valencia and Saleh would remain on the council and would each serve as Bell's mayor. Walker left Bell and took a job in the entertainment industry in Los Angeles, and Rodarte continues to run her vintage clothing store in Echo Park.

LESSONS

What can BASTA teach activists? Local movements require politically savvy leaders but not necessarily a lot of money.

Garcia and Saleh took the lead in developing tactics for mobilizing a "get the bums out" effort. In addition to choosing a catchy name—BASTA (enough! in Spanish)—that residents and the media found appealing, the pragmatic, cash-strapped organizers used decidedly low-tech techniques to rally Bell's citizens. They distributed 8 × 10 black and white flyers publicizing the *Times'* corruption stories and announcing meetings, waking at 3 a.m. and walking Bell's streets to place a flyer on the front porch or front door of every house and apartment in the city. BASTA volunteers put up large yard signs announcing meetings of BASTA and the city council and wrote messages with soap bars on the windows of cars, which they parked in high traffic areas where advertising signs would have been cost prohibitive. One BASTA organizer drew interest with a Facebook page, but it was the group's inescapable, low-tech presence that gave the movement traction.

- BASTA successfully built a political movement from the *L.A. Times* city manager story. They understood the importance of timing. They had the entire city flyered before the first city council meeting.
- BASTA built a huge volunteer base of ordinary people and gave them something to do. The recall effort required personal sacrifice and significant effort. In addition to going to meetings, all were involved in taking action (i.e., the 3 a.m. flyer runs, gathering signatures, making signs, registering people to vote, and ensuring that they did.)
- BASTA's leaders turned to professional advisors for legal and tactical advice to ensure the recall was successful.
- They kept the struggle in the news through careful management of the media.
- They presented a united front by building familiarity and trust between an unlikely coalition of Latinos and Lebanese.
- They stayed clear of partisan competition and stayed focused on their main objective: the recall.
- They did all they could to heal divisions among the resistance factions (i.e., the Bell Residents Club).

Their efforts paid off. The recall was successful, and this cohort of first-generation Americans took the helm of their government.

ENDNOTES

1   BASTA flyer.
2   Jeff Gottlieb and Ruben Vives, "Is A City Manager Worth $800,000?" *L.A. Times.* July 15, 2010. Retrieved from http://articles.latimes.com/2010/jul/15/local/la-me-bell-salary-20100715.
3   Interview with Cristina Garcia.
4   Interview with Nestor Valencia.

5   Cristina Garcia, "Building BASTA," paper delivered at the City of Bell Scandal Revisited, Chapman University, February 19, 2015.

6   Hector Becerra, "Campaigns in Bell and Cudahy Get Ugly," *L.A. Times*. March 5, 2009, para. 4. Retrieved from: http://articles.latimes.com/2009/mar/05/local/me-southeast5.

7   Mike Moodian, "Unity Through Crisis: How a Latino and Lebanese American Coalition Helped Save Democracy in the City of Bell," paper presented at the City of Bell Scandal Revisited, Chapman University, February 19, 2015. Retrieved from http://digitalcommons.chapman.edu/cgi/viewcontent.cgi?article=1203&context=localgovernmentreconsidered.

8   Tammy Audi, "In One City, an Islamic Center Unifies," *Wall Street Journal*. September 20, 2010. See, http://www.wsj.com/articles/SB10001424052748704644404575482001778588866.

9   Personal interview with Ali Saleh.

10 Hector Becerra, "Campaigns in Bell and Cudahy Get Ugly," *L.A. Times*. March 5, 2009. Retrieved from: http://articles.latimes.com/2009/mar/05/local/me-southeast5.

11 City of Bell Resolution 2009-07. Exhibit "A" City Clerk Certificate of Canvas. March 16, 2009. Email from Bell City Clerk, Angela Bustamante.

12 Ali Saleh, personal communication with Mike Moodian, as cited in "Unity Through Crisis: How a Latino and Lebanese American Coalition Helped Save Democracy in the City of Bell" delivered at City of Bell Scandal Revisited, Chapman University, February 19, 2015.

13 Jeff Gottlieb and Ruben Vives, "DA investigating why Bell council members get nearly $100,000 a year for a part-time job." Jun 24, 2010. *L.A. Times*. Retrieved from: http://articles.latimes.com/2010/jun/24/local/la-me-0624-maywood-20100624

14 Denise Rodarte, personal communication.

15 See, http://basta4bell.com/about/. Retrieved April 18, 2016.

16 Interview with Cristina Garcia.

17 Nestor Valencia personal communication February 5, 2015. See, Cornia Knoll, "Bell residents question city's grass-roots organization, *L.A. Times*. September 18, 2010. Retrieved from: http://articles.latimes.com/2010/sep/18/local/la-me-basta-20100918.

18 Mike Moodian, "Unity Through Crisis: How a Latino and Lebanese American Coalition Helped Save Democracy in the City of Bell," paper presented

at the City of Bell Scandal Revisited, Chapman University, February 19, 2015. Retrieved from http://digitalcommons.chapman.edu/cgi/viewcontent. cgi?article=1203&context=localgovernmentreconsidered.

19 Ibid.

20 Ali Saleh, personal communication.

21 John Myers, "Political Road Map: Just 3% of California recall elections actually work. They have one thing in common." *L.A. Times.* October 15, 2017. Retrieved from: http://www.latimes.com/politics/la-pol-ca-road-map-recall-elections-california-20171015-story.html

22 Christopher Goffard and Paloma Esquivel, "Bell voters cast out the old and opt for the new," *L.A. Times*, March 9, 2011. Retrieved from http://articles.latimes.com/2011/mar/09/local/la-me-bell-elections-20110308.

23 Ibid.

24 Ibid.

CREDIT

- Fig. 6.1: Copyright © by BASTA. Reprinted with permission.

CHAPTER SEVEN

Complicit Dupes: The City Council Trial

"These people were crooks; they belonged in prison."

—BASTA co-founder, Ali Saleh[1]

"Council members were either part of the scam or too dumb to realize Rizzo worked for them, not the other way around."

—Jeff Gottlieb[2]

THE *L.A. TIMES'* stories not only set off the recall effort but they sparked a series of investigations by at least ten agencies:

- The U.S. Department of Justice investigated whether Bell police violated the civil rights of residents through aggressive towing of cars and code enforcement.[3]
- The California Department of Corporations investigated various grants the city had received.
- The FBI considered public corruption charges including voter fraud.
- The IRS examined Rizzo's taxes.
- The U.S. Security and Exchange Commission investigated the $100 million-dollar bond sale.

- The California Attorney General's office explored municipal corruption charges.
- The State Controller's Office audited the city's books.
- CalPERS (the state retirement fund) reviewed Rizzo's and Spaccia's outrageous pensions.
- The bond-rating agencies wanted to know how risky it was to loan the nearly bankrupt city money.
- And the Los Angeles District Attorney's Office compiled criminal charges.

It is important to note that up until this time, NO ONE had seriously looked at Bell in a sustained way for years. Now everyone was.

The most important of these investigations was the criminal case brought by the Los Angeles District Attorney, Steve Cooley.

In early September 2010, the DA filed a criminal complaint with the Los Angeles Superior Court that alleged that city officials had stolen $5.5 million from Bell's blue-collar residents. Of this amount, his complaint argued, $1.3 million was stolen by the council for serving on four Bell boards that did little, if any, work but paid council members extravagantly. "We're alleging they used tax dollars collected from the hard-working citizens of Bell as their own piggy bank," Cooley said. "This is corruption on steroids."[4]

Bell residents wanted the court to hand down stiff prison sentences for Rizzo and company. They also wanted them to pay back all the money they had stolen. They expected an open-and-shut case. But they were mistaken. They soon learned that it wasn't going to be easy. This became apparent during the trial. Unlike the recall, which was over in a mere nine months, the judicial process went on for years. Also, it became evident that what was seen as ethically wrong may not have been illegal. This led to frustration and tears by the Bell residents. The legal process in such cases demands patience and stamina and a thick skin since huge disappointments and reversals are inevitable.

On September 21, 2010, in an early morning raid, about 40 armed investigators fanned out across the city and arrested and hauled off to jail Robert Rizzo, Angela Spaccia, and city council members Teresa Jacobo, George Cole, George Mirabal, Victor Bello, Luis Artiga, and Oscar Hernandez. The city council "Bell Six" went on trial in January 2013. Rizzo and Spaccia went on trial later that year.

Teresa Jacobo

Barely five-feet tall, Jacobo, 60, was still in her pajamas cooking breakfast when four cruisers pulled up in front of her house. Five police officers came to her door. They cuffed her in front of her husband and, while neighbors watched, took her to one of the cars parked across the street from her modest home. "It was humiliating. They wouldn't even let me change out of my pajamas or put on a jacket or take my blood pressure medication," she said.[5] She was confused and disoriented. She had worked so hard, struggled her whole life, and saw herself as a hardworking and dedicated public servant. "What is happening?" she asked herself.

Jacobo came to the United States from Mexico when she was a year old. She came with her father, who was then a farm laborer. She grew up in East Los Angeles, the daughter of a welder and a seamstress. When she was 14, she started spending her summers working in a garment factory. She didn't go to college after graduating from high school. "In my family, there was a lot of poverty and I had to work."[6]

After her first marriage didn't work out, she enrolled in a community college where she earned her Associate of Arts degree in accounting. She leased an apartment in Bell; the rents were cheap, and she was a single mother with two children. She married again, had two more children, became a real estate agent, and volunteered at Bell's public schools. Friendly and popular with parents, she was hired by the school district to run a parenting program. That is where she met long-time Councilman George Cole, who was also involved with the public schools. She soon became Cole's protégé and was appointed, with Rizzo's support, to the Bell City Council in 2000 and elected in 2001, as the only woman and the first woman in 22 years.

George Cole

George Cole, a retired steelworker, was a member of the Bell City Council for 24 years. Cole was elected in 1984, at the age of 34, pledging to clean up city hall in the wake of the indictment and conviction of City Manager John Pitts and former Mayor and Councilman Pete Werrlein for accepting bribes and having a secret ownership interest in the California Bell Club. He served until October 2008 when he retired after a falling out with Rizzo and was replaced by Luis Artiga, a local pastor.

Cole had been active in the community and in local politics throughout the Southeast. The son of a minister and medical social worker, fluent in Spanish, he headed a nonprofit called the Steelworkers Oldtimers Foundation which provided more than 1,500 meals each day and other services to seniors throughout the Bell region.[7] Cole had a reputation as a wheeler-dealer and "go-to" guy for local government issues. He was an advocate for Bell's schools, at-risk youth, the immigrant community, and the elderly. Cole had a mini-stroke and a massive heart attack in 2005 but returned to the council after recovering. He had been off the council for two years when he was arrested at his home, cuffed in front of his wife, and taken to the L.A. County Jail.

Oscar Hernandez

Police used a battering ram to knock down the front door of the home of Mayor Oscar Hernandez, 65.[8] Judge Kathleen Kennedy, who presided over the Bell trials, said he exemplified the American dream. He left school after the sixth grade in Mexico and came to the United States when he was a teenager. He was an agriculture worker at first, then, took a job in a foundry. He then married and had four children. In 1980, he purchased a small grocery store in Bell.[9] The city later purchased land he owned adjacent to his store to build Little Bear Park. He also owned rental property in Bell.

Hernandez became a community activist when the city threatened to take his store through eminent domain. Charismatic and talkative, everyone referred to him by his first name, "Oscar." In 2002, at Rizzo's urging, he was appointed to the city council, replacing George Bass. He was elected to a four-year term in 2003. He served the city for eight years, including three times as mayor, a position rotated among the council. According to his lawyer, Stanley Friedman, Hernandez couldn't read or write English. Friedman said he wasn't scholarly, but was elected for his heart. Others, such as political activist and future mayor, Nestor Valencia, who saw Hernandez driving around Bell in a high-end Mercedes, suggested that the "dumb act" was a disguise. Shortly after being taken into custody, Hernandez, who originally was a staunch defender of Rizzo's $800,000 salary, confessed that he and other Bell council members had paid themselves huge salaries for sitting on boards that often never met.[10]

George Mirabal

George Mirabal's family ran funeral homes in Bell, and he was active in the community. Mirabal served on the council from 1986 to 1990 and then worked one year as Bell's clerk. In April 1993, Jay Price, a council stalwart who was first elected in 1958, died at the age of 78. Mirabal, 65, was appointed to finish his term. At the time he was appointed, all of the other council members were Anglo even though 86% of the city's residents were now Latino.[11] He was elected in 1994 and served until being recalled in 2011. He was considered one of the more thoughtful members of the council by city staff, according to trial testimony.

Victor Bello

Victor Bello was born in Cuba and arrived in the United States in 1987. His father had committed suicide. He was divorced, had two daughters, and shared a small apartment with his elderly mother, whom he cared for. Bello worked as a telephone jack installer, but was only sporadically employed. Bello had a language disorder and was on disability for mental health issues, including anxiety and depression. Bello was appointed to the council in 1997 and served until 2009, when he resigned. He served as mayor from 2002-2003. Bello often butted heads with Rizzo and his council colleagues, and starting in 2005, had been banned from city hall by Rizzo other than to attend council meetings.

Nearly a year before the scandal exploded, Victor Bello, 54, had written a letter to the D.A.'s office alleging corruption in Bell. Bello thought his letter would immediately set off an investigation of Rizzo. But when the investigators finally came around for interviews, Bello triggered an investigation of council salaries. Bello told PID investigators that he was still getting his councilman's salary—nearly $100,000 a year—while he was working for the city's food bank, a job Rizzo had created for him. This led Deputy District Attorney Dave Demerjian to subpoena payroll and other records. Rizzo stonewalled, but he eventually got the documents, and they revealed Bell's exorbitant salaries. Demerjian concluded that crimes had been committed but took no further action until the *L.A. Times'* city manager story came out in July 2010.

Bello was placed on a suicide watch shortly after being arrested. He stayed in jail for more than five months because he was unable to post a bond. Bello was the only defendant willing to plead guilty after the 2011 preliminary hearings and was ready to serve two years in state prison. The deal was rejected by the District Attorney's Office.[12]

Luis Artiga

Luis Artiga was a pastor at Bell Community Church. He'd emigrated from El Salvador in 1979 and was appointed by the council in October 2008, following George Cole's retirement. He was elected to the Bell City Council in March 2009 and resigned October 4, 2010, a month after he was arrested and five months before the recall. He was the council's newest member and most of the disputed decisions had taken place before he was on the council. Artiga said he thought the over-the-top salary he had received was a "gift from God."[13] He was the only one of the eight former city officials to be exonerated on all counts. He did not have to return any of the $130,000 he had received for his nearly two years on the council. He had not been on the council long enough to earn any retirement.

THE PRELIMINARY HEARING

Five months after their arrest, the Bell Six faced a preliminary hearing before Los Angeles Superior Court Judge Henry Hall.[14]

A preliminary hearing is a "minitrial" in which a judge determines if there is sufficient evidence that the defendant(s) committed the crime and, therefore, warrant a trial. The prosecutor presents witnesses and evidence, subject to cross-examination by the defense. There's no jury.

If there's probable cause a crime was committed, an arraignment in which the defendants would be required to be *"held to answer"* for specific charges is held. If there's not, the case is dismissed, and everyone goes home.

The preliminary hearing lasted seven days. Judge Hall said the evidence showed that the defendants violated their duty to provide honest and transparent governance. "The allegations are, in my estimation, appalling ... [T]hese people may not be involved in the running of that city in any way, shape, or form ... [They] are to stay at least 100 yards away from Bell city hall. They are not to participate in any community or governmental function relating to the city of Bell. [The defendants] have demonstrated that they cannot and will not act in a responsible way to protect the people of Bell."[15]

THE TRIAL

The trial began January 24, 2013. Judge Kathleen Kennedy presided over all the Bell trials. During her more than 25 years on the bench, she had faced rapists, drug dealers, and murderers. Her courtroom, Department No. 109, was on the ninth floor of the Clara Shortridge Foltz Criminal Justice Center in downtown Los Angeles right next to Judge Lance Ito's from the OJ Simpson trial.[16] She was described as tough but fair.[17]

Kennedy's courtroom looked like most of the other courtrooms in the building—purposeful, with high ceilings, fluorescent lights, and wood-paneled walls. There was a glass-walled holding cell for defendants, and there were marshals with guns. Clerks sat at desks piled high with stacks of manila files.

On this day in January, the defendants' family and friends, the press, and residents of Bell—mostly Latinos—filled the rows of seats behind a banister in the back. In front of the banister were the defendants and their lawyers, crowded around two tables. On the judge's left was a witness stand and jury box. There was a podium for the attorneys to address the court and a large monitor.

THE PROSECUTION

Deputy District Attorney Edward ("Ed") Miller was the lead prosecutor.[18] Miller grew up in the L.A. area and attended UCLA for his bachelor's and USC for his law degree. After graduating from law school and passing the bar, Miller took a job with the District Attorney's Office in 1986 after a friend from law school talked about how she loved working there. He figured he'd work there for a few years and then move on to private practice but became hooked. Miller moved over to the Public Integrity Division (PID) in 2008. He hated corrupt elected officials and knew that the Southeast had more than its share. "The public has a right to have honest public officials, and our office, by aggressively pursuing these matters, helps ensure that they do," he said.

GROUP PORTRAIT

At the council trial, the prosecution and the defense painted different portraits of the defendants. The defense said the defendants —a pastor, a former real estate agent, a steelworker, a telephone installer, a funeral director, and the owner of a mom and pop grocery store —were "bumbling bumpkins" who were manipulated by a strongman city manager. Only one was born in the United States, and only one had a four-year college degree. Spanish was the first language for all but Cole.[19]

The prosecution, on the other hand, said they were "sophisticated manipulators" who knew they were ripping off the people of Bell. Cole ran multiple nonprofit organizations. Jacobo was a real estate agent who had to pass a tough exam to get her license. The well-spoken and thoughtful Mirabal ran a funeral business and had served as city clerk for one year and councilmember for many years. Hernandez ran a business and rented out properties. Even the emotionally challenged Bello negotiated a good deal, retaining his nearly $100,000 council salary when he took a cushy job at a city food bank, unlike his co-workers who were volunteers.

The trial highlighted some of the qualities council members should have. An important quality of council members is that they should not be intimidated by people with more education or better social standing, such as staff, consultants, or developers.

The council that hired Rizzo consisted of a college administrator, a high school assistant principal, a fire chief, a federal bureaucrat, and a steelworker. The last three were retired and received generous pensions. They were all Anglo and native-born and held managerial positions in middle-to-large bureaucracies and were economically secure. Two held two masters degrees, and a third graduated from a local community college. As a group, they were not easily intimidated by Rizzo. Rolf Janssen, who left the council in 2003, said, "I found you had to be very direct with him or else he would take off on his own. He needed to know who ran the city."[20]

In contrast, the "scandal" council was ill-prepared to challenge Rizzo. All but one had emigrated from an impoverished country, and despite some success, all struggled financially at some point. Artiga escaped war-torn El Salvador with nothing and was a pastor to the poor. Hernandez picked crops as a teenager and now ran a small grocery store. Bello was mostly out of work and on public assistance. Before remarrying, Jacobo was a single mother with two children who came to Bell because the rent was cheap. Cole had earned blue-collar wages as a factory worker. Mirabal was slightly better off, running a mortuary.

They had limited formal education. Hernandez left school after the sixth grade and couldn't read or write English especially well. Bello, Artiga, and Cole's formal education ended at high school. Mirabal had an associate's degree in mortuary science. Jacobo earned her bachelor's degree online from a for-profit college while on the council. The monthly check, lifetime health insurance, and pension they received for serving on the council were irresistible.[21]

"The salary and benefits were a big draw," Jacobo said.[22] After serving only six years, she was slated to receive a lifetime pension of $57,000 per year.[23]

But more importantly, they lacked the confidence to assert themselves and question the doings of a person they perceived to be better-educated and of higher economic status, who owned a beautiful home by the ocean and a horse ranch in Washington. They willingly abdicated authority to Rizzo—The Wizard—a well respected, experienced city manager who appeared to know the law and municipal finance—in exchange for their $100,000-a-year salaries plus lucrative benefits.

In short, they needed the job and didn't care to push back against a very determined Rizzo. Those who challenged him were quickly shown the door. Bello, who was banished from city hall when he pushed back, said "He likes to be in control ... You don't talk back to him—that's the way it goes."[24]

Rizzo convinced the uncooperative Bello to leave the council by offering him a plum job at the food bank that paid him his council salary, $100,000. He went underground and challenged Rizzo by going to the district attorney, the press, and the FBI.

Cole was different. He had been on the council for more than two decades and was one of the people who'd hired Rizzo. He had a separate income from his steelworker's pension and from a private charity—the "Oldtimers"—he headed and was a seasoned veteran of Southeast's bare-fisted politics. Cole wasn't afraid to stand up to Rizzo, but he was growing weary. He had suffered a serious heart attack and several strokes, and though he despised Rizzo (the feeling was mutual), Cole knew he didn't have the support on the council—even though he had recruited Artiga and Jacobo—to challenge the city manager if he wanted to. But he didn't really want to because he didn't want to jeopardize his $80,000 pension or his favorite city programs which Rizzo controlled. Instead, he retired in 2008, two years before the scandal blew.

As he had in Hesperia, Rizzo dominated the Bell City Council. His overpowering personality and his willingness to get rid of anyone who stood in his way were intimidating. Yet, Rizzo was an "at-will" employee: he could be fired without cause by a majority of the council. Nevertheless, he was able to keep his job for 17 years—more than twice as long as the average tenure for city managers. "We could never get the three votes," Mirabal said.[25]

And why was that? Because the council members had never had it so good; they didn't want to give up a job that paid an inflated $100,000 a year salary and included a generous pension and health insurance. At the Spaccia trial (next chapter), Deputy District Attorney Max Huntsman had called them "fat, dumb, and happy." They didn't want to rock the boat. Also, they were content to let Rizzo run the city.

THE CHARGE

The defendants were charged with multiple counts of public corruption.[26] Specifically, that they had violated Penal Code 424, which essentially says that public funds must be used for legitimate public purposes. The original interpretation of the law was that a public official's intentions or ignorance of the law were not valid excuses. For example, if you park in a no parking zone, you get a ticket regardless of having a good excuse or not knowing it was illegal. Similarly, the courts have repeatedly rejected the argument that public officials who break the law were "just following orders," "relying on the decision-making expertise of others," or "just unaware of what was going on."[27]

OMAR BRADLEY

Consider the case of Omar Bradley, who referred to himself as "gangster mayor" of Compton, California. Bradley grew up in Compton and had a reputation for hard-ball politics, shady dealings, public rants, and intemperate remarks. With a 50-inch chest and 20-inch arms, the flamboyant Bradley was an imposing character who once told a political opponent that "someone may die in this campaign." Another time, he defended a high school football player—his nephew—for punching a referee. Also, Bradley once told a rapper during a council meeting that "he was being exploited by people of a 'specific ethnic group' who were ruining the image of blacks while 'having a bar mitzvah at the same time.'" The Jewish community was appalled.[28]

In May of 2004, the DA's Public Integrity Division brought corruption charges against Bradley for using his city-issued credit card to pay for golf fees, hotel rooms, clothing, and obtaining cash advances and other personal items. The amount involved was about $7,000, spread over two years.

Bradley said he thought these were legitimate business expenses since he was wooing folks he thought could bring new business to Compton. He also said he was not aware that he was breaking the law and that the city manager said that what he was doing was okay.

But the court said that what Bradley was thinking didn't matter: ignorance of the law was no excuse. Bradley was convicted of felony corruption and was sentenced to three years in state prison.

The question arose, does the defendant's state of mind matter? What if the defendant didn't know that he or she was breaking the law? What if he or she was trying to do the right thing but had made an honest mistake in his or her official duties? Is it really reasonable to expect the generalists who are elected to city council to know the chapter and verse of Penal Code 424? What if the people they look to for legal advice, such as the city attorney, got it wrong? Who would ever want to serve in public office if he or she could be sent to state prison for two or more years for decisions made in good faith?

The California Supreme Court considered these questions when it reviewed the case of Robert Stark. On August 1, 2011, two years before the start of the Bell council trial, it ruled that the accused public official's state of mind *does* matter.[29]

THE STARK DECISION

Robert E. Stark was the auditor controller for Sutter County, which is just north of Sacramento. The auditor controller is the chief accounting officer of the county. He or she is responsible for budget control, disbursements and receipts, and financial reporting. It's an elected position which Stark had held since 1985.[30]

In 2004, Stark was charged with violating various parts of Penal Code 424, "including filing the final budget for fiscal year 2003–2004 six and a half months late, claiming authority to approve rates of services to various county departments, independently amending the county budget without the board's required approval, withholding overtime pay to the county firefighters, and unilaterally transferring money from the county's general fund to another district without approval."[31]

Stark was unpopular with Sutter officials and bureaucrats, to be sure, but he never profited personally, and the county never lost any money because of any of his financial transactions. Stark argued that he didn't know he was breaking the law, and he certainly had no criminal intent. As the chief budgetary officer, he felt it was necessary to shift funds around and not pay certain bills to balance the budget. In other words, he was just doing his job.[32]

The case ultimately wound up in the California Supreme Court, which held that "strong public policy supports a rule requiring either *actual knowledge or criminal negligence* [author's italics] in failing to know the legal requirements underlying the section 424 charges."[33]

The court decided that Stark was innocent of the charges because it was not *reasonable for him to think* he was breaking the law. Stark's professional judgment about financial transactions didn't jibe with Sutter county's chief administrative officer's. He never benefited personally from these transactions. He wasn't a criminal. He certainly didn't deserve to be sent to jail. In August of 2012, as a result of the Stark decision, Mayor Omar Bradley's conviction was reversed. This was less than a half year before the Bell trial.

The Stark decision made the prosecution's burden in the Bell case much more difficult. Not only did the prosecutor have to prove the defendants broke the law but that they *knew* what they were doing was illegal or that it was reasonable to expect that they should have known.

DEFENDANTS' INTENT

Everyone agreed that the Bell Six were horrible elected officials who deserved to be turned out of office. But were they criminals who should go to jail? What exact laws did they break?

Bell's charter says that council members were to "receive compensation not to exceed the amount which council members of general law cities of similar population would receive under State law."[34] Their *legal* salary was $673 per month or $8,076 dollars per year.[35] However, what pushed the council salaries to nearly $100,000 a year were the stipends they voted for themselves for sitting on the boards of four authorities that did little or no work: the Community Housing Authority, the Surplus Property Authority, the Public Financing Authority, and the Solid Waste and Recycling Authority. Sitting on these authorities was part and parcel of being on the council.

Three of the authorities had been around for years. The Surplus Property Authority was established in 1975 when the City of Bell wanted to purchase federally owned land near the city. The Community Housing Authority was created in 1995 so the city could provide low-income housing to Bell residents. The Public Financing Authority issued bonds that were separate from the bonds issued by the housing authority or the city itself. This allowed the city to have access to larger amounts of capital at lower costs. It was created in 1991.

The first three authorities were legitimate; getting *paid* (especially such huge amounts) for sitting on them—which amounted to being paid for doing the same work they were doing as members of the council—was not.

Miller said the Solid Waste and Recycling Authority which the council created was a complete fraud. It was created for the purpose of "acquiring, constructing, maintaining, or operating an enterprise for the collection, treatment or disposal of waste." There was nothing for this authority to do, however, because during all the years that it existed, Bell contracted out garbage collection and recycling to a private company. No staff was hired and no waste facilities were ever built.

Miller argued that these authorities were a "sham." Their only purpose was to provide a means to boost council members' pay. Money from the city's general fund was put into the accounts for each authority, and council monthly stipends were paid from these accounts.

The meetings for the boards of the authorities were held at the same time as the regular city council meetings and in the same room. "The city council members didn't even change their seats."[36] The council would adjourn the city council meeting and then open a meeting for one of the authorities, which they adjourned after a few minutes. They'd then restart the city council meeting. Miller showed the jury an excerpt of the city council meeting for February 6, 2006. "As you can see, the Solid Waste and Recycling Authority met only for two minutes. The meeting started at 8:00 p.m. and it ended at 8:02 p.m. The evidence will show that the brevity of this meeting was not an isolated occurrence. In fact, three of these boards went years where they did absolutely no work at all. They didn't meet. They did zero work. But that did not stop the defendants from taking their full salaries for those authorities."[37]

In all of 2006, for example, the Public Financing Authority met for six minutes. The surplus property authority met for five minutes. The Solid Waste and Recycling Authority met for just two minutes." The two minutes for the Solid Waste Authority meeting was just to pass the resolution that established their pay. It did nothing else that year," Miller said.[38] The boards didn't need to meet for very long because they didn't do anything except to vote themselves raises, which passed unanimously, he argued. Miller said that the council voted for 12% raises for sitting on the boards even in years when they never met again after their one meeting to raise their salaries.

The total amount of time the four authorities met between January 1, 2006, and June 29, 2008—two and one half years—was a total of 72 minutes. Yet they paid themselves $1,900 dollars a month for each of the four authorities.[39]

Miller then showed the jury the resolutions passed by the council to provide them with stipends for sitting on each of these fake boards. Council members received a check every two weeks for their service on the council, plus, by 2009–2010, $1,900 a month for sitting on each of the four pseudo boards ($7,600 per month). These stipends, plus their council salaries, came to $99,276 annually which was many times more than their counterparts in other comparable cities received.[40] This did not include retirement, which were "perhaps the highest pensions of any non-public safety officials in the state, council members would have been receiving pensions of $100,000 a year" for the rest of their lives.[41]

THE PROSECUTION'S ARGUMENT: CRIMINAL NEGLIGENCE

Given the Stark decision, Miller had to show that the council members knew what they were doing, or it was reasonable to expect that someone in their position should have known. He argued the council members didn't want to know the law because if they did, they would have to give up their fat paychecks.

In her instructions to the jury, Judge Kennedy said, "The negligence must be aggravated, culpable, gross, or reckless. Criminal negligence is measured by what is objectively reasonable for the particular person in the defendant's position. Public officials have a duty to act in compliance with the law, and must take necessary steps to determine the appropriateness of their conduct. Those who willfully accept the responsibility to manage or handle public money cannot remain recklessly ignorant of the law regulating their actions."[42]

In his closing remarks, Miller said that negligence is based on what a reasonable person would do in similar circumstances. Miller said to the jury, "Say you were just elected as a city councilmember for the city of Bell. Somebody tells you everything the defendants did and then tells you, 'Hey, go ahead and do what they did.' Criminal negligence ... is negligence so extraordinary that the conduct, when you hear about it, horrifies you. You gasp."[43]

Miller argued that their actions were "aggravated, culpable, gross, or reckless" because as public officials they had a duty to obey the law, and if they didn't know the law, they should have taken reasonable affirmative steps to ensure that they were in compliance with the law. "The law doesn't say that you can just assume that everything is okay," Miller said.

"A GUILTY MIND"

But how do we know what people are thinking or what their mental state is? Miller argued that their actions illustrated that they had a "guilty mind." He presented three witnesses to show that the council members were in on the scam, that they knew exactly what they were doing, and weren't being led around by their noses by Rizzo, who, the defense lawyers argued, kept them in the dark.[44]

ROGER RAMIREZ

The word on the street in 2008 was that Rizzo was making $400,000, and the council members were making $80,000. Long-time Bell resident Roger Ramirez, a paramedic in his late 50s, was one of a handful of citizens who attended city council meetings regularly.[45] At a council meeting in early September 2008, he stood at the microphone facing the council and Rizzo, and he asked Rizzo if he was making over $400,000 year. Rizzo responded, "Hey, if I can make $400,000 a year, I wouldn't be here in Bell." He then turned to the council members and asked how much they were making. Ramirez said he had heard that the city council were making an exorbitant amount, $80,000 per year.[46] No one said a thing. No one answered.[47] After a four or five-second silence, Mirabal finally told Ramirez, "You can get that information by making a public records request." Ramirez said he knew he could do this, but he wanted to hear the city council members address the salary question.

Miller argued to the jury that the length of the silence was telling: "When you think of four or five seconds in the abstract, it doesn't really sound like a long time, does it? Someone tells you, 'I will be there in four or five seconds.' That means immediately. But how about, 'Dear, my darling wife, have you always been faithful to me?' One Thousand, Two Thousand, Three Thousand, Four thousand, Five thousand. 'Yes.'"

On September 9, 2008, Ramirez went to city hall and filled out a public records request form. He wanted to know the salary of the city council members, the mayor, and the city manager. He handed it to Rebecca Valdez, the city clerk.

A week later, Valdez called Ramirez and told him he could pick up the city's response to his public records request. Valdez gave Ramirez a document that said the council members were making $673 a month, or $8,076 a year. No mention was made of the stipends they received for sitting on the four authorities, which boosted their salaries to $92,000. And Rizzo's salary was also misrepresented. Ramirez was told Rizzo was making $15,478 per month, or $185,736 a year, when he was actually making $632,700 a year, not counting the numerous weeks of vacation and sick pay he cashed out.[48]

"When she approached me, she handed it to me. And she was quiet. And I looked at it to see if those were the figures that I had been told. And when I told her that this was not ... the figures I had been told that they are receiving, [the] ... expression on her face was concerned. And she looked around kind of with her eyes ... [fearing] that someone might hear if she were to say anything. Because right next door is another department where they can hear anything going on," Ramirez said.[49] Rizzo's office was about 15 feet from the counter.

Valdez grew up in Bell. At 14, she was hired as an unpaid student intern to do clerical work. She held various city hall jobs before becoming an account clerk who processed invoices for the city.[50] In 2000, when she was a senior at Bell High School, she was hired full time. Rizzo appointed her to city clerk in 2005.[51] She was making about $5,000 a month plus benefits. It was a solid job for any young person but especially for a kid from a poor Bell family. She'd also received a $48,000 illegal loan from Rizzo for the down payment on the house she bought after getting married. Valdez testified that she would lose her job if she didn't do what Rizzo told her to do even if it was wrong.[52]

"Valdez said she complied with Rizzo's directive to give a document listing just a fraction of city officials' salaries to a resident who had filed a public records request because she feared that her job was in jeopardy. Later, she followed Rizzo's order to slip his doctored contracts into a stack of papers to be signed by the then-Mayor Oscar Hernandez," the *L.A. Times* reported.[53]

VICTOR BELLO'S SALARY

Another example of secrecy and deception involved Bello. In August of 2009, after butting heads with his council colleagues and Rizzo and having been banished from city hall by the city manager for everything except council meetings, Bello decided to leave the council. He stopped going to council meetings. Rizzo told the council he was being "reassigned" and said the council should start interviewing people to replace him. None of the members asked any questions of Rizzo about the fate of their long-term colleague.[54]

Bell has a city-run food bank where volunteers distribute free food to the city's many poor residents. It was headed by Ricardo Gonzalez, who was Bell's director of business development. Rizzo created a new position for Bello, "assistant food bank coordinator." Bello would keep his council salary; his contract with the food bank was set to end when his council term was over. Of course, it is illegal to "reassign" an elected official to an administrative job, which is probably why there was no formal announcement. Gonzalez was under the impression that Bello—who worked only 4–5 hours a week—was a volunteer like all the others and was shocked to learn later that he was being paid.

LORENZO VELEZ: THE ONE HONEST COUNCILMEMBER

The council appointed Lorenzo Velez, a heavy-equipment operator for the City of Los Angeles, and a friend of George Cole, to take Bello's place. Velez, who emigrated from Mexico, had been a volunteer at the food bank.

Rizzo directed that he be paid $673 per month, although he did everything all the other council members did, including attending all of the meetings and council functions. Velez was unaware of the exorbitant salaries being paid to Rizzo, the council, and Bello, and was shocked when the salaries were revealed. When the "$800,000" story appeared in the L.A. Times, the other council members left him voice messages saying that it was urgent that they talk.[55]

"Constantly, constantly, constantly they were calling me," in the days after the scandal became public, Velez said. "They were trying to strategize, to bring me in. I wouldn't do it."[56] Miller argued that they didn't tell Velez how much they were making because they feared he might blow the whistle on them. When the scandal blew up, they were terrified by the fact that he had no incentive to stay quiet. This was further evidence of their guilty minds.

THE DEFENSE

The six former council members were tried together, but the jury would consider each person's culpability separately, which is why each of the defendants had their own attorney.[57] Together they argued that (1) the corruption stopped with Rizzo, who ran everything and kept the council in the dark; (2) the defendants weren't aware that they were breaking the law; (3) Ed Lee, the city's attorney, failed to alert them that their actions weren't authorized by the law, and the city's auditing firm, Meyer Hoffman McCann, failed to red-flag financial irregularities; (4) the four authorities did real work that was not reflected in the minutes; (5) the defendants put in dozens of hours each week for the community and deserved the compensation they received; and (6) they didn't break the law because Bell's charter allowed the city to pay the council people for sitting on the authorities. A final argument, advanced by Artiga's attorney, was that he simply wasn't on the council when the other council members voted to raise their salaries. He'd be the only defendant acquitted of all charges.[58]

1. THE CORRUPTION STOPPED WITH RIZZO

The most important argument advanced by the defense was that their clients were not guilty because the corruption started and stopped with Rizzo. The attorneys argued that the prosecutor was overreaching when he attempted to make their clients pay for Rizzo's transgressions. Rizzo was a strongman, who manipulated the council to do his bidding. Rizzo was a control freak and a micromanager who ordered the staff not to talk to the city council members and the council not to speak to the staff. He bullied and manipulated the staff and the council; he made Jacobo "feel like a child" when she asked what he thought were too many questions. He had Bello banished from city hall when he couldn't control him. He also butted heads with Cole. Cole said he voted for a 12% annual pay raise Rizzo proposed for fear that the vindictive Rizzo would gut his favorite programs if he didn't.

Rizzo ordered Valdez, the city clerk, to give false salary information to Ramirez, the citizen who filed the Public Records Request. He had resolutions drafted with unnecessarily complex language to intimidate and confuse the council. He lied to the council and kept information from them. He directed that the resolutions giving him salary increases be sent to Hernandez—rather than the more knowledgeable Mirabal—because he knew Hernandez couldn't read them and would sign whatever Rizzo put in front of him. He set the council agenda and made sure that salary increases were put on the consent calendar. Items placed on the consent calendar are passed with one motion and are not discussed unless one of the members "pulls" the item for separate discussion.

Rizzo gave out city money as loans without council authorization to staff and council, which kept people loyal and quiet. The council were terrorized by this unethical and ruthless city manager just like the citizens of Bell. Nevertheless, three members of the council could have fired Rizzo at any time during his 17-year tenure at Bell but they didn't.

2. EXPERTS FAILED TO WARN THEM

Time and again the defense attorneys pointed to the city's attorney, Ed Lee, of Best, Best, and Krieger, one of the largest municipal law firms in the state, as the one who should be charged, not their clients. Lee had been with the city since 1995. Well educated and well spoken, Lee was an authoritative figure in the council's eyes. He was in charge of drafting contracts, resolutions, and the city charter. His firm received a stipend of at least $10,000 per month. Lee—or his substitute—attended every council meeting and did not hesitate to speak up when he felt the council might be doing something that violated the law. "Why didn't Lee speak up?" the defense asked when he saw them voting to give themselves illegal raises. Lee's silence was interpreted by the defendants as approval. Jacobo testified she had a meeting with Rizzo and Lee. Rizzo told her she was going to get a full-time salary, so she could quit her real estate job and devote herself full time to city affairs. She said she asked if this was legal, and Rizzo assured her that it was, and Lee nodded in the affirmative. The defense also asked why the city's accounting firm Mayer Hoffman McCann didn't issue any red-flags when they audited Bell's books. "The auditor looked at the salaries ... And never, never did the auditor raise a red flag. Never," Ron Kaye, Cole's attorney insisted. The California Public Employee Retiree System (CalPERS) also reviewed all the salaries but raised no warnings or concerns. In short, the attorneys argued, the defendants weren't aware that they were breaking the law or that anything was amiss in Bell because no one—not the city attorney or their auditor or the retirement system or staff—told them. Miller countered that the buck stopped with the council, and it was their responsibility to the public to not take the word of professionals at face value and to investigate further.

3. THE AUTHORITIES DID REAL WORK

The Bell defendants were charged with stealing from the people of Bell and breaking the law because they paid themselves handsomely for sitting on authorities that seldom, if ever, met and did little, if any, work. The primary means for establishing how much work the authorities did were the "minutes." Ron Kaye, Cole's attorney, argued that the minutes didn't reflect all of the work that the defendants did for those authorities, work that did not take place in meetings—on issues such as surplus property, garbage pickup, and affordable housing. Why should they go to meetings when much of the work that needed to be done was out in the community, Kaye argued.

4. THEY DIDN'T BREAK THE LAW

The defense argued that the voter-approved charter permitted the council members to be paid for serving on the authorities. Several of the defense attorneys argued that their clients didn't break the law. The argument went like this: The voters of Bell voted for the city to become a charter city in 2005. The city charter said, in section 502, which deals with compensation, that while the council members must receive salaries comparable to what other general law cities of similar size receive, the council shall receive "compensation for their services as may be prescribed by ordinance or resolution."[59] Shepard Kopp, Jacobo's attorney, argued that the resolutions and ordinances that the council passed in open meetings "provided lawful authority for the payments." The new charter may have placed a limitation on base pay, but "it didn't limit what members of the council could be paid for their service on the various authorities that they also served on, and the new charter specifically recognized that there were going to be these separate authorities and that the council members would be paid for being on them. In addition, Alex Kessel, Mirabal's attorney said, "So what we have here is that their own charter allows them to give themselves salary—through ordinance and resolution." He argued that the city records showed that the defendants were "full-time" employees.[60] But prosecutor Miller said that council members automatically serve on the four authorities, and no one but a councilmember could serve on them. This meant that service on these authorities was part of the job as a councilmember and couldn't be separately compensated.

5. THEY EARNED EVERY CENT

Then the defense attorneys listed all of the work their clients did for the community outside of their official council duties at night and on weekends. They pointed out that council members didn't have staff and had to pay for things like photocopying out of their own pockets. They worked long hours—40, 50, and sometimes 60 hours each week trying to make Bell better—meeting with Bell's citizens, attending ceremonies, reviewing stacks of materials, and going to meetings and conferences throughout the Southeast. Jacobo visited the city's mobile home parks and dozens of other units that the city rented out to poor people and seniors. She was frequently called upon to mediate problems at all hours of the night and on weekends. Jacobo testified, "I thought I was doing a very good job to be able to earn that, yes."[61]

Cole's attorney argued that his client put in many hours on education and health care issues. Even Velez, whom Miller called the "one honest councilman," said he was putting in more than 35 hours a week on council business. The defense argued it was absurd to expect this much effort for $673 dollars a month. One attorney estimated that his client was making $45 an hour, which is high compared to the monthly income of most of the people who lived in Bell but not outrageously so. Moreover, the council salaries were a fraction of what the city paid lower-level staff such as Lourdes Garcia who was making $422,000 total compensation a year as the city's director of administrative services.[62]

JURY DELIBERATIONS

The four-week trial went to the jury on February 22, 2013. After the judge read them additional instructions and admonitions, the jury of seven women and five men, a representative cross section of the people who lived in downtown Los Angeles, retired to the jury room next to the courtroom with their jury instructions, all exhibits that had been admitted into evidence, and the verdict forms. They selected a foreman, who moderated the deliberations.

It wasn't long before fighting broke out. One juror, an older woman who was in tears, asked to be excused because she was being picked on by the other jurors and pleaded with the judge to excuse her. Kennedy refused. She was later excused for misconduct.[63] Deliberations had to start anew when she was replaced with an alternate. Deliberations were halted again when another juror got sick, and everyone was sent home. The jurors sent notes to the judge claiming that they had become hopelessly deadlocked and that there were fundamental disagreements, that some jurors were ignoring the jury instructions, and that things had become "very, very tense." They asked for the testimony to be read back to them and for instructions to be clarified. They asked for documents regarding salaries for serving on authorities, the city charter, and the State Constitution.

Finally, after deliberating behind closed doors for 17 days, the jury was ready to report their verdicts.[64] The jury found Jacobo, Cole, Bello, Hernandez, and Mirabal guilty of about half the counts. "Defendants were acquitted on charges related to their pay for the Public Finance Authority, but were convicted (five counts) for the money they received for sitting on the Solid Waste and Recycling Authority. That board was established in 2005, after the charter had passed, when the city already had an outside contractor for trash services."[65] The foreman said the jury was deadlocked 9–3 in favor of guilty.

Hernandez, Jacobo, and Mirabal were each found guilty of five counts of misappropriation of funds relating to the Solid Waste and Recycling Authority between January 1, 2006, and July 26, 2010. These were felonies which could result in 2–4 years in state prison for each count.

Cole and Bello also were found guilty of misappropriation of public funds from the same authority: Cole of two counts between January 1, 2006, and December 31, 2009, and Bello of four counts between January 1, 2006, and December 31, 2009.[66]

"The jury did not reach a decision on misappropriation of public funds charges related to the Community Housing Authority and the Surplus Property Authority."[67] The jury foreman said the jury was deadlocked 9–3 in favor of guilty on the charges they couldn't resolve.[68] These were felony convictions which could result in 2–4 years of prison for each count. Artiga, who joined the counsel after the disputed salary votes were cast, was found not guilty on all counts. "The pastor wept and looked heavenward as the 'not guilty' counts were read."[69] The others were also "emotional, some were teary-eyed, as they left the courtroom with their families, unsure of their final fates."[70]

The judge read the verdicts in court and, to the surprise of some expert trial watchers, the defense did not exercise its option to poll the individual jurors. Kennedy then ordered the jury to continue deliberating on the remaining counts.

MISTRIAL

And then, things got weird. Kennedy reported that she had received five notes from the jury. One anonymous juror wrote that he or she wanted to rethink his or her verdict because of the "stress and pressure" of the deliberation process.

Another note said that she believed the jury is "getting away from your instructions" and possibly misunderstanding a law on "several levels."[71] Yet another juror wrote the judge that he or she wanted to know more about City Attorney Ed Lee—who was not charged and did not testify—in order to be sure "beyond a reasonable doubt."[72]

Alex Keesel, defense attorney, said the juror who was excused earlier also complained about coercion from another juror. The judge denied the requests to reconsider the verdicts. Another note said, "I respectfully ask if you could remind the jury to remain respectful and not to make false accusations and insults to one another." Still another note, from a different juror, said the jury remained deadlocked. One of the jurors, who was in favor of guilt said, "We had some jurors who just kind of didn't care what the instructions were and what the judge said and that was just that."[73]

Nevertheless, the judge ordered them to continue deliberating. But a half hour later, it was clear that the jurors were done with one another, and Kennedy returned them to the courtroom. An exasperated Kennedy said to the jury and the assembled attorneys, "It seems to me all hell has broken loose ... I'm getting the sense that the lines of communication have broken down between each and every one of you." She declared a mistrial on the undecided counts.

The attorneys were stunned. "I have never heard of anything like this in my 40 years of law," said Robert Sheahen, a veteran Los Angeles criminal defense attorney. "What is going on now is nothing short of bizarre. To go back and ask to reexamine verdicts doesn't happen."[74]

The district attorney decided to retry the case on the remaining counts. To avoid a second trial, and the possibility of up to eight years or more in prison, all five council members accepted the prosecutor's offer of a maximum prison sentence of four years in exchange for a guilty plea on the remaining corruption charges.[75]

In the summer of 2014, in separate hearings, Kennedy sentenced the defendants.

Mirabal, Bello, and Hernandez were sentenced to a year in county jail and a year of probation. The judge also gave the defendants a four-year prison term. The sentences were suspended, which means if the defendant violates probation, he or she goes straight to prison to serve out his or her term. Each was ordered to perform hundreds of hours of community service and pay restitution. They ended up serving only a few weeks in county jail because of credit for time served and early release because of overcrowding.[76]

Cole was sentenced to 180 days of home confinement and five years probation. His attorney had argued that he was in poor health and had several heart attacks, strokes, diabetes and kidney disease, conditions which would be exacerbated if he were incarcerated. Cole was bitter and said that if he saw Rizzo lying on the ground in the desert, dying of thirst, he wouldn't help him. "He ruined me."[77]

The judge denied Jacobo probation and sentenced her to two years in prison. This was the harshest sentence given to any of the council people. Only ringleaders Rizzo and Spaccia got more. Kennedy said Jacobo should have known better because the former real estate agent dealt with contracts and other legal matters. Kennedy also said Jacobo had displayed a "defiant attitude" throughout the court proceedings.

In a soft, trembling voice she said, "... with all my heart, I apologize to the people of Bell."[78]

"I think that she is sorry now that she has to pay the consequences," the no-nonsense Kennedy countered.

Jacobo sat back down, covered her face with one hand, and sobbed. Jacobo's friends and family filled the back rows of the courtroom. Her daughter screamed "Fuck you" at the judge and threatened Jeff Gottlieb, the *Times'* reporter who broke the story.

Someone else in the audience yelled, "You're dead" to one of the attorneys. The marshals jumped up and approached the remaining spectators and restored order.

Jacobo was given 30 days to get her affairs in order. She reported back to the same court early one morning; she was handcuffed, put in a cell for several hours, and given a peanut butter sandwich.

In the late afternoon, she was taken to Central California Women's Facility in Chowchilla, California—270 miles north of Bell—to begin serving her sentence. She was released nine months later.

Artiga, the pastor, who was exonerated on all counts, said he wished he had never served on the council.

Bello, unemployed and on state mental health disability, returned to the small apartment he shared with his mother. In a letter to the court, Mirabal blamed Rizzo and City Attorney Ed Lee. "I never dreamed that any one person could create such havoc as Rizzo did, but I was wrong," he wrote. "In another time, another ethic, I would have fallen on my sword; my disappointment was all that encompassing."[79] Mirabal spent about a month in jail and returned to his home in Bell. "When I tell people I am from Bell, they say, 'Oh that's where those crooks are from.' I know they are talking about me. I'm in seclusion now."[80]

Former Mayor Oscar Hernandez, one of Rizzo's biggest defenders, also became a pariah. The words "Go Away" and an image of Rizzo with horns were spray painted on the outside walls of the once-popular mayor's grocery store. He moved to a trailer in a city about 10 miles from Bell.[81]

At his sentencing hearing, Hernandez said, "I just want to say I'm sorry ... And I take all the blame; I put the blame on myself." His son, Agustin, broke down in tears as he pleaded with Kennedy for a reduced sentence for his father. Hernandez reached over to comfort him. He then covered his face with his hands, leaned on the table, and wept.

"If you didn't have the ability and skills to do the job, then you shouldn't have run for the job," Judge Kennedy said. "Do I think you are the absolute worst of the worst? No, I think you've done wrong. I think there were others that were far more manipulative and got far more ill-gotten gains than you did,"[82] she said.

CONCLUSION

The trial of the Bell Six council defendants raised the question: Is it a crime for elected officials to go along with illegal activities they don't understand or question? The Bell verdicts said, "Yes."

The defense said the defendants were "bumbling bumpkins" who were manipulated by a strongman city manager, and, therefore, not criminals who deserved to go to jail.

But the prosecution argued that they were "sophisticated manipulators" who knew they were ripping off the people of Bell. The defense countered that the corruption stopped with Rizzo, who ran everything and kept the council in the dark. The members of the council weren't aware that they were breaking the law, their lawyers argued, and Ed Lee, the city's attorney, failed to alert them that they were taking unauthorized actions by okaying the pay scheme. The defense also argued that the council couldn't be blamed for taking so much money because of the following: the city's auditing firm, Mayer Hoffman McCann, never red-flagged any financial irregularities; the four authorities did real work that was not reflected in the minutes; the council members put in dozens of hours each week for the community and deserved the compensation they received; and, for good measure, they didn't break the law because Bell's charter, they argued, allowed the city to pay the council people for sitting on the authorities.

LESSONS

What was clear to Bell's angry leaders and residents who had launched the recall—that the former council members ripped them off for millions and deserved stiff prison terms—was much less clear legally. This is evidenced by how long deliberations took—17 days, nearly as long as the length of the actual trial—and the fact that even after exhaustive discussion, they were able to come to a unanimous decision on only *half* the counts but remained deadlocked on the others.

Another key takeaway for those considering public service, or evaluating those who serve them, is that the ignorance defense didn't fly. Jurors did not buy the defense's argument that the council members were not guilty because they were in over their heads and that they received bad advice from the city attorney and Rizzo. As elected representatives of the people, they were responsible for acting ethically, thinking critically about what they were doing, asking questions when they didn't understand, and considering the implications of their decisions. And if they didn't, they were criminally liable for the consequences—something citizens can take comfort in.

Rizzo had helped pack the council with manifestly unqualified people—one did not know English and others seemed completely unaware that Rizzo reported to them or that they bore responsibility for his actions and those of his administration. But the council-manager system, in particular, hinges on the council getting the training it needs, insisting on clarity, and not falling asleep at the wheel. The verdicts in the case were a potent reminder that the buck stops with the elected officials.

ENDNOTES

1   Ali Saleh, personal interview.

2   Jeff Gottlieb "Bell: A Total Breakdown," paper delivered at the City of Bell Scandal Revisited, Chapman University, February 19, 2015.

3   Ruben Vives and Jeff Gottlieb, "Memo Suggests that Bell city police turned ticketing, impounding cars into a game." L.A. Times. Blog. February 28, 2011. Retrieved from: http://latimesblogs.latimes.com/lanow/2011/02/memo-suggests-bell-police-turn-ticketing-impounding-cars-into-baseball-game.html.

4   Frank C. Girardot, "Cooley terms Bell Scandal "Corruption on Steroids." Los Angles Daily News. September 21, 2010. Retrieved from: http://latimesblogs.latimes.com/lanow/2011/02/memo-suggests-bell-police-turn-ticketing-impounding-cars-into-baseball-game.html.

5   Personal interview with Teresa Jacobo.

6   Ibid.

7   Abby Sewell, "Longtime nonprofit for seniors may lose is $2 million contract with L.A. County." *L.A. Times.* August 24, 2015. Retrieved from: http://www.latimes.com/local/california/la-me-oldtimers-20150824-story.html.

8   Dan Whitcomb, "Mayor, officials arrested in California pay scandal," Reuters. September 22, 2010. Retrieved from: https://www.reuters.com/article/us-california-payscandal-arrests/mayor-officials-arrested-in-california-pay-scandal-idUSTRE68K40N20100922

9   Called the "Korner Market" on Corona avenue in Bell.

10 Corina Knoll, "Former Bell Mayor sentenced to year in jail in corruption case." *L.A. Times.* August 1, 2014. Retrieved from: http://www.latimes.com/local/la-me-bell-mayor-jail-20140801-story.html.

11 Joseph Raymond served from 1964 to 1976, but according to some, kept quiet about his Latino ethnicity.

12 Corina Knoll, "Final Bell Council Member Sentenced," *L.A. Times,* August 1, 2014. Retrieved from http://www.latimes.com/local/politics/la-me-0802-bell-finale-20140802-story.html.

13 Ruben Vives and Jeff Gottlieb, "Bell Councilman Luis Artiga Resigns." *L.A. Times.* October 4, 2010. Retrieved from http://latimesblogs.latimes.com/lanow/2010/10/bell-councilman-luis-artiga-resigns.html.

14 The preliminary hearing lasted from February 7 through February 16, 2011.

15 Reporter's transcript of proceedings, February 16, 2011, preliminary hearing for case no. BA376025-05, pp. 173–175.

16 Kennedy was the judge who ordered OJ Simpson to stand trial.

17 Paul Feldman, "Kathleen Kennedy Powell" *L.A. Times.* July 1, 1994. Retrieved from: http://articles.latimes.com/keyword/kathleen-kennedy-powell.

18 Ed Miller prosecuted the council defendants; Sean Hassett and Max Huntsman prosecuted Spaccia and Rizzo.

19 Cole also spoke Spanish as a second language.

20 Personal interview with Rolf Janssen.

21 Health coverage for the councilmember for life and for their families for as long as they were on the council.

22 Personal interview with Teresa Jacobo.

23 City funds were also used to pay for Hernandez's hair plugs, and $10,000 was used for Cole to go to a weight loss camp. See, Jeff Gottlieb and Ruben Vives, "D.A.: Bell paid for mayor's hair plugs, councilman's weight loss camp." *L.A. Times* November 7, 2013. Retrieved from: http://www.latimes.com/local/lanow/la-me-ln-da-bell-paid-for-mayors-hair-plugs-20131107-story.html.

24 Paul Pringle, Corina Knoll, and Kim Murphy, "Rizzo's Horse Had Come In," *L.A. Times*, August 22, 2010. Retrieved from http://www.latimes.com/local/la-me-rizzos-horse-had-come-in-08222010-m-story.html.

25 George Mirabal, phone conversation with author. August 17, 2016. See, https://en.wikipedia.org/wiki/City_manager. See also, https://localgov.fsu.edu/publication_files/turnover.pdf.

26 PC 424 was enacted in 1872. It says: (a) Each officer of this state, or of any county, city, town, or district of this state, and every other person charged with the receipt, safekeeping, transfer, or disbursement of public moneys, who either: 1. Without authority of law, appropriates the same, or any portion thereof, to his or her own use, or to the use of another; or, 2. Loans the same or any portion thereof; makes any profit out of, or uses the same for any purpose not authorized by law; or, 3. Knowingly keeps any false account, or makes any false entry or erasure in any account of or relating to the same; or, 4. Fraudulently alters, falsifies, conceals, destroys, or obliterates any account; or, 5. Willfully refuses or omits to pay over, on demand, any public moneys in his or her hands, upon the presentation of a draft, order, or warrant drawn upon these moneys by competent authority; or, 6. Willfully omits to transfer the same, when transfer is required by law; or, 7. Willfully omits or refuses to pay over to any officer or person authorized by law to receive the same, any money received by him or her under any duty imposed by law so to pay over the same;—Is punishable by imprisonment in the state prison for two, three, or four years, and is disqualified from holding any office in this state. (b) As used in this section, "public moneys" includes the proceeds derived from the sale of bonds or other evidence or indebtedness authorized by the legislative body of any city, county, district, or public agency. (c) This section does not apply to the incidental and minimal use of public resources authorized by Section 8314 of the Government Code. See California Penal Code: http://www.leginfo.ca.gov/cgi-bin/displaycode?section=pen&group=00001-01000&file=424-440. "Here is a breakdown of the charges filed against eight current and former Bell city officials:—Former City Manager Robert Rizzo, 56, is charged with 53 felony counts, including 44 counts of misappropriation of public funds between July 1,

2005, and July 22, 2010; six counts of falsification of public records by an official custodian; and three counts of conflict of interest. The charges include an
allegation that he "took, damaged and destroyed property of a value exceeding
$2.5 million.'—Mayor Oscar Hernandez, 63, is charged with 21 felony counts
of misappropriation of public funds between Jan. 1, 2006, and July 26, 2010.
The criminal complaint alleges that he took more than $262,000.—Vice Mayor
Teresa Jacobo, 52, is charged with 20 felony counts of misappropriation of public
funds between Jan. 1, 2006, and July 26, 2010. The criminal complaint alleges
that more than $262,000 was taken.—City Councilman George Mirabal, 60, is
charged with 20 felony counts of misappropriation of public funds between Jan.
1, 2006, and July 26, 2010, along with the allegation that more than $262,000 was
taken.—City Councilman Luis Artiga, 49, is charged with 13 felony counts of
misappropriation of public funds between June 1, 2008, and July 26, 2010, and is
accused of taking just over $129,000.—Former City Councilman Victor Bello, 51,
is charged with 16 felony counts of misappropriation of public funds between Jan.
1, 2006, and Dec. 31, 2009. The criminal complaint alleges that he took more than
$193,000.—Former City Councilman George Cole, 60, is charged with 12 felony
counts of misappropriation of public funds between Jan. 1, 2006, and Dec. 31,
2008. He is accused of taking more than $133,000.—Former Assistant City Man-
ager Angela Spaccia, 52, is charged with four felony counts of misappropriation
of public funds between July 1, 2005, and July 22, 2010. The criminal complaint
alleges that she took more than $1.3 million." See "Eight City of Bell officials
arrested on alleged salary scandal charges." Retrieved from: http://bhcourier.
com/eight-city-of-bell-officials-arrested-on-alleged-salary-scandal-charges.

27   See, Nina Marino and Blithe Leece, "The Accidental Defendant," *Los Angeles
Lawyer*, March 2015, p. 16–20. Retrieved from http://www.kaplanmarino.com/
wp-content/uploads/2015/08/The-Accidental-Defendant-Article.pdf.

28   Greg Krikorian, "Office Politics." *L.A. Times*, January 12, 1997. Retrieved from
http://articles.latimes.com/1997-01-12/news/ls-17792_1_office-politics/3.

29   See Supreme Court of California. Robert E. STARK, *Petitioner, v. The SUPERIOR
COURT of Sutter County*. No. S145337. Retrieved from http://caselaw.findlaw.com/
ca-supreme-court/1576377.html.

30   The Auditor Controller. Retrieved from http://www.counties.org/county-office/
auditor-controller.

31   Stanford Law School. Citation 52 CAL. 4th 368, 257 p. 3D 41, 128, Cal, RPTR. 3D
611. https://scocal.stanford.edu/opinion/stark-v-super-ct-34000

32   Robert E. Stark vs. Superior Court of Sutter County. Case No. S14537 p.3. http://
      www.courts.ca.gov/documents/s145337-2-petitioners-opening-brief-on-the-mer-
      its.pdf.

33   Stark v. Super. Ct. SCOCAL. Stanford Law School. p. 31. Retrieved from: http://
      scocal.stanford.edu/opinion/stark-v-super-ct-34000.

34   Section 502. Compensation, of the Bell City charter. Retrieved from: http://www.
      cityofbell.org/home/showdocument?id=682

35   They were permitted to vote themselves a 5% annual raise.

36   Reporter's transcript of proceedings, January 24, 2013, page 1253.

37   Ibid.

38   Reporter's transcript of proceedings, January 24, 2013, page 1255.

39   Reporter's transcript of proceedings, January 24, 2013, page 1257.

40   Reporter's transcript of proceedings, January 24, 2013, page 1258, $107,712 per
      year. $673+$7600=$8273 per month, X 12 = $99276 per year.

41   Jeff Gottlieb, "Bell Corruption: Former Councilman gets one year term." L.A.
      Times, July 11, 2014. Retrieved from http://www.latimes.com/local/lanow/la-me-
      ln-ex-bell-councilman-sentenced-corruption-20140711-story.html.

42   Reporter's transcript of proceedings, February 20, 2013,
      pp. 6331–6333.

43   Reporter's transcript of proceedings, February 20, 2013,
      pp. 6373.

44   The legal term is Mens Rea, the accused's mental state.

45   City Clerk Rebecca Valdez estimated that around 10 people attended council
      meetings, sometimes as few as three or four. Reporter's transcript of proceedings,
      January 25, 2013, p. 1592.

46   Reporter's transcript of proceedings, February 5, 2013, p. 3707.

47   Reporter's transcript of proceedings, January 24, 2013, p. 1271.

48   Jeff Gottlieb and Cornia Knoll, "Robert Rizzo had Bell salary information fal-
      sified, city clerk testifies." L.A. Times, February 11, 2011. Retrieved from http://
      articles.latimes.com/2011/feb/11/local/la-me-bell-hearing-20110211. See also,
      Corina Knoll, "Bell 8: City Clerk testifies she was following orders in giving out
      false salary information." blog. L.A. Times February 10, 2011. Reporter's tran-
      script of proceedings, January 25, 2013, p. 1695.

49   Reporter's transcript of proceedings, February 5, 2013, volume 11, pp.
      3728–3729.

50   Corina Knoll and Jeff Gottlieb, "Bell City Clerk says 'I couldn't ask any ques-
      tions.'" January 29, 2013. Retrieved from: http://articles.latimes.com/2013/jan/29/

local/la-me-0130-bell-trial-20130130. In 2004, then-City Clerk Teresa Diaz moved out of town, making her ineligible to hold the elected office. Valdez was given her title but continued her job as an account clerk. Diaz continued to act as the record-keeper for the city, but Valdez testified that she was told to sign documents as the city clerk. "I would always try to question her as to what I was signing, and she would get upset if I would ask her questions," Valdez testified. Even after Diaz left at the end of 2007, and Valdez took over the full duties, she said she felt powerless to speak up. Diaz was the daughter-in-law of former Councilman George Bass.

51 Reporter's transcript of proceedings, January 24, 2013, p. 1513.

52 Reporter's transcript of proceedings, January 24, 2013, p. 1691.

53 Corina Knoll and Jeff Gottlieb, "Bell City Clerk says 'I couldn't ask any questions.'" January 29, 2013. Retrieved from: http://articles.latimes.com/2013/jan/29/local/la-me-0130-bell-trial-20130130.

54 Ibid.

55 Hector Becerra and Ruben Vives, "Bell Councilman an accidental hero by staying clear of corruption scandal," October 13, 2010. Retrieved from http://articles.latimes.com/2010/oct/13/local/la-me-bell-councilman-20101009.

56 Ibid.

57 Hernandez was represented by Stanley Friedman; Jacobo, by Sheppard Kopp; Mirabal, by Alex Kessel; Cole was represented by Ronald Kaye; Bello, by Leo Moriarty; and Artiga, by George Mgdesyan. Moriarty would later represent Jacobo, replacing Kopp.

58 "Bell Corruption trial: Luis Artiga acquitted on all charges," ABC7 News. Retrieved from http://abc7.com/archive/9035318/.

59 Ibid. p. 6396.

60 Bell had something called a "personal action report" or PAD for each of its employees that showed how they were paid and whether they were full- or part-time. Reporter's transcript of proceedings, February 21, 2013, p. 6608.

61 Jeff Gottlieb, "Third Council Member to be sentenced; D.A. wants prison time," *L.A. Times*, July 28, 2016. Retrieved from http://www.latimes.com/local/lanow/la-me-ln-bell-council-sentencing-20140724-story.html.

62 Reporter's transcript of proceedings, February 21, 2013, p. 6741.

63 For doing research on the internet related to the case, including consulting a legal website and looking up the word, "coercion."

64   The rule of thumb is a day of deliberation for each week of testimony. There were four weeks to testimony, which would mean 4–5 days of deliberation. This jury deliberated for 17 days.

65   See Corina Knoll, Ruben Vives and Richard Winton. "Five of 6 ex-Bell council members found guilty in corruption trial." L.A. Times. March 20, 2013. Retrieved from: /articles.latimes.com/2013/mar/20/local/la-me-bell-verdict-20130321-1.

66   Brian Hewes, "Cole, Bello, Hernandez, Jacobo, Mirabal Found Guilty In Bell Corruption Trial." Hews Media Group. Retrieved from: http://www.loscerritosnews.net/2013/03/20/cole-bello-hernandez-jacobo-mirabal-found-guilty-in-bell-corruption-trial/?fb_comment_id=153261491503487_325639#f3e6f2a3587bbec

67   Ibid.

68   Richard Winton, Ruben Vives, and Jeff Gottlieb, "'Bell mistrial: prosecutors on steroids,' defense says." L.A. Times, March 21, 2013. Retrieved from: http://latimesblogs.latimes.com/lanow/2013/03/bell-mistrial-prosecutors-on-steroids-defense-says.html.

69   Richard Winton, Corina Knoll, Ruben Vives, Kathe Mather, "Bell Trial: Jury do back in court to discuss undecided charges." L.A. Times. March 21, 2013. Retrieved from: http://latimesblogs.latimes.com/lanow/2013/03/bell-trial-jury-due-back-in-court-to-discuss-undecided-charges.html

70   Cornia Knoll, Ruben Vives, and Richard Winton, "Five of 6 ex-Bell Council members found guilty in corruption trial," L.A. Times. March 20, 2013. Retrieved from http://articles.latimes.com/2013/mar/20/local/la-me-bell-verdict-20130321-1.

71   Corina Knoll, Ruben Vives, Richard Winton, Kate Mather, "Bell Trial: Juror wants to reconsider guilty verdicts, note says." L.A. Times. March 21, 2013. Retrieved from: http://latimesblogs.latimes.com/lanow/2013/03/bell-trial-juror-reconsider-guilty-verdict.html

72   Corina Knoll, Jeff Gottlieb, Ruben Vives, Richard Winton, Kate Mather, "Bell case mistrial after 'all hell has broken loose with Jury." L.A. Times. March 21, 2013. Retrieved from: http://latimesblogs.latimes.com/lanow/2013/03/bell-case-mistrial-after-all-hell-has-broken-loose-with-jury.html.

73   "Bell corruption trial ended with jury intimidation, attorneys say L.A. Times blog," LA Now, March 21, 2013. Retrieved from http://latimesblogs.latimes.com/lanow/2013/03/bell-corruption-trial-ended-with-jury-intimidation-attorneys-say.html.

74   Ibid.

75 Kate Mather and Ruben Vives," Ex-Bell council members agree to plea deal in corruption case." *L.A. Times*, April 9,2014. Retrieved from: http://articles.latimes.com/print/2014/apr/09/local/la-me-ln-bell-council-sentence-20140408.

76 Restitution: Cole, $77,643, plus $200, 000 in retirement money; Mirabal, $242,294; Bello, $177,000; Hernandez, $241,000, and Jacobo, $242,000. Hernandez and Mirabal were required to do 1,000 hours of community service, Bello was required to do 500 hours of community service.

77 Personal interview with George Cole.

78 Corina Knoll, "Former Councilwoman Teresa Jacobo gets two-year prison sentence," *L.A. Times* July 25, 2014. Retrieved from http://www.latimes.com/local/la-me-bell-sentence-20140726-story.html.

79 Jeff Gottlieb, "Bell Corruption: Former councilman gets one year in jail," *L.A. Times*, July 11, 2014. Retrieved from http://www.latimes.com/local/lanow/la-me-ln-ex-bell-councilman-sentenced-corruption-20140711-story.html.

80 Personal interview with George Mirabal.

81 Ruben Vives, "Ex-Bell Mayor's Store is vandalized with graffiti after sentencing." *L.A. Times*. August 1, 2014. Retrieved from: http://www.latimes.com/local/lanow/la-me-ln-ex-bell-mayor-store-graffiti-20140801-story.html.

82 Corina Knoll, "Former Bell Mayor sentenced to year in jail in corruption case." *L.A. Times*. August 1, 2014. Retrieved from: http://www.latimes.com/local/la-me-bell-mayor-jail-20140801-story.html.

CHAPTER EIGHT

The Mechanics of Graft:
The Spaccia Trial

*"I'm not saying that Ms. Spaccia is a horrible person;
I think she's a con artist. It's all about the
money, and it was all about greed."*

—*Judge Kathleen Kennedy*[1]

ROBERT RIZZO WASN'T Bell's only crook. Angela Spaccia was also stealing from Bell's poor residents. She was forced to resign—along with Rizzo and Adams—a week after the *L.A. Times* city manager story came out.

As Bell's assistant city manager, she is best known for an infamous email chain that epitomized the greed at the heart of the Bell scandal.[2] She was finishing up a contract for incoming police chief and long-time friend Randy Adams when Adams wrote: "I am looking forward to seeing you and taking all of Bell's money?! Okay ... just a share of it!!"

Spaccia responded: "LOL ... well you can take your share of the pie ... just like us!!! We will all get fat together ... Bob [Robert Rizzo] has an expression he likes to use on occasion. Pigs get fat ... Hogs get slaughtered!!! So as long as we're not Hogs ... all is well!"[3]

The emails were damning. They helped send her to prison for 11 years and eight months. She was also ordered to pay nearly $8 million in restitution.

The Spaccia trial provided a close-up look at how the assistant city manager handled the mechanics of Rizzo's graft, hiding salary increases and pension boosts, keeping separate sets of books, using obtuse accounting methods, and writing contracts that wouldn't be reviewed by the council or the city attorney.

CHILDHOOD

Spaccia was born September 1958 in Elmira, New York. She grew up in Sun Valley, California, in the San Fernando Valley, which is about 25 miles north of Bell. Her mother, Yolanda, was a Shoshone Indian. Her father, Francesco, emigrated from Italy and was a professor who taught Italian at UCLA. She had two brothers and two sisters. When she was eight, her parents divorced. Then, when she was 14, her father died of a sudden heart attack while in Italy. He was only 36. Spaccia and one of her brothers were raised by her grandparents in California.

In 1976, Spaccia graduated from Francis Polytechnic School in California. She then earned her Associate's degree from Ventura Community College and her Bachelor of Arts degree in Business Administration from La Verne University in 1990. She also earned several certificates in finance, accounting, and management.

She was 19 when she took a clerk's job with the city of Ventura on the Pacific coast, 60 miles northwest of Los Angeles. After that, she held a series of jobs in various municipal agencies, including director of finance and management services, North County Transit District, Oceanside, CA; director of management services, Los Angeles County Metropolitan Transportation Authority, CA; chief administrative officer, Kootenai County, Idaho; and assistant chief administrative office, County of Ventura. She became an expert in public money management. Her specialty was finance and accounting, including "accounts payable, payroll, financial reporting, and coordination of independent audits."[4]

Spaccia was hardworking and ambitious and was quickly promoted to positions with increasingly greater responsibility.

Terry Adelman, the City of Ventura's finance director from 1987 to 1996, oversaw Spaccia when she was an accounting manager. He praised her abilities and management style. "She ran an incredible accounting department," Adelman said. "She had outstanding audits each year."[5]

There were problems in her personal life. She'd been divorced three times. Her son, Sean, was in a head-on car accident and later a motorcycle collision that left him with permanent brain damage, requiring constant care. His devastating injuries and the fact that she was a single mother would come up again as the scandal unfolded.

In 2000, Spaccia started in Bell as a financial consultant. On July 2003, she was hired as a permanent employee of Bell as assistant to the chief administrative officer. In her deposition and during the trial she said her primary job was to mentor Lourdes Garcia, a young woman whom Rizzo was grooming to become director of finance.

Spaccia had previously worked with Bell's police chief Randy Adams at the City of Ventura in the mid-1970s. He was 21 when he joined the Ventura police department in 1972. It was his first job. Born in California, Adams had his bachelor's degree in police science and administration from California State University, Los Angeles. He would go on to be the police chief at Simi Valley and Glendale before retiring. Now, Spaccia wanted Adams to leave retirement and become Bell's chief of police.[6]

Spaccia seemed always aware of how people perceived her. Spaccia was very attractive and was a fitness buff who worked out daily, dressed professionally at work, often in pants suits, and exuded charm and self-confidence. Soft-spoken, yet deliberate in her speech, she knew how to get what she wanted. She parked her black high-end Mercedes Benz behind the police station in a fenced-off lot that required a special code to get in. The lot was only for police "black and white" cruisers; hers was the only private car there. She wanted people to know she had power, and she was special.[7]

The reclusive Rizzo, on the other hand, liked to park his vehicle at a rear exit to his office "so he could make a quick getaway," he had once said to former Bell Police Sergeant and whistle-blower James Corcoran. During his first decade there, Rizzo drove a Cadillac Seville, but always when he purchased a new one, it was the same model and color, "so people didn't think he had just purchased a new car," he told former Bell Police Chief Mike Trevis.

They complemented each other well. Where Rizzo was an introvert, Spaccia was outgoing and personable. Rizzo, who deplored attention, made Spaccia the public face of the city, but he never relinquished control, said Corcoran. Also, unlike Rizzo, Spaccia was a "numbers" person who knew the details of municipal finance.

"There wasn't a mastermind in this case. There was a *master* and a *mind*. Mr. Rizzo was in charge. He was the boss. He had the power. He had the authority. But Miss Spaccia made what he wanted to have happen, happen. She was the mind," said prosecuting attorney Max Huntsman in his closing remarks at her trial.[8]

THE TRIAL

Judge Kennedy insisted that Rizzo and Spaccia be tried together, but Rizzo shocked everyone when he pled no contest for all 69 counts a few days before he and Spaccia were to go on trial. Spaccia would now be tried alone.

PROSECUTION

Deputy District Attorneys Max Huntsman and Sean Hassett from the Public Integrity Division (PID) prosecuted the case. The erudite and intellectual Huntsman grew up in Los Angeles and attended public schools. He graduated from the University of California, Santa Cruz, and then earned his law degree at Yale.

Hassett, who was of Irish descent, graduated from Loyola Law School and joined the District Attorney's Office in 1994.

He was a streetfighter who wasn't afraid to get his hand's dirty. Hassett was tough, loud, and tended to raise his voice and wave his arms when making a point. He toned things down in court but not all that much. One attorney accused him of using "beer-hall jingoisms" when he spoke to the jury. Hassett liked the accusation so much he had it framed and hung on his office wall. He'd worked in the Public Integrity Division since 2010. He and Huntsman had a long history prosecuting local elected officials. Huntsman did the opening argument; Hassett closed.

Spaccia's trial took place before the same judge, Kennedy, and in the same courtroom as the Bell City Council trial. It started October 23, 2013, about seven months after the close of the Bell City Council trial. The trial would go to the jury on November 21, 2013.

SALARY

Spaccia was charged with 13 counts of misappropriation of public funds, conflict of interest, and keeping the official record secret. By the summer of 2010, Spaccia was making $564,000 a year.[9] Getting such a fat paycheck isn't against the law. But the way she got it is.

Contracts were supposed to be written by the city's attorney, Ed Lee, but Rizzo said he was delegating this to Spaccia "to save attorney's fees." However, it is against the law for employees to write their own contracts. This law is on the books to prevent officials from looting the public treasury. Spaccia crafted her own employment contract and wrote contracts for other highly paid employees. She gave herself and the others huge raises and other financial perks. All of this was kept secret, hidden from the council and the public. And all of it was illegal.

Spaccia worked hard to keep these salaries secret. She was clearly worried that the council and the public would not look kindly on what she called "insane" paychecks. She writes Adams, Bell's police chief, "We have crafted our agreements carefully, so we do not draw attention to our pay periods. The word Pay Period is used and not defined to protect you from someone taking the time to add up your salary."[10]

A "pay period" was approximately every two weeks, but someone reading this contract could easily assume the term meant a month.[11] To see someone's yearly salary, a councilmember would have to multiply the figure in the pay period column in the budget spreadsheets by roughly 26. A bump in a "pay period" didn't attract attention, but it could mean a big increase in yearly salary.

Spaccia's contract, which she authored and only Rizzo approved, guaranteed her a minimum 12% pay increase each year. In some years, the percent was much higher.

During the trial, prosecutor Hassett asked Spaccia what she did to deserve a 42% pay increase in 2005, which skyrocketed her annual pay from roughly $185,000 to $245,000. Spaccia said the big raise was to make up for the salary cut she took when she came to work full time for Bell. Spaccia said she was "grateful" for the raise. "I just did what I was told and accepted it," she said.[12]

She also made it next to impossible to figure out Rizzo's salary. To prove the point to the jury, Hassett asked Spaccia to find Rizzo's salary in the budget she had prepared and the council had approved. "Spaccia started on a page-flipping journey through the budget, first pointing to a section that listed all the positions in the city. Then she turned to another page that listed a salary for the chief administrative officer position. When Hassett asked whether that was Rizzo's salary, she pointed to a column that she said showed the figure listed was actually only 35% of his full salary. When Hassett again asked how someone could find out Rizzo's salary, Spaccia replied, "This is where it gets complicated." Spaccia said they would have to look at another city document, called a personnel action report, which was not part of the budget packet.[13]

All employment contracts were legally required to be signed by the mayor and the city's attorney, Ed Lee, to be legal. But Lee said that he did not recall signing them and was chagrined when he saw his signature on them. Bell City Clerk Rebecca Valdez said she slipped the contracts into stacks of myriad documents, such as resolutions, that mayors typically sign.[14]

Also, all employment contracts for top Bell officials have to be discussed at public meetings and approved by a majority of the council. This never happened because the contracts were never put on the council's agenda.[15] Instead, the council approved the entire budget, which included pay increases for all salaried employees.[16] The reason neither the council nor the city attorney ever saw a separate employment contract was because Rizzo falsely claimed that the council had delegated to him the power to negotiate employment contracts without council approval. The contract signature line was changed at Spaccia's request from "Mayor" to "Chief Administrative Officer."[17] The resolution that supposedly gave Rizzo the power to negotiate contracts had been altered to include language that did not appear in the resolution that the council had approved.

The biggest pay spike took place in 2008—when Spaccia authored a resolution that gave her and Rizzo a week off for every two weeks that they worked. They never took the additional time off. Instead they cashed in the accrued vacation/sick days for a second check. This resulted in a 50% jump in compensation. This conversion was never approved by the council. The council, whom prosecutor Huntsman had called "fat, dumb, and happy" were collecting their own inflated $100,000-a-year salaries and were not asking any questions.[18]

PENSION

By the summer of 2010, Rizzo was making $1,180,000 a year, and Spaccia was making $564,000 total compensation. Both wanted to retire from Bell with as close to their full salaries as they could engineer, which they would *receive for the rest of their lives.*

Alan Pennington, an actuary from Nashville who worked for a subsidiary of Wells Fargo bank, set up Bell's pension plan. He testified for the prosecution. Pennington testified that Spaccia asked him to devise a retirement plan that would benefit only her and Rizzo.

There are two types of employees at Bell: safety employees (police) and non-safety employees. After 9/11, the city agreed to give safety employees what is known as "3 percent at 50," which means that they could retire at any age after 50 and receive 3% of their last year's salary times the number of years they had worked. So, for example, a police officer who had worked 30 years and was over 50 could retire with 90% of his or her final pay.

Non-safety employees received "2 percent at 55." This means they could retire at age 55 and get 2% of their highest year's pay for each year they had worked. So, if "Ms. Jones" worked for Bell for 25 years, and in her last year she made $100,000, she would get 50,000 each year for the rest of her life. Two percent was the highest percentage offered by CalPERS, which is the retirement program for California's public employees.[19]

The city wanted 41 of its selected non-safety employees, including the council, to get 3% too. So, Spaccia instructed Pennington to create an additional 1% pension plan, which was called the *Supplemental Plan*."[20]

Now, Rizzo and Spaccia wanted this 1% increase for themselves too. But there was a problem. Bell's pension program was regulated by a federal law, The Employee Retirement Income Security Act of 1974 (ERISA).

ERISA was put in place to protect people who had worked for a company their entire lives from losing their pensions if the company went bankrupt. Technically, the law only provides insurance protection for pensions. If your employer goes bankrupt, you still get your pension. ERISA has a number of restrictions, including a cap on the amount of pensionable pay. The salary cap was around $250,000.[21] However, several Bell employees, including Rizzo, Spaccia and Adams, were earning hundreds of thousands of dollars over this limit. So, Spaccia asked Pennington to develop a "*Replacement Plan*" so these "high compensation" administrators could get the additional 1%, too. This part of their pension was not insured by the federal government.

Sure enough, Spaccia and Pennington, through their private Wells Fargo consultant, developed a formula so that somebody who made above the salary cap would be able to get the same benefit as if he or she were getting the 1% benefit. This was done by *replacing* the 1% with a much larger percentage on the monies above the capped figure. The "*Replacement Plan*" was so complicated that even Judge Kennedy had trouble understanding how it worked and broke into Pennington's testimony and said, "I don't know about the jury, but I am having a lot of difficulty following this, and I don't think I am getting it."[22]

Here's how it worked: If a person were making $500,000 a year and they received the full 3% (2% from CalPERS, plus the 1% supplemental), and they worked 25 years, their yearly pension would be $375,000. That is, 3% × $500,000 × 25.

However, the salaries above the cutoff, say, $250,000, would not get the benefit of the 1% increase. Instead, they would get 2% up to the cutoff point, $250,000, and 1% of the monies above the cutoff. This comes out to $187,000. That is $250,000 × 2% × 25, or $125,000 *plus* $250,000 × 1% × 25, or $62,5000.

That's a difference of $188,000 per year *for life*. Spaccia and Rizzo didn't want to leave such a huge chunk of change on the table.

To get the full benefit of the additional 1%, the *Replacement Plan* increased the percentage for salary above the ERISA cap. In this example, that would be 4%. The first $250,000 benefit (from CalPERS) would be $125,000 ($250,000 × 2% × 25 years), and the benefit covered by the *Replacement Plan* above the cutoff ($250,000 × 4% × 25 years) would be $250,000 for a total of $375,000.

Rizzo was confident that he could get the council to approve the *Replacement Plan* because he felt he could sell it to them as the *fair* thing to do. He wanted to get the same 1% benefit that everyone else was getting.

The replacement percentage had to be readjusted periodically for Rizzo and Spaccia because of raises, increased years in service, an increase in the ERISA salary cap, and other factors. The end result was that it boosted their yearly pensions by at least $375,000 per year above their already hefty CalPERS payouts.[23] The bottom line is had they not been forced out of their jobs, Rizzo would have gotten nearly a million dollars a year in pension benefits and Spaccia half a million dollars, every year, for the rest of their lives.[24]

Had it been funded, the *Replacement Plan* was going to cost the city $15.5 million for Rizzo and Spaccia alone.[25] This was a huge sum, especially for one of the poorest cities in Los Angeles County.

Spaccia knew that the pension liability would go through the roof if other highly compensated employees, such as Finance Director Lourdes Garcia, were included. This worried Spaccia. She emailed Pennington, "My fear is that our finance director will get the hang of it and try to change the eligibility ... to something that suits her once Bob leaves. It would create an incredible burden for the future generation ... "[26] Or, perhaps, the city would go brankrupt and she wouldn't be paid.

So, Spaccia tailored the *Replacement Plan* so only she and Rizzo could benefit. To keep Garcia and others out, the plan was closed to anyone hired after July 1, 2003—the very date Spaccia was hired. Also, the plan would disappear entirely after they both retired so that future employees couldn't petition the council for the same benefit and, therefore, draw unwanted attention to their exorbitant pensions.[27]

Spaccia also was worried that someone with more on the ball, such as city critic Nestor Valencia, might get elected, or someone from the public, like a Roger Ramirez, would start nosing around. So, she asked Pennington to change the signature line on any proposed adjustments from the mayor to the city manager, Rizzo.[28] This was against the law.

Pennington testified that he had never seen such outrageous public-sector salaries or pension benefits or a pension plan crafted to benefit just two people and tried to warn Spaccia of potential blowback if their over-the-top salary and pensions became public. He sent Spaccia a news story about the outrage over the $900,000 salary and $500,000 pension Bruce Malkenhorst, Vernon's city manager and Rizzo's buddy, was receiving—a yearly pension of $500,000, the highest pension paid by CalPERS. He also warned Spaccia that if a future council challenged the plan in court, a judge may not look favorably on the pensioner "when the member is a highly paid person that had a significant role in developing a plan in which he is the largest beneficiary."[29]

Pennington sent Spaccia an email that said, "I guess the spotlight on the City of Bell could show up [once] you and Bob have retired. Not sure there's anything you should do or anything anyone else could do (to reduce future benefits) but thought you might find it interesting none-the-less."

Spaccia replied, "Yes we have discussed it as well. You are right, there is nothing to do then [sic] watch and see how it plays out."[30]

These outrageous pensions paid to those who had inflated salaries came at the expense of the poor and working-class people of Bell. As retirement costs grew, there was less money in the budget for parks, libraries, street repairs, and the other things cities spend money on. The city's pension obligations for all its retirees would help bring the city to the edge of bankruptcy.

The council offset the impact on the budget by charging residents a separate "retirement tax." The council continued to increase this tax until the state controller, at the height of the scandal, said the tax had been illegally raised and ordered the city to refund $2.9 million and roll back the tax.[31]

Most retirement plans require employees to contribute a percentage of their paycheck to their retirement—with the employer paying the rest. Not so in Bell. Bell's taxpayers funded the entire contribution, including the supplemental. The city administrator who benefited from these decisions would be long gone before citizens finally caught on.[32]

LOANS AND OTHER THINGS

In addition to her exorbitant salary, Spaccia received loans from the city on a regular basis. She received her first loan of $77,000 immediately after she started. The loan was supposed to be in lieu of vacation or sick days. However, she hadn't been at the city long enough to accrue enough sick or vacation days to justify this amount of money. So, she modified her contract to show she had been working at Bell for years. This first loan was a "flat out gift of public funds."[33]

These monies weren't part of a formal loan program. Legitimate loan programs are authorized by the council. There are rules regarding such things as eligibility and payment terms and interest rates and penalties. Official records are kept and are accessible to the public.

Instead, Rizzo—as a "Godfather"—ran an informal loan program in which he lent out city money to about 40 administrators and others as he pleased.[34] Sometimes people paid the "loans" back; sometimes they didn't. "Spaccia said she didn't know if she'd repaid a $77,500 loan she received when she was hired in October 2003. "I didn't keep track of this stuff at all," she, the city's finance person, said."[35] Neither did the city. She ended up receiving a total of $350,000 in loans, none of which were approved by the council.

Prosecutor Hassett said, "The loans were not actually loans. It is only a loan if you intend to pay it back. Spaccia 'repaid' her 'loans' using her sick and vacation time. The only problem is, she didn't have any sick or vacation time. When she took her first 'loan,' she had just started working for the city.

So, how did she resolve this dilemma? She created her own employment contract, giving herself vacation time as if she were a 20+ year employee. However, this still wasn't enough vacation time to 'repay' her 'loan.' So, she and Rizzo created resolutions *doubling and tripling the amount of sick and vacation* time they were accruing. Eventually, they stopped taking 'loans' and just started cashing out their sick and vacation time as they accrued it, resulting in their receiving a second paycheck equal to 50% of their already grossly inflated and completely illegal salary."[36]

But, there is more: Spaccia had the city pay all of her FICA contributions for Medicare and Social Security in 2008; she gave herself a 20% raise after her last raise in 2008; she gave herself an additional $200 per "pay period" in 2006; and she also gave herself the maximum amount of severance pay allowed by law if she were fired. Finally, Spaccia devised a scheme to get the city to pay her entire contribution to her 401 K Deferred Compensation Retirement Savings Plan, worth $45,000 per year. They did this for Rizzo, too: $90,000 a year for the two of them for the three years until they got caught. This in addition to her CalPERS retirement! [37]

In addition, during her seven years at Bell, Spaccia took a total of a year and a half off work to deal with family members who had medical problems. She went to Idaho to care for her grandfather. She also cared for her son who had had a serious motorcycle accident. Nevertheless, she continued to receive her full salary and she never used a single sick or vacation day. Instead, she continued to garner more paid days off.[38] Rizzo had done this for other employees, and she said she was grateful for his generosity and didn't think she was doing anything wrong accepting this "benefit."[39]

To avoid paying income tax, Spaccia and Rizzo set up dummy corporations which reported fake losses. They were charged with filing false tax returns.[40]

LAYOFFS AND MAYWOOD

In 2008, the economy began to sour, and Bell faced a huge cash shortfall as the impact of the cheating began to kick in. There was a brief discussion by the council of reducing their excessive pay and benefits, but they decided not to. Instead, on Christmas Eve, the city fired 40 part-time workers from the Parks Department to make ends meet.[41]

This was when Rizzo approached Maywood. Maywood was going bankrupt and was unable to get insurance because of excessive claims made against its police department, which it was looking to disband. Maywood also provided policing for the City of Cudahy (pop. 24,000), a city of mostly Latino immigrants on Bell's southern border. Rizzo offered to run Maywood and create a "super" police department that would patrol the three cities, with the intent of bringing in new revenue to Bell. He sent Spaccia over to Maywood to work for free as its city manager (chief administrative officer). She stayed only seven months because of death threats she said she received as a result of her efforts to fix gang-infested Cudahy, which she concluded was "unsalvageable."[42] When the scandal erupted, any talk of consolidation ended.

DEFENSE

Spaccia reached out to Harland Braun, 73, to represent her. Braun is a Los Angeles criminal defense attorney known for his list of high-profile celebrity clients and for his theatrical manner in the courtroom.

Braun alleged this was a politically motivated prosecution. Jerry Brown, the attorney general, was running for governor; Steve Cooley, the Los Angeles County district attorney, was running for attorney general; and John Chiang was running for reelection as state controller. Each launched an investigation and brought charges against Spaccia and others. All this received a significant amount of publicity. Spaccia, he argued, was being used to further their political ambitions, and, as a result, there was a rush to judgment. Finance Director Lourdes Garcia, not Spaccia, should have been charged, he said. But instead, Garcia was given immunity and became one of the prosecution's star witnesses against Spaccia. Garcia, he argued, was Rizzo's "go-to person" when he wanted contracts written and backdated; Garcia, not Spaccia, wrote the false memorandum regarding salaries that was given to Roger Ramirez. The defense also argued that none of the city's attorneys told Spaccia that she was breaking the law. In fact, at times, the attorneys even told her that Rizzo had the authority to do things that were later found to be illegal.[43]

Defense attorney Braun said it was all Rizzo's fault. Braun told the jury, "… At the end of the day, despite all the publicity, and all the smears and all the politics, Angela Spaccia, like a lot of people, was a victim of Robert Rizzo."[44]

Braun portrayed Spaccia as a typist who had no managerial experience and no special expertise in municipal finance. She had no responsibility over the budget, no involvement with the council agenda, and no idea what was going on. Instead, Spaccia, like everyone else, did what Rizzo told her to do. For example, Rizzo, Braun argued, dictated the terms of Randy Adams's compensation package and asked Spaccia to present them to Adams.

Spaccia claimed she didn't even want a huge salary but that Rizzo more or less forced her to take it. When she started at Bell, she said she told Rizzo that all she wanted was a $200,000-a-year salary, so she could retire at age 50 at $100,000 a year.[45]

CLOSING

It is not a crime to make a lot of money. But it is against the law to join with one or more people to develop a secret plan to do something unlawful. This is called a conspiracy.

It is also against the law to tailor a retirement plan to benefit you and just one other person, Robert Rizzo. This is called a conflict of interest.

And it is also against the law to write employment contracts for exorbitant amounts of money for yourself ($564,000), your boss, Rizzo ($1,180,000), and your long-time friend, incoming Police Chief Randy Adams ($457,000) and not have them approved by the council. This is called a misappropriation of public funds.

Finally, it is against the law to destroy, mutilate, or alter or secrete (make secret) a public record. This is called secretion of the official record. Spaccia did this when she gave Police Chief Randy Adams a document on city letterhead acknowledging a yet-to-be-determined work-related disability. Adams could then turn around and use this letter to avoid paying federal taxes on his pension. This document was never approved by the city council, and Spaccia did not make a copy for the files. Spaccia altered other documents, to the benefit of herself and Rizzo.

VERDICT AND SENTENCING

On December 9, 2013, after ten days of deliberation, the jury found Spaccia guilty on 11 of the 13 charging counts. "She was accused of writing illegal contracts, receiving $350,000 of illegal loans from the city, and hiding an agreement that allowed the police chief to retire with a medical disability. The jury was unable to reach a verdict on one count of misappropriating public funds and found her not guilty on one charge related to secretion of public records."[46]

On April 10, 2014, Spaccia appeared before Judge Kennedy to be sentenced. She'd been in jail since being convicted in December; Kennedy had rejected Braun's request for bail and a new trial. Braun had accused Kennedy of being biased against his client.

Judge Kennedy gave Spaccia the second harshest sentence of any of the Bell defendants—11 years and eight months in state prison. She also ordered her to pay more than $8 million in restitution to the city.

"I think [Spaccia] is a con artist," said an incensed Judge Kennedy during the sentencing hearing. "It's all about the money, and it was all about greed."

"Her weapon is not the weapon that I usually see in cases that come before me. It's not a gun, it's not a knife. It's the trust that people had in her," Kennedy said. "She is charming, she is attractive, she is well educated. She is not someone that you think is stealing you blind."

"Ms. Spaccia likes to portray herself as somehow a victim of Mr. Rizzo. She is no victim. ... She got unbelievable amounts of money. ... And so now the day of reckoning is finally here. ... Ultimately what happened is that both Rizzo and Spaccia were not content with being pigs," Kennedy said. "They were hogs and they basically got slaughtered because you can't keep these kinds of things hidden forever."[47]

Spaccia stood silent and shook her head as Kennedy berated her. The four months in jail had taken their toll. She was heavier now and her good looks had faded. Unlike the other defendants, she never apologized or showed remorse. Bell's former second-in-command, wearing an orange jumpsuit, was handcuffed and taken directly to prison.

LESSONS

In the end, Spaccia received a prison term of 11 years and 8 months and was required to repay $8.2 million to Bell. The judge called her a "con artist." But the details that surfaced also exposed the hands-off, pass-the-buck, the "professionals know better" system that prevailed in the city, and the broken, inadequate regulatory system that allowed it to flourish.

Angela Spaccia showed what's possible when safeguards are lax. Cities across the country would do well to let that awareness guide them in creating stronger standards for ethics, legal review, and accounting, which are spelled out in the final chapter. Without them, as it became clear during the trial, there are few restraints on the power of unelected bureaucrats—especially when the mayor and city council they work for aren't vigilant overseers, and the administrators heavily influenced who was on the council.

The council, the city attorney, the city's auditor, members of CalPERS (the state retirement system), and Bell's top paid employees all knew things were terribly wrong, but because there were few negative consequences for them personally, they chose to stay quiet. All of them bore responsibility for allowing Spaccia and Rizzo's schemes to flourish.

Could Bell's activists have cut through the wall of obfuscation that protected Rizzo without the *L.A. Times*? They were on the right track in discussing Public Records Requests. Citizens have a right to see their city's financial information, audits, and records of meetings, and they have a right to explanations, though they may need the help of a CPA to unearth questionable data. Even though it's fairly certain that requests in Bell would've been met with the same stonewalling that Rizzo tried with the press, a blocked request is one of the red flags that can rouse state watchdogs, interest a grand jury, and help set higher-level scrutiny in motion.

ENDNOTES

1   Corina Knoll and Kate Mather, "Former Bell second-in-command gets 11 years for corruption. *L.A. Times*. April 10, 2014. Retrieved from http://articles.latimes.com/2014/apr/10/local/la-me-spaccia-sentencing-20140411.

2   Spaccia said she was joking. See Jeff Gottlieb and Ruben Vives, "'Pigs get Fat' email was a joke, Spaccia testifies at her trial," *L.A. Times,* November 13, 2013.

3   Jeff Gottlieb, "Huge Bell Salaries based on 'secret formula,' prosecutor tells jury." *L.A. Times*. October 23, 2013. Retrieved from: https://www.latimes.com/local/lanow/la-me-ln-spaccia-trial-opens-20131023-story.html

4   Deposition of Pier'Angela Spaccia, Thursday, February 21, 2013, p. 28.

5   Arlene Martinez, "Angela Spaccia, former Ventura employee embroiled in Bell pay scandal, maintains innocence," *Ventura County Star*, February 6, 2013. Retrieved from http://www.vcstar.com/news/angela-spaccia-former-ventura-employee-embroiled-in-bell-pay-scandal-maintains-innocence-video-ep-29-351808801.html.

6   Adams said in a personal communication to the author that he was receiving a $260,000 pension. He'd have to give this up if he became chief. He wanted Bell to pay him the $260,000 plus a chief's salary of about $200,000, which resulted in $457,000, a figure he said he never thought Bell would agree to. Adams was not going to replace two supervisors, which may have made the deal more attractive to the city.

7 Interview with Bell police officer James Corcoran.

8 Assistant District Attorney Max Huntsman, closing remarks. Reporter's transcript of proceedings of *People versus Pier' Angela Spaccia*, November 20, 2013, p. 7086.

9 Reporter's transcript of proceedings of *People versus Pier' Angela Spaccia*, October 23, 2013, p. 1232.

10 Reporter's transcript of proceedings of *People versus Pier' Angela Spaccia*, October 23, 2013, p. 1242.

11 The city had been using Pay Period long before Spaccia arrived.

12 Reporter's transcript of proceedings of *People versus Pier' Angela Spaccia*, November 14, 2013, p. 5796.

13 Jeff Gottlieb and Ruben Vives, "In corruption trial, Bell's Spaccia struggles to explain high salaries." *L.A. Times*. November 14, 2013. Retrieved from http://articles.latimes.com/2013/nov/14/local/la-me-1115-spaccia-20131115.

14 Jeff Gottlieb, "Bell mayor tricked into signing Rizzo, Spaccia contracts, clerk says," *L.A. Times*. October 13, 2013. Retrieved from http://articles.latimes.com/2013/oct/31/local/la-me-ln-bell-mayor-tricked-contracts-rizzo-spaccia-20131031.

15 Jeff Gottlieb, "Ex-Bell city attorney unsure how his signature got on contracts." *L.A. Times*. October 28, 2013. Retrieved from http://articles.latimes.com/2013/oct/28/local/la-me-ln-bell-city-attorney-signature-20131028.

16 This was when a few hundred voters approved the city's change from a general law to a charter city, affirming to Rizzo that no one was watching.

17 Reporter's transcript of proceedings of *People versus Pier' Angela Spaccia*, November 20, 2013, p. 7107.

18 Jeff Gottlieb, "Prosecution begins closing argument in Angela Spaccia trial," *L.A. Times*, November 20, 2013. Retrieved from http://articles.latimes.com/2013/nov/20/local/la-me-1121-angela-spaccia-20131121.

19 THE CalPERS limit would eventually be raised to 2.7%. So, Bell employees received the un-heard of rate of 3.7% at 55. See, Jeff Gottlieb, "Pensions for Rizzo, 40 other Bell employees will be larger than first estimated." *L.A. Times*. September 30, 2010. Retrieved from: http://articles.latimes.com/2010/sep/30/local/la-me-rizzo-pensions-20100930.

20 So now the yearly pension for "Jones" if she worked 25 years would be $75,000 (3 times 25). And if she worked 30 years, she'd get $90,000 for the rest of her life. Many employees benefit from "pension spiking." If someone was making $100,000 a year and wanted to keep making his or her final year's salary as his

or her pension, he or she would get a 10% pay raise his or her final year. CalPERS would use that person's final year to determine his or her pension; 90% of $110,000 is nearly $99,000.

21   The number was adjusted up each year.

22   Reporter's transcript of proceedings for *People versus Pier' Angela Spaccia*, October 24, 2013, p. 1535.

23   Jeff Gottlieb, "Bell's Spaccia was set to make an extra $8 million, expert testifies." *L.A. Times.* October 24, 2013. http://articles. latimes.com/2013/oct/24/local/la-me-ln-bell-spaccia-8-million-20131024.

24   These are rough estimates. Final retirement would depend on the cap, the years worked, and the final year's compensation.

25   Reporter's transcript of proceedings for *People versus Pier' Angela Spaccia*, October 23, 2013, p. 1237.

26   Email contained in Exhibit 18.

27   Reporter's transcript of proceedings for *People versus Pier' Angela Spaccia*, October 23, 2013, p. 1240.

28   Reporter's transcript of proceedings for *People versus Pier' Angela Spaccia*, October 23, 2013, p. 1241.

29   Reporter's transcript of proceedings for *People versus Pier' Angela Spaccia*, October 24, 2013, p. 1551.

30   Jeff Gottlieb, "Pensions for Rizzo, 40 other employees will be larger than first estimated." *L.A. Times.* September 30, 2010. Retrieved from http://articles.latimes. com/2010/sep/30/local/la-me-rizzo-pensions-20100930.

31   Ibid.

32   IBGYBG means: "I be gone, you be gone."

33   Sean Hassett, closing. Reporter's trial transcript of *People versus Pier' Angela Spaccia*, November 21, 2013, p. 7214.

34   Sean Hassett, closing. Reporter's trial transcript of *People versus Pier' Angela Spaccia*, November 21, 2013, p. 7215.

35   See Jeff Gottlieb and Ruben Vives, "Several documents point to questionable action in Bell," *L.A. Times,* November 15, 2013. Retrieved from http://articles. latimes.com/2013/nov/15/local/la-me-angela-spaccia-20131116.

36   Personal interview with Sean Hassett.

37   Reporter's trial transcript of *People versus Pier' Angela Spaccia*, November 21, 2013, p. 7266.

38 Jeff Gottlieb, "In Spaccia defense, a simple premise: Her high pay wasn't a crime." *L.A. Times.* November 22, 2013. Retrieved from http://www.latimes.com/local/la-me-1123-angela-spaccia-20131123-story.html.

39 Reporter's trial transcript of People versus Pier 'Angela Spaccia,' November 21, 2013, page 7314

40 Jeff Gottlieb and Ruben Vives, "Rizzo, Spaccia discussed falsifying tax returns, prosecutor says." *L.A. Times.* November 8, 2013. Retrieved from http://articles.latimes.com/2013/nov/08/local/la-me-spaccia-20131109.

41 Reporter's transcript of proceedings for *People versus Pier' Angela Spaccia*, November 21, 2013, p. 7222.

42 Harland Braun, opening statement, reporter's transcript of proceedings of *People versus Pier' Angela Spaccia*, October 23, 2013, p. 1275. The Mongols and the 18th Street Gang dominate the city. Her son was severely beaten up in a parking lot outside a restaurant. He isn't robbed. Spaccia attributes beating to her work in Cudahy.

43 Jeff Gottlieb, "In Spaccia defense, a simple premise: Her high pay wasn't a crime." *L.A. Times.* November 22, 2013. Retrieved from http://www.latimes.com/local/la-me-1123-angela-spaccia-20131123-story.html. Retrieved from http://www.latimes.com/local/la-me-1123-angela-spaccia-20131123-story.html.

44 Harland Braun, opening statement, reporter's transcript of proceedings of *People versus Pier' Angela Spaccia*, October 23, 2013, p. 1332.

45 Jeff Gottlieb, "In Spaccia defense, a simple premise: Her high pay wasn't a crime." *L.A. Times.* November 22, 2013. Retrieved from http://www.latimes.com/local/la-me-1123-angela-spaccia-20131123-story.html. Retrieved from http://www.latimes.com/local/la-me-1123-angela-spaccia-20131123-story.html.

46 Jeff Gottlieb and Ruben Vives, "Angela Spaccia found guilty in Bell corruption case." *L.A. Times.* December 9, 2013. Retrieved from: http://articles.latimes.com/2013/dec/09/local/la-me-ln-spaccia-verdict—20131209.

47 Corina Knoll and Kate Mather, "Former Bell second-in-command gets 11 years in prison for corruption," *L.A. Times*, April 10, 2014. Retrieved from http://articles.latimes.com/2014/apr/10/local/la-me-spaccia-sentencing-20140411.

CHAPTER NINE

Taking on Rizzo

"Mr. Rizzo, you did some very,
very bad things for a very long time."[1]

—*Judge Kathleen Kennedy*

ROBERT RIZZO WAS charged with 69 counts, including misappropriation of public funds, engaging in a conflict of interest, falsifying public records, perjury, and conspiracy.[2]

But he never went before a jury: Rizzo shocked everyone when he pled no contest a few days before he and Spaccia were to go to trial together in October of 2013. Underlying that decision were three years of legal decisions and political machinations that not only had a bearing on Rizzo's case, but that also serve as a window into how various government entities handle city corruption cases.

Rizzo's lawyer, Jim Spertus, a former federal prosecutor, was looking forward to seeing him have his day in court, but three things came together that caused Spertus to urge his client to plead no contest.

Spertus didn't think Rizzo could get a fair trial in Los Angeles. He'd become the poster child for public greed and corruption. His face was plastered all over town, on the cover of newspapers, and featured in TV news programs. Spertus argued this saturation coverage made it impossible to find a neutral pool of jurors. He was the perfect villain for the district attorney and the attorney general, both of whom were campaigning for higher office. Spertus filed a change of venue motion, but Kennedy denied it.[3]

Spertus felt the most serious charge against his client was the misappropriation of public funds—spending public money without legal authority. To prove Rizzo had done that, the prosecution would have to show he'd acted with criminal intent: that is, that Rizzo had *intentionally* tried to deceive the council when it voted on the pay increases. Spertus was confident that he could persuade the jury that Rizzo acted straightforwardly.

But the Stark case (Chapter 7) changed the rules in midstream, reducing the standard of proof in municipal corruption cases to *criminal negligence*. Instead of being asked whether Rizzo *intended* to hoodwink the council, now the jury would be asked whether Rizzo *should have known* that he was breaking the law. Conviction was much more likely in that scenario, and Rizzo, theoretically, could have faced being sentenced to six consecutive years for each of the 69 counts against him. By contrast, the judge told Spertus that a no-contest plea would likely get Rizzo 10 to 12 years, of which he might serve 40% to 50%: five to six years.

Rizzo also faced federal charges for claiming hundreds of thousands of dollars in phony losses to lower his tax liability.[4] Knowing that his client was likely to receive a multi-year prison sentence for tax fraud from federal court, Spertus shrewdly asked Judge Kennedy if the state court sentence she was going to impose could be served concurrently with his federal sentence.

Federal prisons are far nicer than state prisons. They're filled with white-collar criminals who sleep in dormitory-like rooms, not cages. State prisons are overcrowded hell holes filled with gangbangers and other violent felons. They also have horrible medical care, which was a big problem because Rizzo, now 60, was in poor health.[5] Also, the federal prison he would likely be sent to would be closer to his wife and daughter.

The judge agreed with the concurrent sentence request. Spertus' plan was for Rizzo to do the federal time first. This reduced the amount of time he'd spend in state prison. Spertus even goaded federal prosecutors to give his client even *more* time for tax fraud. Spertus was privately thrilled and proud of his legal skills.[6] Others took notice, especially when Angela Spaccia, Bell's Number 2, ended up getting more time in state prison.

Given the failure of the change of venue motion, the Stark decision, and Judge Kennedy's indicated sentence, Rizzo decided to plead no contest. So, in October 2013, three days before he was set to go on trial with Spaccia, Rizzo shocked everyone and pled "no contest" to all 69 counts. By not going on trial, Rizzo, unlike Spaccia, avoided the enumeration and public retelling of his myriad crooked schemes. Now, all that remained was for him to be sentenced.

On April 16, 2014, Rizzo stood before Judge Kennedy. He'd always been heavy, but now he was obese; while walking from his car to the court, Rizzo tripped on a curb and broke his leg. His face was pale and puffy. His thinning hair, now all gray, was combed back. He pressed his hands on the table to steady himself, and in a "small, halting, scratchy voice" addressed the court.[7]

"Your honor, I started in Bell in 1992. For the first 12 years, we ran a very good tight ship because we didn't have any issues. And beginning in the 13th year, I breached the public's confidence by starting to look at the position more towards myself than towards the community. I'm very, very sorry for that. I apologize for that. If I could go back and make changes, I would. I have done it a million times in my own mind. All I can do today is ask you to please understand that I'm sorry. I will never do anything like this again. I will never have an opportunity, but I did breach the public's confidence, and I do apologize."[8]

Everyone knew that the sentence would be between 10–12 years because that is what Judge Kennedy indicated she would give Rizzo if he pled no contest. Nevertheless, Hassett, the prosecutor, asked for a longer sentence. Spertus argued that a sentence closer to five years was more appropriate since he hadn't been in trouble before. He had admitted his crimes had apologized, and had been cooperative. Judge Kennedy called Spertus' request "ridiculous."

Now it was the public's turn. Several citizens from Bell spoke, urging the judge to impose the harshest sentence possible. Alfred Areyan, 57, who has lived in Bell for four decades and monitored much of the criminal proceedings against Bell's former leaders, described Rizzo as the mastermind of the wide-ranging corruption. "He was the black widow that created the web," Areyan said.[9]

Another Bell resident, Donna Gannon, who has lived in Bell since 1941 and attended nearly all of the trial, said, "Feel sorry for Rizzo? I don't. He preyed on the naive people and the uneducated people in the city of Bell. And he deserves as much as he can get. ..."[10] Violeta Alvarez, who was elected to the council in the recall election said, "Even in 30 years we are still going to be paying for the wrongdoing of Mr. Rizzo."[11]

Judge Kennedy, presided over all the Bell trials, called Rizzo a "Godfather" who abused his power. "Power tends to corrupt, and absolute power corrupts absolutely ... That is the theme of what happened in Bell ... There were no checks and balances to control Mr. Rizzo and those that were in power in the city .... Nobody wanted to upset the apple cart because they were being paid so well," she said.[12]

Judge Kennedy sentenced him to 12 years in state prison and ordered him to repay $8.8 million in restitution. Unlike Spaccia, who was cuffed and taken off right after she was sentenced, Rizzo was given a month to get his affairs in order before reporting to the U.S. Marshal's Office in downtown Los Angeles. From there he was taken to federal prison in Lompoc, California.

THE POLITICAL CONTEXT

Politics entered the picture in a dramatic way on September 15, 2010. A week before the Los Angeles County District Attorney Steve Cooley was set to file criminal charges against the eight defendants—the council defendants, George Cole, Oscar Hernandez, Victor Bello, Luis Artiga, George Mirabal, and Teresa Jacobo plus the city manager and his assistant, Robert Rizzo,

Angela Spaccia—Jerry Brown, then California's attorney general, upstaged Cooley with a civil action ("AG lawsuit") against the eight that alleged "violations of various state laws pertaining to the waste of public funds, conflict of interest, breach of fiduciary duty, and violation of public trust."[13]

The AG lawsuit raised important questions about who should be handling the Bell case: the state government and Attorney General Jerry Brown or Los Angeles County and District Attorney Steve Cooley, or both?

Both Brown and Cooley were running for higher office in 2010, and getting tough on the Rizzo gang was a way to capitalize on a notorious public case. Brown was in a tight race for governor, and with the election less than two months away, he pounded the Bell issue to help him hold his slim lead over Meg Whitman, the multibillionaire ex-Hewlett-Packard CEO, who had poured $140 million of her own money into her campaign.[14]

Cooley, who was running to replace Brown as attorney general, felt Brown was trying to "duke his way"[15] into a high-profile case, but Brown argued that as the chief law officer of the state, the attorney general not only had the power to act but also an urgent need to do so because the members of the Bell City Council who committed the abuse were still in power and were not going to authorize any legal action against themselves or their now-former city manager with whom they allegedly conspired.

In addition to jurisdiction, the case also raised the question of separation of powers: Can the judicial branch review compensation decisions made by a legislative body? In other words, if the city council wants to pay outrageous salaries to its city manager, isn't that its business (and the voters who elected the council members), not the court?

Brown's lawsuit was heard by Los Angeles County Superior Court Judge Ralph W. Dau, who was 73 at the time.[16] Dau had been on the bench since 1995 and had a reputation for integrity, hard work, and attention to detail. His decisions were rarely overturned.

Done in a rush, the attorney general's complaint was poorly written and had the appearance to him of being a "political lawsuit," Dau said in his decision to dismiss the attorney general's complaint.[17] The decision to pay outrageous salaries was a "legislative" act, he wrote, and the legislature, in this case, was the Bell City Council. Therefore, the attorney general was violating "separation of powers" by getting involved. Also, Dau said, there was no need for the state to step into what he argued was a local matter. The attorney general, in short, should butt out.[18] Finally, Dau argued that the individual council members could not be held liable for their joint decision to pay Rizzo an outrageous salary. This is called legislative immunity.

Brown's office appealed the trial court's decision to the court of appeals. In the meantime, Cooley's case moved forward.

In the two-plus years it took for the appellate decision to come back, much changed in Bell and California. Brown took office as governor. Cooley lost his attorney general bid. The council members accused of corruption were recalled from office in March 2011, and the city was under new management. Under the old regime, Bell had opposed the AG lawsuit, but the city's new officials worked with the new Attorney General, Kamala Harris, to reverse Dau's decision and make it possible for the attorney general to pursue litigation on behalf of the financially strapped city. Bell's new leadership team welcomed the chance to have a second set of lawyers it didn't have to pay for to help gain restitution from the defendants.

The attorney general's appeal was heard by Judge Walter Croskey, 78. Croskey had served as an appellate court judge for more than 25 years. He was one of four judges who served on the appellate panel and, like Dau, was widely admired and respected. He was also one of the court's most prolific authors of published legal opinions. A published opinion can be "cited as binding legal precedent within the State of California and the United States."[19] Croskey would consult with the other justices on the appellate panel, but the ruling was his.[20]

The decision in the appeal of Dau's decision came down on March 20, 2013, the same day five of the six council defendants were found guilty of the corruption case that Cooley had filed.[21]

The court found that the attorney general has the right to step into city affairs in cases of funds misappropriation and conflicts of interest, acts that fall outside the city's charter—a decision that will be useful in other California cities plagued by corruption.

With his legal bills piling up, Rizzo, on October 15, 2010, about one month after the attorney general's lawsuit was filed, asked the city to pay *his* legal fees and costs in defending the lawsuits filed against him by the district attorney, the attorney general, and the city of Bell.[22]

In addition, Rizzo argued that his employment contract specified that he was not personally liable for administrative decisions he made as city manager.[23] In his deposition, Bell's Attorney Ed Lee said that Rizzo's employment contract said the city would pay his legal fees if he got sued doing city business.

This provision is included in most city manager contracts to protect them from being held liable for, say, buying a police car that had a faulty airbag that hurt the driver.

To many, this was the height of chutzpah: Rizzo was demanding that the city that he had ripped off for millions pay for his defense against those, including the city, who were suing him! Also, city officials felt that the demand that Bell should pay damages due itself that the court might impose on him was ridiculous.

Not surprisingly, the city refused to pay for Rizzo's defense. Nor would they indemnify him against the cost of any judgments made against him.[24]

Judge Ralph Dau agreed that the city was responsible for Rizzo's defense. But he did *not* rule that Rizzo's contract indemnified him. This would have ended the matter. However, Dau had just been reversed by the appellate court on the AG lawsuit. He was certainly aware of the blowback he'd get if he ruled against the City, that Bell must pay Rizzo's defense bills.

So, Dau decided to proceed cautiously. Instead, he said there should be a trial about what the contract says. This was highly unusual because a contract is a matter of law, and a judge should be able to rule whether the Rizzo contract was valid and whether it does or does not grant immunity, according to Rizzo's lawyer, Jim Spertus.

However, Judge Dau wanted this to be a "bench trial" in which both sides would prepare briefs and argue their cases, and he'd render a decision. That way, he'd have a suitable paper trail to buttress an unpopular decision.

The city's attorney, Anthony Taylor, saw where this was going: the city would end up having to pay millions to defend Rizzo—a costly and embarrassing setback. So, to prevent that from happening, Taylor asked the judge to make this a jury trial rather than a bench trial.

Taylor thought there was little chance a jury would decide that the unpopular Rizzo's contract required the city to pay his legal costs. Rizzo's lawyer, Spertus, argued that this was a legal issue that Judge Dau, not a jury, should decide. Dau agreed; there would be no jury trial.

Taylor then threw the legal equivalent of a "Hail Mary" pass. Normally, attorneys file appeals to the appellate court *after* the trial court has concluded its business. Taylor wanted the appeals court—again Judge Croskey—to get involved immediately and to rule that the city was entitled to a jury trial regarding Rizzo's contract.

Taylor filed an interlocutory writ which is a request for the appeals court to consider a ruling by a trial court judge *while* the case is being heard in trial court. The standard for granting an interlocutory writ or appeal is that there would be irreparable injury if the appeal takes place *after* the trial court has acted. This was a highly unusual move with a very low probability of success.

But Taylor hit the jackpot. He was only asking for the appeals court to order the trial court to hold a jury trial about Rizzo's contract. But the appeals court, meaning Croskey, ignored this question and on October 4, 2013, dismissed the case entirely. He ruled that the city did not have to pay for the defense of an employee charged with a crime, regardless of any contract. Period. Spertus, Rizzo's attorney, who could possibly be out millions in legal fees, was—not suprising—shocked.

Taylor, explaining the opinion, said the "city would have to pay for Rizzo's defense in a case where a developer sued the city manager because its proposed shopping mall was turned down,"[25] but not when the city manager was accused of criminal activity or when the city or the attorney general was taking action against him.

The appellate court also ruled that the attorney general can pursue litigation on behalf of a city.

In 2014, both Jerry Brown and Kamala Harris were reelected by huge margins. In March of 2015, the attorney general's civil case against Rizzo was quietly dismissed. However, the order by Judge Kennedy for Rizzo and other defendants to pay restitution to the city stood.

LESSONS

The upshot for those who want to see justice done after they've rooted out local corruption is that politics can be an ally, but they need to be aware of the political context in which they are doing battle. "Being tough on crime" and "going after the crooks stealing the public's money" reliably produce political capital for elected prosecutors at the county and state level. In this case, both the attorney general and the district attorney were going after the bad guys with suspicions and evidence of wrongdoing. The more potential scrutiny, the better.

The Bell case established two important legal precedents. First, the Courts of Appeal decided that the attorney general can pursue claims against former corrupt officials. Before that decision was issued, the trial court had taken the view that the attorney general could not pursue such litigation, according to Bell attorneys David Aleshire and Anthony Taylor.[26] This gives reformers a powerful potential ally—the attorney general—in their fight against local corruption.[27] "City officials and state officials can now work together through the court system to obtain justice," say David Aleshire and Anthony Taylor, Bell's attorneys. From a practical standpoint, this is especially significant because "local government entities that have been looted by corrupt officials often do not have the necessary financial resources to fight their legal battles alone."[28]

The Bell case also established the precedent that public agencies do not have to pay for an employee's legal fees and costs in lawsuits filed by the attorney general or district attorney or indemnify from them other lawsuits when the employee's actions were outside their prescribed duties. "The Court of Appeals' [sic] decision allows public agencies to pursue claims against public officials without the official turning around and claiming that the victimized public agency pay for its own recovery efforts," wrote Aleshire and Taylor."[29]

ENDNOTES

1   Jeff Gottlieb, Corina Knoll, and Christopher Goffard, "Bell's Rizzo sentenced to 12 years in prison," *L.A. Times*, April 16, 2014. Retrieved from http://www.latimes.com/local/la-me-0417-rizzo-prison-20140417-story.html.

2   This chapter is based on interviews with the prosecuting and defense attorneys, the trial transcripts and press accounts, and the paper written by Bell city attorneys David J. Aleshire and Anthony Taylor, "Corruption on Steroids: The Bell Scandal from the Legal Perspective," paper presented at the City of Bell Scandal Revisited, Chapman University, February 19, 2015. I also attended the various Bell trials and spoke with Bell residents there. Misappropriation of public funds is the appropriation of public money without legal authorization. The prosecution alleged that Rizzo broke this law when he (and Spaccia) asked a representative of a Wells Fargo subsidiary to devise the Bell Supplemental Retirement and Replacement Benefit Program and when he directed Lourdes Garcia to create a policy that would increase his and Spaccia's sick and vacation time. The policy would only benefit the two of them but without appearing so. Conflict of interest occurs when a person is in a position to derive personal benefit from actions or decisions made in his or her official capacity. Rizzo broke this law when he wrote his own employment contract which hiked his pay without council approval. This one was complicated because the council did approve Rizzo's pay increases, but they did not post an agenda 72 hours before the council meeting, which is required by the Brown Act. See the transcript. It is against the law to steal, remove, or secrete (keep secret); destroy, mutilate, or deface; or alter or falsify any public record. This is known as Secretion of Official Record. But is commonly referred to as falsifying public records. Rizzo

broke this law when he instructed a Bell employee to give Roger Ramirez false payroll information and when he and Spaccia had an official letter prepared for Police Chief Randy Adams that said, "Mr. Adams qualifies for and will be filing for, a medical disability retirement, in conjunction with his service retirement, when he retires from the City of Bell." This letter was not entered into the city's official records, but it was given to Randy Adams to use when he retired. Perjury occurs when someone willfully and contrary to his or her oath states as true any material matter which he or she knows to be false. Rizzo perjured himself when he filed a false statement (California Form 700) of his economic interests. A conspiracy occurs when two or more people agree to commit a criminal act. Rizzo was guilty of conspiring to break the law by colluding with Spaccia to commit these illegal acts.

3   Interview with Jim Spertus.

4   Jeff Gottlieb, "Bell corruption: Rizzo gets 33 months for tax fraud," *L.A. Times*, April 14, 2014. Retrieved from http://articles.latimes.com/2014/apr/14/local/la-me-ln-rizzo-prison-tax-fraud-20140414.

5   Due to his obesity and addiction to alcohol and stress.

6   Interview with Jim Spertus.

7   Jeff Gottlieb, Corina Knoll, and Christopher Goffard, "Bell's Rizzo sentenced to 12 years in prison," *L.A. Times*, April 16, 2014. Retrieved from http://www.latimes.com/local/la-me-0417-rizzo-prison-20140417-story.html.

8   Reporter's trial transcript of *The People versus Robert Adrian Rizzo*, April 16, 2014, p. 14.

9   Jeff Gottlieb, Corina Knoll, and Christopher Goffard, "Bell's Rizzo sentenced to 12 years in prison," *L.A. Times*, April 16, 2014. Retrieved from http://www.latimes.com/local/la-me-0417-rizzo-prison-20140417-story.html.

10   Personal interview with Donna Gannon.

11   Personal interview with Violeta Alvarez.

12   Op. cit.

13   David J. Aleshire and Anthony Taylor, "Corruption on Steroids: The Bell Scandal from the Legal Perspective," paper presented at the City of Bell Scandal Revisited, Chapman University, February 19, 2015.

14   California Gubernatorial Election, 2010. https://en.wikipedia.org/wiki/California_gubernatorial_election,_2010.

15   Personal interview with Steve Cooley.

16   The AG's complaint contained seven causes of action: (1) The first charge was the one that charged the entire council with waste of public funds (Code of Civil

Procedure section 526a), with respect to the excessive compensation paid all defendants; (2,3) The second and third causes of actions were that the council was negligent in authorizing the wasteful expenditures of public funds. It is alleged that the councilmember defendants negligently failed to exercise due care and reasonable diligence in approving the employment contracts of Rizzo and Spaccia; (4,5) The fourth and fifth causes of action against Rizzo and the councilmember defendants alleged fraud regarding the issuing of a misleading ordinance. By publication in the council meeting minutes, councilmember defendants affirmatively misrepresented to the public that Ordinance 1158 was to limit their compensation. In fact, the ordinance nearly doubled their salaries, the AG said; (6) A sixth cause of action charges Rizzo and Spaccia with entering into a contract in which they have a personal financial interest; and (7) Finally, the seventh cause of action was breach of fiduciary duty and violation of public trust. Defendants, as officers and employees of the city, violated the public trust and breached their fiduciary responsibilities to the city and its citizens when they awarded themselves and each other excessive and wasteful compensation that were not commensurate with their respective duties and responsibilities. *The People ex rel. Edward G. Brown v. Robert Rizzo et al.* Superior Court State of California. Retrieved from https://oag.ca.gov/system/files/attachments/press_releases/n1988_document_3.pdf

17 Richard Winton, "Attorney general's lawsuit against Bell officials could be in jeopardy; Rizzo's attorney says case is 'dead,'" *L.A. Times*, November 10, 2010. Retrieved from http://latimesblogs.latimes.com/lanow/2010/11/attorney-generals-lawsuit-against-bell-8-could-be-in-jeopardy-rizzos-attorney-says-case-is-dead-.html.

18 "The powers of state government are legislative, executive, and judicial. Persons charged with the exercise of one power may not exercise either of the others except as permitted by this Constitution. (CAl. Const., art III $ 3).

19 David J. Aleshire and Anthony Taylor, "Corruption on Steroids: The Bell Scandal from the Legal Perspective," paper presented at the City of Bell Scandal Revisited, Chapman University, February 19, 2015.

20 *The People ex rel. Kamala D. Harris v. Robert Rizzo et al.* In the Court of Appeals of the State of California Second Appellate District, Division Three, March 20, 2013.

21 *The People ex rel. Kamala D. Harris v. Robert Rizzo et al.* In the Court of Appeals of the State of California Second Appellate District, division three, March 20, 2013.

22   David J. Aleshire and Anthony Taylor, "Corruption on Steroids: The Bell Scandal from the Legal Perspective," paper presented at the City of Bell Scandal Revisited, Chapman University, February 19, 2015.

23   The contract reads: "City shall defend, hold harmless and indemnify Employee against any claim, demand, judgment or action, of any type or kind, arising out of any act or failure to act, by Employee, if such act or failure to act was within the course and scope of Employee's employment. The City may compromise and settle any such claim or suit provided City bear the entire cost of any such settlement." Croskey, Second Appellate Decision, p. 5, footnote 7.

24   *City of Bell v. Superior Court of the State of California*, County of Los Angeles Court of Appeals of the State of California Second Appellate District, Division Three, p. 4. This was Croskey's second appeal. This created an interesting dilemma: if the city had to provide Rizzo a defense, then whatever monies the city might be able to get from Rizzo would be offset by the monies it would have to pay defending him. In short, the harder if fought to achieve justice and restitution, the more it cost. This cross-complaint, in turn, prompted the city, on November 24, 2010, to bring its own cross-complaint against Rizzo.

25   Jeff Gottlieb, "Bell won't have to pay Rizzo's legal bill, court rules" *L.A. Times*, October 4, 2013. Retrieved from: http://articles.latimes.com/2013/oct/04/local/la-me-ln-bell-rizzo-legal-bill-20131004.

26   See David J. Aleshire and Anthony Taylor, "Corruption on Steroids: The Bell Scandal from the Legal Perspective," paper presented at the City of Bell Scandal Revisited, Chapman University, February 19, 2015.

27   This is the case in California, and possibly in other states, if the published appellate court decision is followed.

28   David J. Aleshire and Anthony Taylor, "Corruption on Steroids: The Bell Scandal from the Legal Perspective," paper presented at the City of Bell Scandal Revisited, Chapman University, February 19, 2015, p. 13.

29   Ibid. p. 14.

CHAPTER TEN

Rebuilding Bell

"The place was a total disaster."[1]

—Pedro Carrillo, interim city manager

ALL HELL BROKE loose when the *L.A. Times* began publishing its Bell investigation stories in print on July 15, 2010.[2] In the following months, the scandal was featured on local, national, and international news outlets. The obscure little city, which City Manager Robert Rizzo had tried so hard to keep out of the spotlight, was now world famous.[3]

Bell's mostly low-income citizens were enraged when they found out their city manager was making twice the U.S. President's salary. Hundreds gathered at Bell's city hall carrying signs with photos of Rizzo and the words "Justice," "Resignation," and "Recall." The 85-seat council chamber, built in 1957, wasn't big enough to hold the heckling crowds, so they moved the council meeting to the larger community center next door.

Speaker after speaker berated the Rizzo-council for ripping off the city.[4] "People were furious. There was just pure rage. There was a mob mentality and I worried there'd be violence," said Pedro Carrillo, the first interim city manager after Rizzo's ouster. "Cities have mutual aid agreements for emergencies. I must have called mutual aid six times in about three weeks. We were trying to prevent rioting," he said.[5]

But while the media and the public fixated on the sky-high salaries, the greatest damage inflicted by Rizzo—the four city managers who followed him insist—came from the absent or rundown government operations, the crippled civic infrastructure, the tons of needless debt the city took on, the deteriorated business climate, and "corruption at its worst."[6] In many ways, the $5.5 million dollars in excessive salaries was the least of Bell's problems.

A week after the *Times* story broke, Robert Rizzo, Assistant City Manager Angela Spaccia, and Police Chief Randy Adams resigned. That night, in a special council meeting that went to nearly 3 a.m., the council appointed Pedro Carrillo, a consultant under Rizzo, interim city manager, despite that he'd never been a city manager or even an assistant city manager.[7] But city hall was in chaos, and the council was desperate.

Bell's finances were in shambles, and the city was hemorrhaging money. Carrillo immediately reached out to State Controller John Chiang, who sent him several auditors to help decipher Bell's books and figure out its financial situation. He then eliminated positions, fired people, retired others, and reduced hours. For months, meetings had to be canceled for lack of a quorum; the council members, fearing enraged residents, just didn't want to come. Carrillo's job became more difficult when, two months after the publication of the *Times* report, all but one of the Rizzo council members were arrested and, following the preliminary hearing, banned from city hall.[8] Carillo was left running the city by himself. "I was working 14-hour days, 6–7 days a week. It seemed like every week we encountered another crisis or investigation," he said.[9]

Far from being perceived as a hero, however, Carrillo was thought of as Rizzo's man.[10] The cuts he made and his desire to save the city millions by shuttering the police department, whose rank and file had funded the recall, made him deeply unpopular.[11] So, following the recall election, which swept away the Rizzo council and put a new group of reformers in office, the new council immediately asked Carrillo to do a search for a permanent city manager.

Carrillo opened a search, but no one applied. The deadline was extended, but still no applications came in.[12] Carrillo left the day his contract ended, and Bell was again without a city manager. At this point, Ali Saleh, the newly elected mayor and BASTA co-founder, stepped in as city manager even though he had absolutely no experience in municipal government. The fact that a city councilperson was also the city manager is highly inappropriate, not to mention utterly bizarre. But the city had no choice.

The International City Manager's Association (ICMA) was deeply embarrassed by Rizzo and the damage he had caused.[13] When Kevin Duggan, the director of ICMA's West Coast Division (Cal-ICMA) learned that Bell had not received any applications, he contacted Saleh and offered to organize, pro bono, an effort to find an interim city manager. Duggan worked with the League of Cities and the California City Management Foundation to find an interim city manager. That turned out to be Ken Hampian.[14]

San Luis Obispo is 212 miles north and a four-hour drive from Bell. Ken Hampian had been its city manager for ten years before retiring. He'd thought of applying for the interim city manager job in Bell, but didn't want to move away from home for 10 months, which is about how long he thought it would take to hire a full-time city manager. "I was proud to have been a city manager, and I was completely offended that Rizzo sullied the reputation of all public servants," Hampian said. At the urging of Duggan and other colleagues, he moved to the area and worked for the city for a month (pro bono).

As word got out that Hampian was volunteering in Bell, other retired public servants stepped forward to volunteer time and even equipment. Santa Monica's deputy chief of police used vacation time to help out. Among Hampian's priorities was to find a capable longer-term interim manager. With the help of Duggan and others, Arne Croce was recruited and appointed by the Bell City Council to serve as interim city manager for the next several months.

Croce had been San Mateo's city manager for 18 years before retiring. He was also furious with Rizzo for giving the profession he loved a black eye and felt obligated to help put Bell back on track. Croce put through the first honest and transparent budget the city had seen in years, and included the public, for the first time ever, in setting community priorities. He spent considerable time sharing the benefit of his experience with the new city council, including best practices for serving as an elected local government official. He renegotiated the massive bond debt incurred by Rizzo and found a path out of the burdensome obligations. Croce dealt with some difficult remaining personnel issues and helped the city recruit Doug Willmore, who became Bell's first permanent city manager since Rizzo.

Prior to coming to Bell, Willmore was the city manager of the City of El Segundo, also in Los Angeles County. He was fired after only 10 months on the job when he alleged that Chevron owed the city millions in back taxes and proposed a tax hike on the politically powerful oil company. He successfully sued the city for violating antiretaliation and whistle-blower laws.[15] Willmore's integrity, calm, openness, and toughness were especially attractive to the new Bell council which was bent on reform and wanted to distance itself from Rizzo[16] "The problems that Bell faced at that time were massive, and many were unknown. And they were about to become even worse," he said.[17]

All four post-Rizzo city managers faced several big challenges:

FISCAL EMERGENCY

No one had a clear picture of the city's finances. Willmore had no idea, for example, what the city's assets and liabilities were; what it owed, and to whom; and how much money it had. There was a huge backlog of financial transactions which hadn't been booked. The city hadn't reconciled bank statements in three years. "They deposited checks in the bank, but you didn't know what they were for," he said. "The city was virtually insolvent without even knowing it," Willmore said.[18] Also, Willmore found that the city hadn't been properly audited for years.

Auditors keep cities honest and financially sound. A good auditor looks for conflicts of interest and overcharges and reports these and other problems to the city manager. The city manager then reports the auditor's findings and concerns to the city council, along with proposed fixes. This never happened under Rizzo. Instead, the city's longtime auditor—Mayer Hoffman McCann—had always given it a clean bill of health.

State Controller John Chiang strongly disagreed with their assessment. Chiang said the city's auditors were a "rubber stamp."[19] He found very serious problems, including that "the City's internal controls did not comply with audit standards resulting in excessive compensation, illegal taxes, mismanaged bond funds, and questionable contracts and land practices."[20]

Chiang said the auditor failed to catch that Rizzo had the city buy property owned by Mayor Oscar Hernandez for an above-market price; that it overpaid by millions of dollars for a building owned by another ex-councilman; that Rizzo had a side business with a private contractor who was also the city's planning director; and that the city paid "more than $1 million to a law firm that employed Rizzo's soon-to-be second wife."[21] Ultimately, when the proper audits were done, it was revealed that the city's reserves had disappeared. Instead, it was in the red for $1.5 million.[22]

NO MANAGEMENT TEAM

There were no long-term managers in place. This meant that there was no one in a leadership position who could provide information about how things had been done in the past. Croce found that most of Bell's top managers had left or were under indictment. There was no police chief, finance director, community services director, public works director, or planning director. Moreover, those managers that remained were inexperienced.[23] "Rizzo put loyalty to him above competence when it came to hiring and promotion decisions," Croce said. Croce hired several well-qualified interim department heads who stepped in to begin the rebuilding process. Willmore had to put a competent senior management team in place.

STAFF CHAOS

A well-run city requires well-trained and well-motivated staff. However, Rizzo had run city hall into the ground. Human resources (HR) policies had not been updated since the 1980s despite the enormous changes that had taken place in HR law since that time. There was no training of staff outside of mandatory state-required training. To maintain control, Rizzo discouraged staff from joining professional organizations and participating with their colleagues in professional conferences. Rizzo warned one staff person who did go to a conference, "Don't speak with anyone. Don't participate in any groups. Don't ask any questions. And every time there is a break you call me and give me an update on what you are doing."[24] During Hampian's interim tenure, a councilmember asked for $45 to attend a regional workshop. In searching the budget for training funds, Hampian learned that no money was allocated for training in any city departments except for the police, but only if the training would be state reimbursed. According to former employees, Rizzo's attitude was "everything you need to know we can teach you here."[25] After the scandal broke, the once isolated staff were traumatized by the media spotlight and the tremendous public suspicion of anyone who worked for city hall. Morale was at rock bottom.

RULES AND PROCEDURES

Rizzo loved to quote from *The Godfather* and *The Sopranos*. As the tough guy he fashioned himself to be, Rizzo liked to make seat-of-the-pants decisions based on intuition rather than standardized procedures and policies. For example, he alone decided how much local businesses paid for licenses and fees and for code violations—based on how much he thought the business could afford and whether he liked its owners. Written procedures would only limit his power and discretion. As a result, Bell typically didn't have or adhere to any written rules for such things as purchasing, running council meetings, taking personnel actions, processing development applications, or contracting. One retired volunteer city manager audited city contracts and learned that approximately 75% were expired. This included key contracts like trash collection, graffiti removal, and engineering services. Also, there were no updated job descriptions; several employees had the same job title but much different duties and compensation. There was no salary schedule, or any sort of rational compensation template, or any formal agreements with the city's three main bargaining units.[26]

PHYSICAL INFRASTRUCTURE

City hall had none of the tools that a normal office should have. The 53-year-old building hadn't been maintained and was in disrepair. Its light blue cinder block walls needed painting, and the heating and air conditioning filters had never been replaced. Rizzo would not allow the carpets, which were filthy, to be cleaned, so visitors would think the city was operating on a shoestring budget.[27] Furniture and equipment were worn and outdated. Official city documents—including employment records, contracts, council minutes, and building permits—were stuffed into cardboard storage boxes that were piled up against a wall because there weren't enough filing cabinets.

There had been no effort to invest in technology. "Half the emails I got I couldn't open if they had an attachment because the system was so bad. My phone dropped calls constantly," Hampian said. Croce agreed, saying, "I was told to clear my voice mail messages because if the system was too full, it would slow down 911 coming into the police dispatch."

Finally, the absence of a computerized information management system hurt the city's ability to locate important documents.[28] This undermined the city's ability to defend itself in court and to keep up with countless public records requests.[29]

LAWSUITS

The city faced more than 60 legal claims and administrative actions. Some lawsuits could have bankrupted the city.[30]

Willmore immediately turned to City Attorney David Aleshire, of Aleshire and Wynder (A&W). Dave Aleshire read about the scandal from his office 40 miles away in Irvine, California, and had contacted BASTA and offered to help with the recall pro bono. The firm focused on local government law and was widely known and respected. Following the successful recall, A&W was selected, after a competitive process, to be the city's attorney. A&W attorney Anthony Taylor was put in charge of corruption-related litigation.

Willmore knew he couldn't fight every legal challenge. That would've cost millions, and bankruptcy was a possibility if the city didn't win. It was also possible that litigation would generate additional legal claims against the city. Willmore and A&W decided to divide the cases into three categories: litigate, settle, and defer.

Litigate

Among the first to be sued by the city was former City Attorney Ed Lee. Lee was Bell's long-time city attorney under Rizzo and a partner with the law firm Best, Best and Krieger (BBK). Lee had failed to alert the council, or anyone else, about the legal shenanigans taking place in Bell—the excessive compensation schemes, the improper employee loan program, and fraudulent contracts. Many people, especially the Bell defendants, believe Lee deserves much of the blame for the scandal because they looked to him for guidance regarding the high salaries. He always assured them they weren't breaking the law. The city recovered $2.5 million for legal malpractice from Lee's firm, BBK.

The city also collected $3 million from its former auditor, Mayer Hoffman McCann, for the city's claims against them for the corruption scandal.[31]

Willmore and others were appalled by the lawsuits by ex-employees Rizzo, Spaccia, and Adams.[32] Rizzo and Spaccia said they were improperly terminated and sued the city for millions for unpaid wages and benefits. They claimed that the city should pay their attorney fees. Rizzo, Spaccia, and Adams also sued the city for some $6 million in future unfunded pension benefits. Rizzo said he was due a $600,000-a-year pension based on his final pay in Bell.[33] In addition, he was slated to receive payouts from his 401K retirement plan which once contained more than $1 million, part of it funded by the city, based on his exorbitant salary.

"Many of the criminals that had preyed on Bell before the scandal were back to take another bite out of Bell. The city was never going to pay any of them another dime," Willmore said. He knew that settling would not produce the justice that the citizens deserved. They were determined to fight.[34]

The city won back the improper payments it made into Rizzo's 401K. He only kept the pre-corruption 401K funds that were legally protected. Most importantly, the state appeals court ruled that Bell did not have to pay Rizzo's legal bills. Rizzo's pension was later reduced to $86,598. Spaccia was slated to receive a yearly retirement of nearly $250,000. This was reduced to $23,960. (She would continue to receive a pension from the County of Ventura, where she had formerly worked.) Also, Spaccia was no longer eligible for retiree health coverage from the City of Bell.

Police Chief Adams negotiated a settlement with the city in which the city agreed not to go after him in court. In exchange, "Adams actually repaid the city $215,000 in excessive salary and abandoned his claim for reimbursement of $500,000 in legal fees and for another $800,000 in unpaid wages, benefits, and lifetime medical (total $1.3 million)."[35] He would still receive a pension and health care benefits of more than $200,000 from his previous service elsewhere.

In addition to their state retirement plan, in 2003, Rizzo created a Supplemental Plan for himself and 40 other Bell officials. The plan was terminated in 2011, but the city was still on the hook for nearly $6 million. A total of 40 employees receiving benefits sued the city for the termination of benefits. The court ruled that the plan was not legally established. The city agreed to reduced payouts.

Settle

Rizzo had purchased 25 acres of land in what Willmore calls a "misguided investment scheme" for $38 million.[36] As the scandal was unfolding, the city defaulted on the loan to bond holder Dexia, an international bank. Dexia foreclosed on the property and was expected to seek a judgment for the additional $15 million, which would have bankrupted the city. A&W avoided litigation by selling the property along with 14 other acres for $44 million. This allowed the city to pay off the note and put some sorely needed cash in its account. The developer who bought the property built 500,000 square feet of commercial space, generating 350 jobs and tax revenue for the city.[37]

In another shady deal, in 2009, Rizzo paid $4.6 million for a downtown property—more than twice what it was worth.[38] The property, Western Auto, was owned by mob-connected Pete Werrlein, the ex-councilman and political wheeler-dealer. The city couldn't afford the payments, which would have totaled $7 million with interest by the time the loan was paid off. The city defaulted, and the property owner sought to foreclose on the property. The city filed a lawsuit to stop the foreclosure and won in court when it obtained an injunction to stop it. Thereafter, the city negotiated a settlement that was approved by the court on September 19, 2013, that allowed the city to use redevelopment funds, which are separate from the city's general fund, to purchase the property. The cost to the city's general fund was zero. The city saved $3 million in payments it didn't have to make.

Rizzo did the worst long-term harm when he pushed through a $70 million bond to finance the construction of a sports complex, a new library, and a community theater. The city eventually issued $50 million in bonds, but taxpayers had to pay back $100 million in principal and interest. To avoid raising taxes, the city abandoned the plan to build the sports park, community center, and library and used the unspent bond proceeds to prepay the bonds. The city has been able to avoid a tax increase, but it still owed $30 million.[39]

Deferral

The city was able to defer litigation for most civil matters with the eight ex-officials until the criminal prosecutions were complete. In addition to buying the city time, it allowed Bell's attorneys to benefit from legal work done by the district attorney.

Bell's attorneys also persuaded the federal (e.g., SEC and IRS) and state agencies (e.g., the State Controller, State Attorney General, Department of Corporations) investigating the scandal to help the rebuilding effort rather than take punitive action. The city's attorney urged authorities not to punish the citizens of Bell for the transgressions of past leaders. "Bell is not the criminal; it was the management team and council members in power. Now there is new management, and any penalties or damages assessed now will be paid by the taxpayers and residents of Bell, an impoverished community which has been betrayed once by its leaders, and could now be penalized again by an unthinking rule-obsessed bureaucracy."[40]

For example, the city was set to be penalized by the IRS for $6 million due to not spending the proceeds of the tax-exempt bond issue when it was supposed to, due in part to the scandal. The city agreed to pay only $257,000. The city's attorneys were also able to convince the State Attorney General not to put the city into receivership, but to instead support the city's efforts to get restitution from the Bell defendants.

CIVIC INFRASTRUCTURE

Most well-run cities have numerous opportunities for citizens to participate in local governance. Cities typically have a planning commission, parks and recreation commission, an architectural design and review board, and a whole host of other boards and committees. These are part of what's known as a city's civic infrastructure.

These volunteer groups serve several important functions. First, they lessen the council's workload and can help absorb political heat. The planning commission, for example, takes the first look at a development project and decides whether it merits further consideration by the council. A larger group of residents, beyond the five elected council members, are therefore involved in—and responsible for—major land-use decisions, which are usually controversial. Second, these boards and commissions are a "farm team" for future council members. This is where potential council members develop governing skills and knowledge.

In other cities, service clubs (e.g., Rotary, Kiwanis, YMCA, chambers of commerce, etc.) are venues for the discussion of current events, which includes the performance of local government officials. They often hold candidate debates, which provide an opportunity for candidates outside of city hall to get the exposure they need to mount a successful campaign. It is also a chance for voters to take the measure of potential future elected officials. These clubs are another venue for future leaders to prove they have what it takes to be on the council. Finally, they provide a forum for the council to hear from the community and for the community to connect with the council.

City officials can get feedback from a cross section of the community. Group members, in turn, report back to the community on what's going on at city hall and how well leaders are doing. Service club members can also be a "watchdog" that "barks" when they sense something is wrong, therefore providing an important check on government authorities. The city manager and council members frequently speak to these groups and keep them abreast of what the city plans. Under Rizzo, there were no state-of-the-city addresses, or prayer breakfasts, or other forums in which people could congregate and discuss issues of concern to the community. Civic clubs and organizations had all but ceased to exist in Bell.

There was a chamber of commerce, but it was "owned" by the city: the executive director—typically an independent position—was under the control of Rizzo and never gave any contrary opinions. In fact, Rizzo, for a time, served as the chamber's executive director. Willmore said the chamber of commerce was a pack of "Rizzo stooges." The dissolution of the chamber further crippled Bell's business environment. Big box stores, such as Home Depot and Walmart, whose tax revenues help a city pay its bills, avoided Bell.

Croce said, "The money Rizzo stole was the least damaging thing he did to Bell ... The most damaging thing he did was robbing the community of its civic infrastructure."

The bottom line is that there was no way for any citizen to get involved in city government other than by getting on the council. But since Rizzo wanted to run everything, he had to heavily manage the selection process. He did this by recruiting the people he could intimidate and control and orchestrating the defeat of those whom he thought would oppose him. He played an active role in council discussions regarding who to appoint to the council when unscheduled openings arose. As Rizzo appointed incumbents, officials such as Victor Bello, a telephone installer, and local pastor Luis Artiga enjoyed a significant electoral advantage over any real or potential challengers despite their dubious qualifications. As trial testimony would reveal, Mayor Oscar Hernandez could neither read nor write English and signed nearly everything Rizzo put in front of him. The other council members were unwilling to challenge their city manager or rein him in when questions regarding his behavior arose.[41]

Rizzo didn't want a spark plug like Nestor Valencia, the founder of the Bell Residents Club, or the charismatic and outspoken Ali Saleh, the cofounder of BASTA, asking him tough questions. Valencia and Saleh had grown up in Bell and graduated from Bell High School. They had run for office but lost because they did not have Rizzo's support. Both were elected in the recall and later served as mayor.

Because there was no effort to groom future leaders, there was no bench to go to when there were council vacancies. So, when the recall election came about, none of the people elected had any local government experience. This meant that there was no institutional history which could be passed down from senior members to junior members and to the city manager and city attorney. They were starting from scratch.[42]

NO TRANSPARENCY

Democracy requires a well-informed public. This means city operations must be transparent. Rizzo, however, despised transparency and did all he could to keep city operations secret. He tried to intimidate residents from looking too closely at how the city functioned. He did this by taking note of those who showed up to council meetings, especially if they spoke. When anyone asked for documents or asked tough questions, Rizzo and the council members were not forthcoming, responded with insults, and often lied. Public meetings were not video recorded. For a long time, the city didn't have a website, and when it finally built one, it was poorly done. Rizzo had no interest in following the Public Records Request Act, which guaranteed citizens the right to public documents.

ETHICS PROBLEMS

Obviously, Bell had very serious ethics problems. According to a report by the Center for the Advancement of Public Integrity, small municipalities like Bell are big corruption risks because there isn't proper oversight by county, state, and federal levels of government. The report says that "... Bell did not have any formal anticorruption mechanisms in place—particularly oversight and transparency measures—so no one outside of the small group of decision-makers running Bell had the ability or duty to ensure that the city's leaders were governing with integrity."[43]

TRUST DEFICIT

Rizzo had destroyed citizen trust and confidence. The recall election united the community, and the newly elected council members were, at first, treated as heroes. However, that didn't last long. Soon residents began yelling at the council and saying they were just as corrupt as Rizzo and that they weren't listening. There was a tremendous need to restore trust and inculcate within the community the desire to engage properly with the council and one another—what Alexis de Tocqueville, the author of the classic *Democracy in America*, called the "habits of the heart."

CONCLUSION

In February 2015, four and half years after the scandal first erupted, Willmore, the first permanent city manager after Rizzo, left Bell for another assignment. Bell had largely recovered from the harm inflicted on it by its former top officials due to the hard work of the post-Rizzo city managers and council and its city attorney.

As of January 2017, the city was solvent and had a very healthy $19 million in reserves ($13.2 million annual budget). Audits were done on a regular basis by a respected accounting firm, and there were no outstanding scandal-related lawsuits or pending administrative actions.

As part of the rebuilding effort, the city adopted a strategic plan in May 2016. One of its priorities was that there should be a strong management team. There is now a comprehensive hiring process. Positions are widely advertised and finalists go through a rigorous background check. A rating panel, which includes top managers from other cities, interviews candidates and makes recommendations. Also, the city created the Bell Leadership Academy for continued professional development. The Leadership Academy is an eight-session program (each session is four hours) developed to improve city management. Directors and managers of each department participate in this training.[44]

City employees are now encouraged to go to conferences and participate in their professional associations.

The city has adopted rules and procedures for the acquisition of equipment and services and the conduct of financial affairs. The council adopted formal procedures for the conduct of meetings, which it scrupulously follows. Each department has created or updated its own policies and procedures, and an internal system ensures that contracts don't lapse.

City staff is "hypervigilant" about financial matters given past abuses, the current City Manager Howard Brown said. "If I ask them to move money from one account to another, they'll say we didn't see the council pass a resolution about that at the last city council meeting, which many watch at home online."[45]

City hall has been repainted and carpets have been replaced. New computers, software, and office furniture have been purchased, and a state-of-the-art phone system has been installed. There is a plan in place that ensures computers and other technology are updated in a timely manner.

The strategic plan also emphasized the importance of civic engagement. The city created several committees and task forces (e.g., code enforcement task force, planning commission) and led the effort to create an independent chamber of commerce) that are all comprised of Bell residents and local business owners. The city manager regularly meets with resident groups. The city parks and recreation department created 40 new clubs and organizations for Bell's residents. This is up from just a handful existing under Rizzo.

To better engage the public and foster a more participatory relationship between city hall and its residents, the city held a "Goal-Setting Community Forum" around the city's budget. Residents received a brief overview of the city's finances. Residents then deliberated over budget priorities, with subjects ranging from public safety to business permitting and taxes.[46] The city also hosts community events such as the State-of-the-City Address, Holiday Tree Lighting Ceremony, Mayor's Cleanup, Small Business Development Workshop, and 5K Run/Walk.

Believing that sunlight is the best disinfectant, the city has a state-of-the-art website to provide easily accessible information to the public. The website includes salaries, budget, itemized spending, staff reports, city contracts, council minutes and documents, the city manager's bi-monthly report to the council, and the municipal code. City council meetings are streamed live and videotaped for future viewing. The city's social media outlets (e.g., Facebook, Twitter) transmit updates and promote events. The Sunshine Review, a nonprofit that examines state and local government transparency, gave the new website an "A-" for transparency.[47]

In regard to ethics, the city adopted a Policy for Fraudulent or Unethical Behavior to "cover all employees, management, elected officials, volunteers, vendors, and contractors."[48] After a comprehensive review of the city's ethics reforms, The Center for the Advancement of Public Integrity concluded that a " review of the three cornerstones of municipal integrity—Accountability, Oversight, and Transparency—reveals a concerted effort on the part of Bell to tighten ethics requirements, ensure some level of oversight, and increase transparency."[49]

INTO THE FUTURE

Bell has come a long way, but it still faces some challenges. The city still owes $30 million for the construction bond and the purchase of a downtown business property, which is now worth half of what Rizzo purchased it for. Like most cities, Bell has a huge unfunded pension liability. There is high turnover as officials regularly leave for better paying jobs in wealthier cities. The city is still debating whether to have its own police department or to outsource police services to the county or another city.

Voter turnout, as in the rest of the country, remains a challenge. In the 2013 and 2015 municipal elections, turnout was about 15%. That's down from the 30% that voted in the recall election but above the low teens and single digits in the Rizzo era. In 2013, 11 candidates vied for three slots on the council. That's far better than pre-recall elections when only Rizzo-backed candidates ran, and elections were frequently cancelled for lack of interest. Of course, the city manager stays out of election politicking.

All indicators suggest that Bell has recovered and, in some ways, has become a model for municipal governance.

LESSONS

The Rizzo years had destroyed nearly every structure a city needs to function with efficiency and integrity. For anyone taking the measure of a city they suspect is in the throes of breakdown, the list of essentials the managers found lacking in Bell is a good starting point for assessing what's intact, what's missing, and what might be the most critical issues. Equally useful is the reminder that while Bell was exploited by a corrupt city manager, it was guided back to health by seasoned professionals in the field. The lesson here is to screen the experts for integrity and credentials and insist that they answer to the public.

Building a city from scratch is hard work, but city leadership usually enjoys a healthy reservoir of public support. That was not the case in Bell. The city manager team, which included one volunteer, faced a hostile, seething community disinclined to trust government after what they'd been through. Rebuilding trust was a major priority.

The managers realized they couldn't tackle all of Bell's problems at once, so they prioritized, first addressing issues that threatened the city's existence. There was real fear that the city could go bankrupt or be dissolved by the state, so the team brought in experienced professionals to help them navigate the fiscal and legal morass, starting with an auditor who could show them where the city stood financially and expert attorneys.

As the crises abated, the management team systematically set about restoring Bell's civic and administrative structures. The steps they took, and the map they left for the city manager who stepped in after the scandal, put Bell on the road to recovery.

Taken together, these could serve as a model of best practices for city government, ensuring that a city has all the ingredients that must be in place for the council-manager system—and democracy—to work.

ENDNOTES

1   Personal interview with Pedro Carrillo.

2   Published online July 14, 2010.

3   In addition to appearing in the network evening news programs and major news outlets, such as the *New York Times* and the *World Street Journal*, the story was covered in Europe, the former Soviet Union, Japan, and Africa, according to Gottlieb and Garcia, who were interviewed by or received inquiries from reporters from these countries.

4   Mayor Oscar Hernandez arrived to the meeting with a police escort.

5   Carrillo was the first of four city managers who would help rebuild Bell. Carrillo served a year. He was followed by Ken Hampian, who served a month, Arne Croce (9 months), and finally Doug Willmore, who served from June 1, 2012, until March 1, 2015. He was followed by Jerry Groomes and Howard Brown.

6   James M. Casso, and Jayne W. Williams, Meyers Nave, "Bell—What Happened and How It Happened: The Role of the New Administration and the City Attorney". Paper presented at the League of Cities 2011 Spring Conference at Tenaya Lodge at Yosemite Fish Camp as part of the pane, Crisis Management and Restoring Public Trust after Bell. Friday, May 6, 2011 General Session. 10:45 a.m. - 12:00 p.m. See, http://www.cacities.org/getattachment/6202b6ac-a488-4df1-9653-65a16bb3b2ae/5-2011-Spring-James-Casso-Jayne-Williams-Crisis-Ma.aspx.

7   Carrillo headed a small firm, Urban Associates, that provided temporary department heads and program directors to local governments while they were searching for a permanent person. He was widely known by city managers in the region, and Rizzo had hired him as a consultant.

8   Lorenzo Valez was the one member not arrested or charged. See, Hector Becerra and Ruben Vives, "Bell councilman an accidental hero by staying clear of corruption scandal," *Los Angeles Times*, October 13, 2010. Retrieved from http://articles.latimes.com/2010/oct/13/local/la-me-bell-councilman-20101009. Mayor Oscar Hernandez had complained that he was receiving death threats. See, Jeff Gottlieb, "Bell mayor says death threats keep him from council meetings," *Los Angeles*

Times, February 12, 2011. Retrieved from: http://articles.latimes.com/2011/feb/12/local/la-me-bell-mayor-20110212. Four days later, Los Angeles County Superior Court Judge Henry J. Hall ordered six current and former Bell City Council members to stand trial on charges of looting the city treasury and barred the elected officials from city hall or being involved in any way in running the city. See, http://articles.latimes.com/print/2011/mar/11/local/la-me-bell-hearing-20110311.

9   Personal interview with Pedro Carrillo.

10   See, Jeff Gottlieb, "Interim city administrator leaves Bell," *Los Angeles Times*, July 26, 2011. Retrieved from: http://articles.latimes.com/2011/jul/26/local/la-me-bell-finances-20110726.

11   Ibid.

12   Ken Hampian said, "When you open a search you often get a large number of unqualified people. But with this search, not even delusional people applied. It was utterly toxic." Personal interview. See also, Ruben Vives, "Bell Finds Reform Harder than it Looks," *Los Angeles Times*, July 16, 2011. Retrieved from http://articles.latimes.com/2011/jul/16/local/la-me-bell-manager-20110716.

13   ICMA expelled Rizzo after the scandal broke.

14   See the "Rebirth of Bell," City Manager Foundation. Retrieved from https://www.cacitymanagers.org/rebirth-of-bell/.

15   Megan Barnes," Rancho Palos Verdes hires city manager who helped repair scandal-plagued Bell," *The Daily Breeze*, January 29, 2015. Retrieved from http://www.dailybreeze.com/government-and-politics/20150129/rancho-palos-verdes-hires-city-manager-who-helped-repair-scandal-plagued-bell.

16   Willmore received the Cal-ICMA ethics award in February, 2014. See, http://icma.org/en/ca/newroom/highlights/Article/104193/CalICMA_Honors_Two_Members_WithEthics_Award.

17   Personal interview with Doug Willmore.

18   Megan Barnes," Rancho Palos Verdes hires city manager who helped repair scandal-plagued Bell," *The Daily Breeze*, January 29, 2015. Retrieved from http://www.dailybreeze.com/government-and-politics/20150129/rancho-palos-verdes-hires-city-manager-who-helped-repair-scandal-plagued-bell.

19   Jeff Gottlieb, "California seeks discipline for Bell's auditing firm," *Los Angeles Times*, May 25, 2012. Retrieved from http://articles.latimes.com/2012/may/25/local/la-me-bell-20120525.

20   David Aleshire and Anthony Taylor. "Corruption on Steroids: The Bell Scandal from The Legal Perspective," paper presented at the City of Bell Scandal Revisited, Chapman University, February 19, 2015.

21 Paul Pringle, Corina Knoll, and Kim Murphy, "Rizzo's Horse Had Come In," *Los Angeles Times*, August 22, 2010. Retrieved from http://articles.latimes.com/2010/aug/22/local/la-me-rizzo-20100822.

22 Doug Willmore, "City of Bell—Reformed and Reborn," paper delivered at the City of Bell Scandal Revisited, Chapman University, February 19, 2015.

23 Interview with Arne Croce.

24 Interview with Arne Croce.

25 Interview with Ken Hampian.

26 David Aleshire and Anthony Taylor, "Corruption on Steroids: The Bell Scandal from The Legal Perspective," paper delivered at the City of Bell Scandal Revisited, Chapman University, February 19, 2015.

27 According to Hampian and Croce.

28 Such as documentation regarding Rizzo's final pay that were crucial to determining his pension. Pedro Carrillo, Bell's interim chief administrative officer, said that "much of the documentation simply does not exist," as quoted in see, Kim Christensen, "Rizzo, other former Bell officials won't receive pensions to match huge salaries," *Los Angeles Time*, November 13, 2010. Retrieved from http://articles.latimes.com/2010/nov/13/local/la-me-1113-bell-pensions-20101113.

29 According to City Attorneys David Aleshire and Anthony Taylor. See, David Aleshire and Anthony Taylor. "Corruption on Steroids: The Bell Scandal from The Legal Perspective," paper presented at the City of Bell Scandal Revisited, Chapman University, February 19, 2015.

30 The material in this section draws heavily from David Aleshire and Anthony Taylor, "Corruption on Steroids: The Bell Scandal from The Legal Perspective," paper presented at the City of Bell Scandal Revisited, Chapman University, February 19, 2015. Ed Lee resigned on August 2, 2010. He left his law firm, Best, Best and Krieger, and was fired as city attorney from other cities. Lee was also sued by the eight defendants. Bell hired Meyers Nave to serve as interim city attorney replacing Lee. About a year later, the city hired David Aleshire, whose firm Aleshire and Wynder.

31 Mayer Hoffman McCann were also fined $300,000 by the California Board of Accountancy and placed on two years' probation.

32 Including Eric Engena, who sued the city for $837,000, including compensation for 329 unused sick and vacation days. See Jeff Gottlieb, "Ex-Bell official seeks $837,000 payout," *Los Angeles Times*, August 28, 2012. Retrieved from http://articles.latimes.com/2012/aug/28/local/la-me-bell-20120829.

33   See, Kim Christensen, "Rizzo, other former Bell officials won't receive pensions to match huge salaries," *Los Angeles Times*, November 13, 2010. Retrieved from http://articles.latimes.com/2010/nov/13/local/la-me-1113-bell-pensions-20101113.

34   Doug Willmore, "City of Bell—Reformed and Reborn," Paper delivered at the City of Bell Scandal Revisited, Chapman University, February 19, 2015.

35   Dave Aleshire and Anthony Taylor paper, "Corruption on Steroids: The Bell Scandal from The Legal Perspective." Paper presented at the City of Bell Scandal Revisited, Chapman University, February 19, 2015.

36   Doug Willmore, "City of Bell—Reformed and Reborn," Paper delivered at the City of Bell Scandal Revisited, Chapman University, February 19, 2015.

37   Pat Maio, "City of Bell land bought by L.B. developer," December 27, 2013. Retrieved from http://www.ocregister.com/articles/bell-595012-city-land.html.

38   In 2017, the property is worth $2 million, according to Howard Brown, Bell's city manager.

39   Personal communication with Aleshire and Taylor. According to the city's bond attorney, the city was required to levy taxes each year to pay debt service on the bonds. The city issued two sets of bonds. There was a $15 million bond in 2004 and a $35 million bond in 2007. Their annual debt service on the 2004 bonds (i.e., annual payment of principal and interest) was approximately $1,025,000 and on the 2008 bonds was $2,450,000. Due to the fact that some of the interest was funded in the bond issue from principal (as capitalized interest)—approximately 3–5 years for each issue), there were no required taxes to be levied or payments required out of taxes in the first 3 to 5 years of the bond issue. The city did not start levying the taxes until approximately 2006 and passed a resolution for a few years to ratchet up taxes to the level needed to pay the 2004 issue. By 2010, they had not increased the levy sufficient to pay for debt service on both bond issues, the 2007 bonds were starting to come due, and they started paying more of the taxes from bond proceeds. The city would have had to increase the current taxes on the bonds by 70% in order to pay the debt service on both issues. The city also decided it no longer needed a sports park. Therefore, the city used the unspent bond proceeds (approximately $20 million) to prepay some of the 2007 bonds and avoided having to increase taxes.

40   Dave Aleshire and Anthony Taylor paper, "Corruption on Steroids: The Bell Scandal from The Legal Perspective." Paper presented at the City of Bell Scandal Revisited, Chapman University, February 19, 2015.

41   Judge Kathleen Kennedy, Robert Rizzo sentencing remarks. Reporter's trial transcript of *The People versus Robert Adrian Rizzo*, April 16, 2014, p. 14.

42   Actually, "less than scratch." The council and manager would be starting from scratch if they were starting an entirely new city, in which they would have widespread support from the community. Such support did not exist in Bell.

43   See, Center for Advancement of Public Integrity, "Rebuilding Bell, CA: Review and Recommendations for the Continued Improvement of Accountability, Oversight and Transparency," p. 1., Columbia University Law School paper presented by Jennifer Rodgers at the City of Bell Scandal Revisited, Chapman University, February 19, 2015.

44   The Leadership Academy, an eight-session program (each session is four hours) developed to improve city management, started January 19, 2017. Directors and managers of each department will participate in this training. The training will focus on the following subjects: 1. What is effective communication? 2. Learning the language of leadership; 3. How to successfully communicate, coach, and give feedback; 4. Navigating the 7 Habits of Highly Effective People; 5. How to analyze and determine effective managerial systems, "What works and doesn't work"; 6. How to manage issues and solve problems; 7. Understanding the roles of supervision and management; and 8. How to create culture, building a winning team, and achieve results. This program is directed by Henry T. Garcia of HR Dynamics & Performance Management, Inc. (consulting firm).

45   Interview City Manager Howard Brown.

46   See Pete Peterson, "Liberty ... Bell," *PublicCEO*. Retrieved from http://www.publicceo.com/2012/01/libertybell/.

47   Alisha Green, "Bell, California: Moving from Secrecy to Sunshine" Sunshine Foundation. Retrieved from https://sunlightfoundation.com/2013/03/21/bell-california-movingfrom-secrecy-to-sunshine/. See also, http://www.cacities.org/Top/News/News-Articles/2013/October/League-of-California-Cities-Reinforces-Commitment.

48   See "Policy for Fraudulent and Unethical Behavior." Retrieved from http:www.cityofbell.org/home/showdocument?id=4591.

49   See, Center for Advancement of Public Integrity, "Rebuilding Bell, CA: Review and Recommendations for the Continued Improvement of Accountability, Oversight and Transparency," p. 1., Columbia University Law School paper presented by Jennifer Rodgers at the City of Bell Scandal Revisited, Chapman University, February 19, 2015.

CHAPTER ELEVEN

Making Local Government Harder to Plunder

"The whole art of government consists in the art of being honest."

—*Thomas Jefferson*[1]

THERE HAD BEEN little state oversight of local government before the *Los Angeles Times* pieced together the scope of the corruption in Bell. But in the wake of the scandal, there was a flurry of legislative activity. California legislators introduced at least 16 bills aimed at making it harder for the next Rizzo to hijack a city. Governors Arnold Schwarzenegger and Jerry Brown signed off on nine changes to state law (Table 11.1) which fell into three categories: emergency, transparency, and accountability.

Emergency bills dealt with the immediate crisis. Transparency bills required local government give the public access to information that the public was not previously privy to (such as salaries). Accountability legislation outlawed abuses of power and strengthened the checks on local government.

This chapter first reviews the California legislature's response to the Bell scandal. It then highlights a range of policies aimed at creating ethical standards, accountability, government openness, and citizen involvement—all of which are like kryptonite to kleptocrats. While some of the policies are California-specific, they're widely adaptable across the country.

LEGISLATION

Emergency: dealing with the immediate crisis

Two bills dealt with the immediate crisis in Bell. The recall election simultaneously forced four council members from office and elected five new people. But in order for the newly elected council members to take their seats Bell's city charter required that the city council certify the election results. The problem was that Bell didn't have a functioning city council because a judge had ordered three current city council members to stay at least 100 yards away from Bell city hall following their arrest. The solution, enacted in Assembly Bill 93 (AB 93), allowed for the Los Angeles County Board of Supervisors to certify the results of the recall election and to swear in the new council.[2]

Another Bell-specific emergency bill (AB 900) forced the city to refund millions of dollars in property tax overpayments to Bell taxpayers. These illegal assessments had been used to fund the Rizzo regime's self-dealt outrageous pay and pensions.[3]

Transparency: sunshine is the best disinfectant

Transparency legislation gave all California citizens new access to information about what cities are doing with their money, new safeguards against abuses, and new vehicles for requesting state investigations when they suspect wrongdoing. New legislation required local government officials' salaries be posted online and that a city post the agenda and accompanying materials on their website at least 72 hours before a council meeting. Also, decisions about compensation for city managers (and other local agency executives) must be made at regular city council meetings, not at a special meeting. The public must be given 72-hours notice of this meeting (up from 24).[4]

Accountability: Keeping public officials honest

Among new anti fraud provisions, the legislature created "an agency within the state auditor's office to scrutinize cities, counties, and special districts at high risk of waste, fraud, or abuse; enacted restrictions on automatic raises for managers; required

CalPERS, the state retirement system, to monitor for excessive salary increases; and required employees to repay paid leave or settlements if convicted of a crime related to his or her job."[5] Governor Brown also signed a bill (AB 353) that outlawed the controversial practice in Bell (and other locales) in which cities made tens of millions of dollars towing the cars of sober immigrants from DUI checkpoints because they did not have a valid driver's license. Most of these drivers are undocumented immigrants who are not allowed to obtain a driver's license in California.[6] The legislature also barred cities from imposing unreasonable tax hikes.

Cities, counties, and special districts were ordered to regularly report payroll data to the State Controller's office. These data are placed into searchable employee compensation data base, which have since received thousands of hits.[7]

TABLE 11.1 *Bell Legislation*

	BILL	TYPE	SUMMARY	STATUS
1	AB 93	Emergency	Emergency Election Certification.	Approved by Governor
2	AB 900	Emergency	On Time Tax Refund	Approved by Governor
3	SB 501	Transparency	Local government salaries must be posted.	Approved by Governor
4	AB 1344	Transparency	Cities must post agenda and agenda packages on web. City manager compensation must be discussed at regular, not special meeting. Public must get 72 hours, not 24 hour, notice. Ban employment contracts that include automatic extension clauses and built-in pay raises above cost of living, as well as severance that pays more than 12 months' salary.	Approved by Governor

	BILL	TYPE	SUMMARY	STATUS
5	AB 1350	Accountability	Prevents any unreasonable tax raises from occurring in local jurisdictions.	Approved by Governor
6	AB 340	Accountability	CalPERS required to monitor for any excessive salary increases.	Approved by Governor
7	AB 353	Accountability	Outlaw towing of the cars of sober immigrants from DUI checkpoints if they did not have proper ID.	Approved by Governor
8	AB 2476	Accountability	Strippped pension benefits from public employees who are convicted of a felony.	Approved by Governor
9	AB 187	Accountability	This bill authorizes the state auditor to identify and investigate "high risk" local government entities.	Approved by Governor
10	AB 1987	Accountability	Prevent pension spiking through end-of-career salary increases and bonuses	Vetoed by Governor
11	AB 194	Accountability	Caps total compensation that may be used to calculate a pension benefit.	Vetoed by Governor
12	AB 2064	Transparency	Requires legislative and Constitutional officers to post salaries on the web.	Died
13	AB 192	Accountability	A public employee who takes a job at much higher pay with another public entity increases the pension liabilities of his or or her former employer. This bill would have limited the original cities pension liability.	Died

BILL	TYPE	SUMMARY	STATUS
14 AB 148	Transparency	This bill would require the local agency to post the ethics training record records of all elected members of the local agency on the local agency's Internet Web site.	Died
15 AB 1955	Accountability	Prevent city officials from issuing bonds if the state controllers says council members are overpaid.	Died
16 SB 827	Accountability	This bill would declare the intent of the Legislature to convene a conference committee to reform state and local pension systems.	Died

Good ideas that weren't approved

Other bills proposed but failed to get the necessary votes to pass or were vetoed. Five other bills died in the legislature. AB 1955 would've prevented cities from issuing bonds if the state controller determined city officials were overpaid. It died. A bill that would have required the posting of legislators' and other constitutional officers' salaries also died.

Under the present system, a public agency must pay part of the increase in a public employees' pension if that employee leaves one agency for a better paying job in another agency. AB 192 would have stopped this, but it, too, died in committee.

Governor Brown, who was beholden to the state's public employees unions, vetoed a bill that would have prevented "pension spiking." Pension spiking occurs when public employees get a pay increase right before retiring to ensure they have a more lucrative pension payout. He also vetoed a bill that capped the total compensation that could be used to calculate a pension benefit.

But the reforms stopped short of addressing the deeper causes of the corruption we saw in Bell, the conditions that breed kleptocracy. These are addressed later in this chapter.

CORRUPTION IN OTHER MUNICIPALITIES

In the decades Bell was under siege from kleptocrats, so were numerous other cities in California. The still-growing list includes:

- Vernon: Former City Manager Bruce Malkenhorst engineered for himself a salary of $911,000 per year and more than half a million dollars in yearly pension benefits after he retired in 2005. He was the highest paid retiree in the state.[8]
- South Gate: The city council gave itself a 500% pay increase for serving on boards and commissions that rarely met and fired all the city's longtime department heads, replacing them with unqualified cronies to whom they paid exorbitant salaries and benefits.[9]
- Compton: Mayor Omar Bradley, who referred to himself as a "gangster mayor," was convicted in 2014 of felony corruption charges for "using his city-issued credit card to pay for golf rounds, hotel rooms, clothing and in-room movies, among other things. He also was convicted of taking cash advances for city business expenses and then charging those items to his city credit cards and pocketing the money."[10] In 2017, the city's former treasurer was arrested on embezzlement charges for skimming money from cash payments to the city.
- Palm Springs: Federal prosecutors accused former Mayor Steve Pougnet of accepting $375,000 in bribes from two developers whose projects he promoted.[11]
- Beaumont: Prosecutors charged in 2016 that seven former city officials, including the city manager and finance director, had stolen as much as $43 million from the city over three decades. In 2017, a first-term councilmember was indicted on unrelated bribery and perjury counts.[12]

Corruption is not limited to high-immigration cities, such as those found in the "corridor of corruption," where one could blame poverty, low education levels and a transient population.

It is also occurring in wealthier, better educated, and more settled locales.

- Orange County: This affluent area is 25 miles south of Bell and includes such wealthy, high-income cities as Laguna Beach and Newport Beach. According to a report the Orange County Grand Jury issued in 2013, Orange County is a "hotbed" of corruption: "[There is a] history of impropriety by local officials. Orange County has gained a reputation (among some) for impropriety rivaling that of New York's Tammany Hall or Chicago under Mayor Richard J. Daley ... From 1974–77, an eye-popping 43 Orange County political figures were indicted, among them two congressmen, three supervisors, and the county assessor. "Sadly, the conduct continues today at all levels of Orange County government."[13]

There are scores of local government corruption stories from outside of California as well.

- Dixon, Illinois: Rita Crundwell, a controller, pleaded guilty in 2012 for stealing "more than $53 million dollars from the city since 1990." Crundwell used this money to fund her opulent lifestyle, which included running a quarter-horse farming business that generated a great deal of revenue.[14]
- New Orleans: Mayor Ray Nagin, who gained national fame during the Hurricane Katrina disaster, was found guilty of accepting hundreds of thousands of dollars in bribes from local businessmen. He was convicted of 20 of the 21 counts against him, was sentenced to serve 10 years in prison, and was ordered to pay $84,264 to the IRS.[15]
- Hartford, Connecticut: Mayor Eddie Perez was convicted of attempting to extort money from a developer. Previously, he had been convicted of bribery, conspiracy, and falsifying evidence.[16]
- New York City: Councilman Miguel Martinez stole $106,000 in public funds and in 2009 was sentenced to serve five years in prison.[17]

Preventing Future Bells

Baby Bells are popping up all over the U.S. because the underlying causes of the scandal—character, oversight, and engagement—mentioned in Chapter 1 are not unique to this small California city. What, then, can be done? The rest of this chapter addresses these factors which converged to such an extreme degree in Bell. It also makes suggestions for reform (Table 11.4).

CHARACTER

Moral failure—the conscious decision to do wrong—was at the heart of the Bell scandal. Robert Rizzo was a thief, and so, too, were other high-ranking Bell officials, who were aided by a compliant, ignorant, and greedy council. Establishing and maintaining an environment in which officials and employees display honesty and integrity and act in a moral way must be a city's top priority. Doing so begins with hiring honest people. When looking for people to hire, Warren Buffet says organizations should look for three qualities: "integrity, intelligence, and energy. And if they don't have the first, the other two will kill you."[18]

Buffet's maxim certainly applies to Rizzo. Rizzo was clearly intelligent and energetic but was a person of poor character who lacked integrity. Bell officials who hired Rizzo admit that they failed to properly vet him. Kevin Duggan, a retired city manager, is the head of ICMA's West Coast division. He helped Bell recruit the post-Rizzo city managers. He has also written about ethics issues that confront city managers. When hiring a city manager, he recommends:[19]

ICMA Suggestions

- Cities should use a professional search firm to help attract and screen candidates.
- Councils need to make sure someone does a thorough background check and asks tough questions about candidates.
- Councils need to look beyond technical experience and competencies to the equal (or greater) issue of character/integrity/honesty. Those traits should never be taken for granted.

- Cities should require that the city manager be a member of the International City Manager Association (ICMA) and be compliant with ICMA's code of ethics.
- Cities should require regular performance evaluations that include transparency, openness, good communication, and honesty as factors that are evaluated.

Not only was Rizzo personally corrupt but he was able to create a culture of corruption that ensnared numerous other city officials. Had he faced more push-back from the organization, it is unlikely he would have prevailed. Instead, most were bought off with high salaries, personal loans, promotions, and lucrative consulting contracts which he dangled in front of them. Others lacked the backbone to stand up to the fiercely determined and intimidating city manager.[20]

Ethics Training

In addition to adopting an ethics code and other anti-corruption policies, cities should require ethics training. They should also routinely encourage employees to join various professional organizations and to abide by their codes of ethics. They also should have strong reporting and enforcement mechanisms.

Bell did not have ethics policies or any ongoing ethics training. Rizzo also frowned on employees participating in professional organizations, at which they would have been exposed to ethics policies. Fortunately, the post-scandal council made the adoption of anti-corruption measures a top priority.

Codes of Conduct

One way governments establish a culture of integrity is to adopt codes of conduct for officials and employees. The thinking is that there must be an ongoing effort to combat temptations associated with government. An ethics code wouldn't have dissuaded Rizzo, but it may have emboldened others to confront him and cause them to think twice.

Jennifer Rodgers is the executive director of the Center for the Advancement of Public Integrity (CAPI) at Columbia Law

School. In her review of the anti-corruption policies adopted following the Bell scandal administration, she states "Rizzo may have attempted to fleece the city of Bell even if strict anti-corruption measures were in place ... [T]he hope is that strict measures will at least slow ... officials [like Rizzo] down, limit the damage from their actions, and/or speed detection of their wrongdoing ... [I]f strict expectations for ethical behavior are made clear and are enforced, and the opportunities for corruption are limited" a cultural of integrity will prevail.[21]

Ancient oaths may be helpful today

Oaths are public vows to uphold agreed-upon standards of ethical behavior.[22] An oath is a sacred public promise. The president and other newly appointed office holders, new citizens, lawyers, pharmacists, witnesses at trials, military recruits, and Boy and Girl Scouts, to name a few, take oaths. There should also be an oath for city council persons and employees such as the one taken in ancient Athens.

The Athenian Oath is a pledge taken by the citizens of ancient Athens, Greece to enhance civic virtue. Why not recite it at the start of each council meeting, following the pledge of allegiance? Each time an official (and others) recites the oath he or she would be reminded of his or her promise to uphold the public good. It beautifully illustrates his or her high-minded duties and responsibilities.[23]

> "We will never bring disgrace on this our City by an act of dishonesty or cowardice. We will fight for the ideals and Sacred Things of the City both alone and with many. We will revere and obey the City's laws, and will do our best to incite a like reverence and respect in those above us who are prone to annul them or set them at naught. We will strive unceasingly to quicken the public's sense of civic duty. Thus, in all these ways, we will transmit this City not only, not less, but greater and more beautiful than it was transmitted to us."

Can virtue be taught?

The university also has a responsibility to inculcate virtue. Ethics training is now mandated in most professional schools. Through case studies and moral reflection, students are instructed to understand, to be mindful of, and to feel responsible for the consequences of their actions as public servants. Fundamentally, this is about recognizing that it is the public that is the "boss" in a democratic system. Future public servants must be taught to listen to residents, include them in the decision process, and, above all, to treat them with respect. This is tough going. According to public administration scholar Lewis Mainzer, "Ethics is especially difficult to teach because we can hardly assume that we have succeeded in our goal: making a difference in how students will behave in their actual public administration responsibilities. We can teach about goodness, but we do not know if we can teach" people to be good.[24]

ACCOUNTABILITY

Another condition which fostered the Bell scandal was the lack of effective oversight. Jennifer Rodgers, of the Center for Public Integrity, writes that "Even with appropriate accountability and transparency regulations (which were not present in Bell before the Rizzo scandal), small municipalities like Bell constitute outsized corruption risks because the oversight they rely on at the county, state, and federal levels of government are simply inadequate."[25]

Robert Rizzo thought he could get away with what he did, which included breaking the law, because he was convinced that no one was watching. Those few citizens who did take an interest in local government, came to city meetings and persisted in asking difficult questions could be stonewalled, lied to, or intimidated. As for the rest—complacent council members, consultants, and city staff—they could be bought off, sweet-talked, lied to, or simply ignored. In the case of city staff, this included illegal personal loans and other forms of manipulation, which Rizzo skillfully employed.

Transparency is critical

The California legislature took some steps to strengthen oversight by improving governmental transparency. But it came up short in many other ways.

The legislature required salaries, but not benefits, be posted online. This was a major omission because benefits packages typically account for a third of a city manager's total remuneration, as Barbara Kogerman found in her study of city manager compensation:

> "Unlike the more transparent compensation data involving city manager base salary, their benefits packages are often difficult to ferret out, are obscure to the public, and offer a stealthier way to overly compensate a City Manager without raising public alarm. These added compensation benefits may and often do include such items as management incentives, deferred compensation, contributions to private retirement programs, insurance premiums, paying the employee's portion of payments, physical examinations, home offices, cell phones and computer equipment, autos, auto expenses, moving expenses, payouts for unused sick or vacation leave, greater-than-average vacation leave days, and the like. Many of these benefits will be taken into account when the employee retires, thereby increasing their final compensation as a basis for their retirement pay."[26]

This information is not available to the public online. This matters because Rizzo, you recall, was slated to receive an annual pension of $880,000 per year for life, and Spaccia received one sick day for each day she worked, "a benefit" which effectively doubled her pay.

Strengthen public records requests

The legislature could have strengthened the California Public Records Request Act by having strong penalties for individuals and government entities that deny people the information they are entitled to. Such was the case when Bell Clerk Rebecca Valdez gave Roger Ramirez false salary information and "stonewalled" *L.A. Times* reporters Gottlieb and Vives. The legislature could also have adopted much tougher transparency laws, such as the one in Hamburg, Germany which requires that *all* government information not impacted by privacy issues be posted online. This includes all documents, especially contracts.[27]

This is important because Bell entered into several suspicious agreements that the public was not privy to. These included the purchasing of properties from former officials for much more than the market said they were worth and special deals for Rizzo cronies. As Supreme Court Justice Louis Brandeis said, "Sunlight is the best disinfectant."[28]

Lots of people knew, but kept quiet.

The legislature should have also required the mandatory reporting of wrongdoing by the city attorney and auditor and CalPERS. Ed Lee was Bell's city attorney and legal adviser. He worked for Best, Best and Krieger (BBK), the largest municipal law firm in California. Lee was fully aware of the legal shenanigans taking place in Bell, but he never reported them to the district attorney or attorney general. BBK would settle with Bell for $2.5 million without admitting any wrongdoing. Randy Adams, Bell's chief of police and chief law enforcement officer, who was also in possession of ill-gotten financial benefits (i.e., his outrageous salary and pension), also failed to uphold the law by not alerting authorities.[29]

Mayer Hoffman McCann (MHM) was Bell's longtime auditor.[30] MHM is a pre-eminent accounting firm which audits dozens of California local governments and has 30 offices nationwide. MHM knew about the "excessive compensation, illegal taxes, mismanaged bond funds, and questionable contracts and land practices," but the auditing firm continually gave the city a clean bill of fiscal health. State Controller John Chiang said they were a "rubber stamp" and that the city had not been properly audited in years.[31] The firm received a disciplinary fine of $300,000 (plus $50,000 for the cost of the investigation) and was placed on two years probation by the California Board of Accountancy.[32] They also settled with Bell for $3 million.[33]

CalPERS is the government agency that manages the state's massive pension system. Bell administrators did report the outrageous salaries and pensions to CalPERS. The agency could have balked at the huge pay hikes that result in over-the-top retiree pensions. At minimum, it could have raised a red flag and reported what was going on to the attorney general. It didn't do either; CalPERS is not a "policing" agency. Even as Rizzo's pay eventually grew to nearly $800,000, CalPERS remained silent.[34] This prompted then-Attorney-General Jerry Brown to comment, "A 47% increase in salary should have set off alarm bells ... That kind of jump in pay is shocking and completely unacceptable. CalPERS should have told someone, and the attorney general's office is a good place to start."[35]

At present, cities, counties, and special districts hire a firm each year to conduct an audit. The results are forwarded to the State Controller's Office (SCO). No action is taken unless the audit uncovers serious financial problems or the agency asks the SCO to examine its books.[36]

A *Los Angeles Times* review of state and local records found that the independent audits of public agencies frequently fail to flag cases of fraud and mismanagement. "Many cities that have been troubled by public corruption or mismanagement during the last decade—including San Diego, Compton, and South Gate—got clean audits, even in cases in which public officials were later sent to prison." Bell, they conclude, "is far from being alone."[37] The legislature responded by passing a bill, AB 187, which empowered the state auditor to audit any entity he or she "identifies as being at high risk for the potential of waste, fraud, abuse, or mismanagement." In that same article, Chiang remarked that Bell "*is the tip of the iceberg* (author's italics)." The controller only has the resources to audit just a few dozen each year.

One proposal is to have *every* local government unit audited on a regular basis by the state auditors or the state controller.

This would require a huge increase in the resources budget for these offices, especially the hiring of hundreds, if not thousands, of new auditors and would be opposed by the agencies, the accounting firms they hire, and those in the legislature who see this as an unnecessary duplication of effort.

A related reform is to limit the number of years a private firm may audit a city. This would help ensure an objective and independent assessment of the city's finance. This proposal would also get substantial pushback from local governments and the private accounting firms they pay to audit their books.

Another problem is that the state's 5,000 counties, cities, special districts, and other government agencies do not use the same schema for measuring things, such as revenues, expenditures, assets, and liabilities. Accountants call this a "chart of accounts."

According to Wikipedia, "A chart of accounts (COA) is a created list of the accounts used by an organization to define each class of items for which money or the equivalent is spent or received. It is used to organize the finances of the entity and to segregate expenditures, revenue, assets and liabilities in order to give interested parties a better understanding of the financial health of the entity."[38]

If all public entities used a common chart of accounts (essentially an agency's "checkbook") and if these data were posted online, software could be run that automatically flagged financial outliers—large salaries, pensions, double dipping, and vastly different compensation for individuals with the same job title in nearby localities—for further inspection. In addition to helping to detect fraud, having a uniform online chart of accounts would help improve how the public's money is spent.

Another reform is to increase municipal corruption investigations and prosecutions. Shortly after being elected district attorney in 2000, L.A. District Attorney Steve Cooley established the Public Integrity Division (PID). The PID's mission is to investigate and prosecute local government corruption.

The PID has only eight attorneys and 18 investigators for the 88 cities in Los Angeles County, many of which are riddled with corruption. Most U.S. state and local governments rely on the Justice Department and the FBI to battle local corruption. Cooley believes there should be a public integrity division in the attorney general's office.[39] "The attorney general is very weak in this area. You can't rely on the Feds; they are too selective and their effort isn't sufficient."[40]

Surprise! There is no oversight of local government

One of the Bell scandal's most revealing lessons is that citizens can't rely on the county or state or anyone else to deter corruption. They must be eternally vigilant because no one else is watching. They are on their own.

Bell activists tried to engage the board of supervisors, state legislature, attorney general, and others. They were shocked and frustrated when told that corruption in city government was a local problem, beyond the scope of the respective office. They, like the rest of us, thought higher levels of government oversee lower levels. The state, they thought, oversees counties, which, in turn, along with the state, oversee cities and special districts. This turns out not to be true.

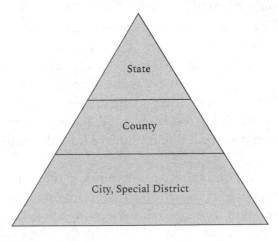

FIGURE 11.1 How People Think California Government is Organized

The reality: cities are on their own

The reality is that state and county agencies do not routinely monitor municipal affairs. As the governor's website states, "Governor Brown *does not have* (author's italics) jurisdiction over local issues. Your elected representatives of local government are in the best position to assist on issues and/or concerns relating to local government. For issues pertaining to city government, you should contact your Mayor and City Council members as applicable ... For issues pertaining to school districts, you should contact your elected school board to express your issues and/or concerns ... For issues pertaining to county government, you should contact your county's Board of Supervisors ..."[41]

State government has not built the capacity to oversee local government. Since 1960, the number or cities and special districts has increased 35% and 54% respectively. (Table 11.2) The state controller has only 277 auditors and produced 515 final reports in the fiscal year 2016-2017.[42] This office does not have the capacity to review the state's more than 5,000 counties, cities and special districts. Local entities are required to submit annual financial reports to the State Controller's Office (SCO). However, these are rarely examined; there are simply too many for the SCO's limited staff.[43] That's why no "red flags" were raised before the story burst onto the front pages of the *L.A. Times*. It is not that the "checks" failed in the Bell scandal, but that there weren't any "checks" to begin with.[44]

State agencies may *choose* to get involved, but they aren't required to, and they usually don't—unless there is some political benefit to be garnered for the agency head. For example, the California State Controller's Office, the California Attorney General, and the Los Angeles District Attorney started seriously investigating Bell *only after* the *Times'* city manager story came out.[45]

TABLE 11.2   *Number of Cities and Special Districts in California has Increased*[46]

	POPULATION IN MILLIONS	COUNTIES	CITIES	SPECIAL DISTRICTS
1960	15.8	58	357	3,123
2015	39.5	58	482	4,800
Increase	150%	0%	35%	54%

And then there is CalPERS, the agency that administers the state's public employee retirement fund. CalPERS officials knew about the outrageous salaries and pensions in Bell, but stayed silent.[47]

Similarly, after the November 2010 election was over, and attorney general Jerry Brown had been elected governor, and Bell was no longer in the headlights, the attorney general's (now Kamala Harris) enthusiasm for prosecuting the Bell defendants quickly evaporated.

Absent legal restrictions and public opinion, cities, especially home rule or "charter" cities, are more or less free to do as they please. Cities are far less fearful of state agencies oversight than, say, taxpayers are of being audited by the IRS.

Why, then, do so many of us think that the state oversees local government? One reason is that since the 1960s, there has been a growing concentration of power in the California state's capitol. State government has taken the lead in civil rights, crime, and environmental legislation. Proposition 13 further concentrated power in Sacramento, the seat of state government, by slashing property taxes. This amounted to a 22% loss of local revenue. This forced the state to financially backfill local municipalities so they could meet their budgeted responsibilities. Local governments became further dependent on Sacramento for funding when, in 2011, Governor Brown axed the state's 400 Redevelopment Agencies, which cut $1.7 billion from local government coffers.[48]

Sacramento's heavy handedness is apparent when the legislature raids local treasuries to make up for shortfalls in state revenue, passes unfunded mandates, and imposes one-size-fits-all protocols, requirements, and policies on an expansive and diverse state.[49]

The controller's website also gives the impression that the state has substantial oversight responsibilities. "The [controller] is responsible for accountability and disbursement of the state's financial resources ... [and] independently audits government agencies that spend state funds ..."[50]

Rizzo knew outside agencies had neither the resources nor the inclination to oversee municipalities, especially an obscure little city like Bell. He took the bold risks he did because he knew there was little chance he'd get caught. And he almost got away with it: Rizzo was just a few years away from retiring. Had he not been outed by the *Times*, he would have retired with an annual payout of $880,000, the highest public pension in California.

As an experienced, financially oriented city manager, Rizzo knew there is no real financial oversight by the state of cities. Rather than being on one of the lower rungs of the ladder of state government, as one would imagine, counties, cities and special districts float like lilies on a pond, only tenuously attached to one another (Figure 11.2). There is no agency above them that ensures that citizens are not being ripped off.[51] It is up to a city's residents to police their city hall. The state has neither the desire nor capacity to do it for them. Rizzo saw that no one was guarding the city's treasury. So, he took what he could. Surely, he is to blame. But what about the system that left the city's vault open?

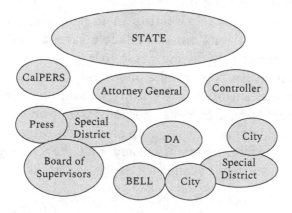

FIGURE 11.2 How California government is really organized

Critical Role of the Press

The Bell scandal also vividly demonstrated the vital role a watchdog press plays in democracy. Despite this, there was no discussion in the legislature of the falloff in press coverage of local government. Nor were there any bills presented that would have strengthened media coverage of local government by, for example, providing public subsidies or tax breaks for private media outlets or some other form of support.[52]

Had the *Times* not stumbled upon the Bell story, the scandal would never have seen the light of day. The press was the only "check" that worked and, then, just barely. Unfortunately, there is no systematic, coordinated coverage of local government in most cities. No reporter, for example, regularly attends city council meetings in Bell or any of the other 87 cities in Los Angeles County. Shrinking newsrooms have made this deficiency even worse.

News coverage of local government is scattershot, hit and miss. *L.A. Times* reporter Ruben Vives was responsible for covering about a dozen cities in the area. He got a tip about the high salaries in Bell while writing about the next door town of Maywood.[53] *L.A. Times* reporter Jeff Gottlieb was on another assignment at the time and was brought in to help Vives out—the point being that it was not inevitable that Rizzo would get caught.

Given the dramatic decline in press coverage of local government, citizens must be made aware, as Bell showed, that we cannot rely on the press to expose wrongdoing in their community. Nor can the public rely on some other government institution at the county or state level or on city consultants (e.g., attorneys and auditors) or on city employees or neighboring cities to stop abuses. Local governments control significant pots of money, and there is significant temptation to steal because there are no checks.

ENGAGEMENT

A disengaged public is the third factor contributing to the scandal.[54]

All the transparency in the world will not do any good unless citizens pay attention, care, and hold public officials accountable by voting.

Unfortunately, political engagement is falling, especially in local government. Blame has been placed on the schools, the council-manager form, and the failure of government to do more to engage people in politics, among other things.

A number of groups blame the education system for the decline in civic engagement.[55] "The California Task Force on K–12 Civic Learning [says] that our state is in the midst of a 'civic education' crisis. ... Los Angeles Mayor Eric Garcetti and William A. Covino, the president of the California State University at Los Angeles, [have called] for a greater emphasis on civics learning and community service at the K–12 and university level."[56]

Surveys repeatedly show students are unaware of their responsibilities as citizens. They lack basic knowledge of democratic values, including the role citizens play in democracy, the role of the press, the rule of law, and the need for an independent judiciary.[57]

In an article in *The Atlantic*, Richard Kahlenberg and Clifford Janey even go so far as to argue that the American education system's failure to teach a "love of liberal democracy" contributed to Donald Trump's victory. "Public schools are failing at what the nation's founders saw as education's most basic purpose: preparing young people ... to resist the appeal of demagogues. In that sense, the Trump phenomenon should be a Sputnik moment for civics education."[58]

The civic engagement crisis is especially bad in city elections. Only about a fifth of eligible voters vote in municipal elections. This percentage continues to decline.[59] Turnout in Bell was typically in the teens and sometimes fell into single digits. Less than

400 people voted in the special election which changed Bell from a general law to a charter city—a pivotal point in the scandal.

Cities must face the challenge to get people involved in civic affairs. This is important because government at the local level is crucial to making democracy work. And as Alexis de Tocqueville reminds us, this is where people first learn to be democratic citizens who are involved in public affairs and pursue the common good.[60]

Civics Education

Just as public schools recognized the need to place emphasis on science, technology, engineering, and math, so-called STEM, courses, which are geared to preparing students for the private marketplace, schools need to put greater emphasis on preparing students to be thoughtful, informed democratic citizens.[61]California requires only one semester of government in high school, which focuses on the Constitution and federal institutions. There's nothing about city and county government. At the university level, courses on local government are missing-in-action across the U.S.

To better train active citizens and future leaders who keep democracy alive, schools should return to offering civic instruction, with an emphasis on local government and active learning in the community. They need to offer debate clubs where students can practice public speaking. The importance of doing so was powerfully illustrated by the poised and eloquent student leaders at Marjorie Stoneman Douglas High School who spoke out for gun control. They were the beneficiaries of a curriculum that emphasized civic awareness, debate, public speaking, theater arts, and journalism.[62]

Consolidating governments

California has 58 counties, 482 cities, and more than 4,800 special districts, as well as thousands of school districts with thousands of elected officials. Fragmented government produces a plethora of nooks and crannies where a culture of corruption can take root and spread. For example, there are four city halls less than four miles from Bell's city hall.[63] These cities have a total population of around 140,000 people. If the cities were combined—they abut one another—there would be five, rather than 25, council members; 1 instead of 5 police chiefs, and so forth. Given the press' limited resources, reducing the number of local government units would make it easier for reporters to do their job keeping citizens informed. Fewer government entities would mean there would be fewer elected officials to monitor. Although somewhat rare, successful municipal consolidation efforts have taken place across the United States.[64]

Make Local Government Responsible for Improving Voter Participation.

Local government also has to do more to improve civic engagement. Detroit, Philadelphia, Chicago, and Austin have launched aggressive public engagement initiatives, according to the National League of Cities.[65] Other cities are experimenting with "city hall web sites, community surveys, neighborhood councils, online forums, participatory budgets, town hall meetings, and community-wide visioning processes."[66] We can also learn a lot from cities outside the U.S. The City of Barcelona, Spain for example, has an entire department responsible for fostering the "active involvement of citizens in the process of creating, executing and evaluating public policy" and "[collaborating] in the creation of community networks to strengthen citizens' capacity to play an active part in collective affairs." It is headed by a Commissioner of Democracy and Active Participation.[67] The Barcelona City Council also "funds projects that propose outstanding innovations in the field of active participation and democracy."[68]

Also in Barcelona, the International Observatory on Participatory Democracy (IOPD) gives out awards annually to recognize efforts by local governments to promote "Best Practice in Citizen Participation."[69] The contest receives entries from all over the globe.[70]

In the U.S., the Participatory Governance Initiative at Arizona State University studies "emerging trends and innovative experiments around the world that are relevant to the realities of governance and public engagement in the 21st century."[71] The project is a great resource for those cities who want to strengthen engagement in their communities. These initiatives are exceptions, however; most cities do very little to engage citizens.

Cities often encourage people to sort their trash and participate in neighborhood watch programs but rarely stress the importance of voting. Doing so would violate the politics-administration dichotomy central to the council-manager form. A muscular "get out the vote" program would likely be criticized for being a waste of money and for encouraging the "wrong" people to vote.[72] This is unfortunate because this is precisely the effort local democracy requires.

The Bell scandal illustrates the critical role of the public in keeping city hall honest. In an editorial about the Bell scandal, the *L.A. Times* wrote, "Bell fell prey to these thieves because government stopped answering to the public, and because an apathetic public failed to question the government. ... the most valuable lesson to be learned is that democracy requires citizens to be involved and to ask questions. There will always be venality and theft, but gadflies, whistle-blowers, and a watchful citizenry are still the best backstop on corruption."[73]

Judge Kennedy said it well at her sentencing of Mayor Oscar Hernandez, "... [a] lot of these things wouldn't have happened ... if there had been more participation by the electorate ... So there is a lot of blame to go around."[74]

Citizens, not Consumers

Although we are often told otherwise, we are citizens, not "consumers of government services" from a government that functions like a business.[75] The word "citizen" has its roots in the word "city"—an inhabitant of a city, a member of a community. Citizens own the government, and it should be responsive to them. We—the people—are the moral force behind government. Government policy must go beyond balancing the books and making a profit, the primary concerns of business. Government policy should be informed by what we value—justice, equity, historic preservation, clean water, and protection of wild spaces, for example.

As consumers, we act alone, prioritizing our own self-interest, looking for an advantage. But when we take the role of citizens, we act in concert with one another, concerned with what is best for the community, which includes people we will never meet, future generations, and people from different walks of life.

We become full citizens by participating in our cities: by voting, by joining groups, expressing opinions, or joining a neighborhood cleanup. Not everyone can or will run for office, join a board, or show up at every city council meeting. But democracy doesn't depend on that. It rests on our paying attention, as citizens, to even one of the myriad details of community life that concerns us—potholes, school matters, local crime, plans to replace run-down parks, graffiti, local taxes—and joining with our neighbors in addressing that issue. When we pay attention and care what happens in our community, we make government personal and bring it alive.

Civic Infrastructure is Vital

There's only one way to resist the kleptocrats, Bell teaches us. We must strengthen the web of connection that ties us to our communities. Civic infrastructure, collective efficacy, and social capital refer to the social connections among average people rather than the actions of elected leaders or voting. A key difference between democratic Bell and Bell the kleptocracy was the health of the civic infrastructure, the web of connection that binds people to their communities and gives life to democracy.

That web, say community engagement experts Jill Blair and Malka Kopell, is "made up of places, policies, programs and practices that enable us to connect with one another, to ... build community and to solve public problems. It is this basis upon which ordinary people are able to participate in ordinary civic life—from joining neighborhood watch groups to entering the voting booth."[76]

When community members have shared values and aspirations, when the bonds among them are strong, when trust is high, and when they are willing to cooperate, quality of life for all increases. Research shows strong correlation between social capital and crime rates, homelessness, risk of hunger, standardized test scores, and voting turnout. This is true even in poorer communities.[77]

The Community Matters organization says, "Civic infrastructure enables citizens to connect with each other, solve problems, make decisions, and build community in both physical and nonphysical ways. By strengthening civic infrastructure, a community can come together to meet whatever challenges it faces and become a more sustainable, vibrant place to live."[78]

Mathew Desmond, the author of *Evicted*, calls this "collective efficacy ... the stuff of loosely linked neighbors who trust one another and share expectations about how to make their community better."[79]

Robert Putnam coined the term "social capital" which he defines as the "connections among individuals—social networks and the norms of reciprocity and trustworthiness that arise from them." According to Putnam and his followers, social capital is a key component to building and maintaining democracy. Similarly, in her classic book, *The Death and Life of Great American Cities*, Jane Jacobs explains how this works, "The first thing to understand is that the public peace—the sidewalk and street peace—of cities is not kept primarily by the police, necessary as the police are. It is kept primarily by an intricate, almost unconscious network of voluntary controls and standards among the people themselves, and enforced by the people themselves."[80]

A robust group of civic clubs and organizations help build and maintain a community's civic infrastructure. Service clubs (e.g., churches, League of United Latin American Citizens, unions, activist groups such as BASTA and the Bell Residents Club, and other groups concerned with growth and development, the environment, historic preservation, seniors etc.) are venues for the discussion of current events, which include the performance of local government officials. These clubs collapsed under Rizzo.

Activist civic groups such as BASTA and the Bell Resident's Club emerged —prompted by revelations reported in the *L.A. Times*—to sweep him and the council members from power. The collapse of a community's civic infrastructure is a warning sign that the kleptocrats may have already moved in, or will, shortly.

One simple way to begin to gauge the health of local democracy—and its ability to resist the incursion of kleptocrats like Bell's Pete Werrlein—is to count the strands of the web, the number of ways the community invites all residents to belong and have a say. Bell, at its strongest, had a proliferation of them:

- Community organizations and service clubs based on common interests and concerns.
- City-sponsored civic activities—parades, movies for families, ceremonies, holiday gatherings, car shows, Halloween parades, and concerts, MLK day, Cinco de Mayo, July 4th celebrations —where the community gathers in the same place doing the same thing.
- Citizen committees that advise the city council.
- Religious, school, and youth groups.

Another metric, of course, is participation in the government itself. It's helpful to ask:

- Are unexpected council vacancies being filled by appointment, rather than election?
- Are elections being cancelled because incumbents aren't being challenged?
- How many qualified people are running for office?
- What percentage of the citizenry is registered to vote and what percentage is showing up at the polls?
- How well does voter registration and turnout reflect the entire community?
- How much of the newly arrived population is registered to vote?
- What sorts of "invitations" to participate—language, citizenship and cooking classes, events, social gatherings—are

being offered to the community's immigrant voters and their children?

- What kind of action plan does the city have for getting *all* citizens involved in the community?

We talk about civic duty and the obligations we have as citizens. But a sense of community isn't automatic. Cities must cultivate the community's web of connection, feeding a greater sense of responsibility in the young and each other. Cities and schools and other organizations must instill in residents a responsibility for shaping the future of the city, and an understanding that its health is in their hands.

Dwindling Participation

Nowhere is the collapse of civic engagement greater than in local government where only about a fifth of eligible voters vote. In the decades prior to the Bell scandal, for example, turnout in Bell's municipal elections rarely rose above the teens and was often in single digits.

Tom Hogen-Esch argues that the council-manager form of government lends itself to corruption in high-immigration cities.[81] This is because the council-manager form deliberately discourages turnout by poor and the newly arrived by having off-year elections, nonpartisan ballots, and at-large rather than district elections.

One of the reasons that turnout in Bell council elections was so low, he argues, is because election day was isolated in March rather than in November when elections for higher offices (e.g., the president, congress and the governor) are held. Also, party labels provide voters an important cue. These cues are absent in municipal elections. At-large elections—where candidates must win votes from the entire city—are too costly and time consuming for anyone but the wealthy and politically connected to launch a successful campaign. Also, at-large elections dilute the power of minorities. In contrast, district elections—which have more walkable jurisdictions and fewer voters—reduces the cost and time involved in running for office and make it possible for people of more modest means to become candidates.

Making election day a holiday or moving it to Saturday and adopting all-mail elections could help improve turnout. The important thing Hogen-Esch says is that cities be able to experiment with "alternative arrangements" to increase voter participation.[82]

Dwindling participation is not confined to Bell. In the 2014 midterm races for Congress, turnout was the lowest in 70 years (36%). And, of course, the United States has the lowest turnout in presidential elections of any industrialized nation (around 55%). These numbers are for registered voters; the percentage for voting-age voters (people who are eligible but fail to register) is often even lower. For example, in the 2016 presidential election, 59% of eligible voters voted, but only 54% of the voting-age population voted.[83]

Disengagement is especially apparent and worrisome among America's youth, who are disconnecting from traditional forms of engagement in public life. Evidence is everywhere.[84] Research has found that 18–24-year-olds are:

- Less knowledgeable about politics.
- Less likely to express traditional forms of patriotism and citizenship.
- Less likely to follow traditional news about government and public affairs.
- Less likely to engage in traditional forms of political participation (such as participating in a campaign, attending a political event, contacting an elected official).
- Less trusting of political institutions and processes.
- Less likely to register with one of the political parties.
- Less likely to register to vote.
- Less likely to vote.

The Harvard Institute for Politics reported that 18–29 year-olds are experiencing a five-year low in their trust in public institutions while their cynicism about the political process has never been higher.[85] Also, according to the Pew Research

Center, "half of Millennials (50%) now describe themselves as political independents ... These are at or near the highest levels of political ... disaffiliation recorded for any generation in the quarter-century that the Pew Research Center has been polling on these topics."[86]

The 2014 midterm congressional election suggests that things are getting worse. Only 8.2% of eligible California youth (18–24) turned out to vote. Furthermore, youth accounted for only 3.9% of all voters in this election even though they make up 14.5% of the eligible electorate.[87] Mindy Romero, the director of the California Civic Engagement project and the author of the report, said in a webinar that the findings matter for at least three reasons.[88] First, voting is habit forming. If young people do not start voting in their teens, they are unlikely to vote as adults, with the result being even more dismal turnout rates for the general population. Second, voting is connected to other forms of community engagement. Voters are more likely to care about their community and quality of life issues, such as schools, environment, and the needs of future generations, and are more willing to engage in the long-term conversations necessary to solve vexing problems. Finally, the fact that youth are so underrepresented has serious consequences for issues that affect young people—such as access to education, gun violence, affordable housing, and the environment. How can their concerns about, say, climate change be addressed when they are not at the table? Today's youth will have to pay the bills being run up by current decision-makers.

As we saw in Bell, when citizens abandon civic life, corruption flourishes. Thieves can arrive unnoticed and steal a government blind, tailoring rules for their own self-dealing purposes and penalizing opponents. Any respect for democratic norms—such as transparency, freedom of the press, the rights of citizens, and the law—disappears when elected and unelected leaders conclude that no one is watching.

A watchful citizenry is key. Citizens need to keep their collective eye on the council and top administrators. The press can be the vehicle for doing this.

Citizens must form groups which keep tabs on local government. If corruption becomes embedded, they need to raise hell. Bell showed us that even political amateurs can band together and drive the crooks from office. Citizens need to be aware that there is a huge talent pool of skilled professionals that specializes in local government (e.g., attorneys, community organizers, recall specialists, political strategists) available for hire or willing to volunteer to help bring about change.

TABLE 11.3 *Reforms*

CONDITION	SUB-PROBLEM	REFORM
CHARACTER	Moral Failure	Ethics training in graduate school and professional development. Greater penalties for public officials that abuse the public trust. Use ICMA hiring protocol and other recommendations.
OVERSIGHT	Transparency	Every document, contract should be accessible online.
	External Review	Regular audits Mandated external oversight by DA or AG.
	Poor Consultants	Limit the number of years auditors can work for a city.
	Press Coverage	Increased news coverage of local government. Subsisize press
	Fragmentated Government	Consolidate governments

CONDITION	SUB-PROBLEM	REFORM
ENGAGEMENT	Low Turnout	Civics Education
		Saturday Voting
		District Elections
		Consolidating governments
		Make Local Government Responsible for Engagement
		Improve Civic Infrastructure
		Experiment with new ways to improve participation

LESSONS

Many of these reforms would require a change in state law, something that is nearly impossible for ordinary citizens to do. But many others could all be put in place locally. Because these provisions challenge a comfortable status quo that protects the privilege of those in power, including those who would skim (or worse) from the public trough, local governments are likely to drag their feet unless they're pressured by the public.

But change can come. Even a small handful of reform-minded people from a community can begin to ask questions, size up the state of their local government, and build a push for better government. They can build on the lessons of Bell's decline, its activist resistance, and its rebirth to begin to rebuild civic life. They can turn out voters to win local elections with reform candidates and use the initiative process to get the openness they seek.

The ideas are there. Bell has demonstrated the urgency of *acting* on them. Without such changes, future Bell scandals are inevitable.

ENDNOTES

1   Extract from Thomas Jefferson's "A Summary View of the Rights of British America." The Jefferson Monticello. Jefferson Quotes and Family Letters. Retrieved from: http://tjrs.monticello.org/letter/1272.

2   Authored by Senator Lou Correa. Also included are stipends, automobile allowances and incentive and bonus payments. Significantly, the value of benefits is not included. The Resolution of the Board of Supervisors of the County of Los Angeles certifying the Bell election results can be found at: http://file.lacounty.gov/ SDSInter/bos/supdocs/60009.pdf. The new council was Ali Saleh, Nestor Valencia, Violeta Alvarez, Danny Harber, and Anna-Marie Quintano.

3   Patrick McGreevy, "Legislators offer plan to refund Bell property tax overcharges," *L.A. Times*, August 19, 2010. Retrieved from http://articles.latimes.com/2010/aug/19/local/la-me-bell-legislature-20100819, and Karen Wilkinson, "California Cities and Counties Mandated to Disclose Public Employees' Salaries, August 11, 2010. Originally, the salaries had to be posted on the state controller's website. Subsequent legislation required that salaries be posted on city-run websites. Retrieved from http:// www.govtech.com/dc/articles/California-Cities-and-Counties-Mandated-to. htmlhttp://www.govtech.com/dc/articles/California-Cities-and-Counties-Mandated-to.html.

4   Howard A. Friedman and Lyndsy B. Rogers, "AB 1344 Enacts New Transparency and Accountability Measures for Public Agency Executive Contracts," Fagen Friedman & Fulfrost LLP website. Analysis if legislation. Retrieved from https:// www.f3law.com/newsflash.php?nf=318.

5   "The lesson of Bell: A watchful citizenry is still crucial." Editorial: *L.A. Times*. December 11, 2013. Retrieved from: http://www.latimes.com/opinion/editorials/ la-ed-bell-trial-20131211-story.html

6   Ryan Gabrielson, "California Checkpoint impounds to stop under new law signed by Gov. Brown" *Huffington Post*. December 11, 2011. Retrieved from: https://www.huffingtonpost.com/2011/10/11/ california-checkpoint-impound_n_1005607.html

7   "The lesson of Bell: A watchful citizenry is still crucial." Editorial *L.A. Times*. December 11, 2013. Retrieved from: http://www.latimes.com/opinion/editorials/ la-ed-bell-trial-20131211-story.html

8   Editorial "Vernon's nervy ex-manager suing city after defrauding it." August 28, 2017. https://www.dailynews.com/2013/07/29/vernons-nervy-ex-manager-suing-city-after-defrauding-it-editorial/

9   Sam Quinones,"The Savage Politics of South Gate" Los Angeles Times. July 8, 2001. Retrieved from: http://articles.latimes.com/2001/jul/08/magazine/tm-19647

10 Benjamin Oreskes, "Former Compton Mayor Omar Bradley Sentenced to 36 months' probation for misappropriation of public funds." August 30, 2017. Retrieved from: http://www.latimes.com/local/lanow/la-me-ln-omar-bradley-sentencing-20170830-story.html

11 Richard Winton, "Ex Palm Springs Mayor and 2 developers charged with corruption" Los Angeles Times. February 16, 2017. Retrieved from: http://www.latimes.com/local/california/la-me-ln-palm-springs-investigation-20170216-story.html

12 Colin Atagi, "Beaumont officials plead guilty in $43M embezzlement case, get probation and fines." Desert Sun. December 20, 2017. Retrieved from: https://www.desertsun.com/story/news/crime_courts/2017/12/19/beaumont-almost-brought-its-knees-officials-plead-guilty-43-million-embezzlement-case/963714001/

13 Orange County Grand Jury Report, 2012-2013. "A Call for Ethical Standards: Corruption in Orange County," Retrieved from: http://www.ocgrandjury.org/pdfs/2012_2013_reports/Corruption-in-OC04152013.pdf

14 Former Dixon Comptroller Rita Crundwell Pleads Guilty to Federal Fraud Charge, Admits Stealing $53 Million from City." *FBI.* FBI, 14 Nov. 2012. Web. 03 June 2017. <https://archives.fbi.gov/archives/chicago/press-releases/2012/former-dixon-comptroller-rita-crundwell-pleads-guilty-to-federal-fraud-charge-admits-stealing-53-million-from-city>.

15 "Ex-New Orleans mayor Nagin gets 10 years in prison." *CNN.* Cable News Network, 09 July 2014. Web. 05 June 2017. <http://www.cnn.com/2014/07/09/justice/ray-nagin-sentencing/index.html>.

16 Lynnley Browning, "Hartford Mayor Arrested for Second Time This Year." *The New York Times.* The New York Times, 02 Sept. 2009. Web. 07 June 2017. <http://www.nytimes.com/2009/09/03/nyregion/03hartford.html>. Helen Ubiñas "Mayor Eddie Perez's Conviction Yet Another Chance To Learn From Scandal." *Courant Community.* N.p., 25 June 2010. Web. 07 June 2017. <http://www.courant.com/community/hartford/eddie-perez/hc-ubinas-perez0620-20100619-column.html>.

17 Alice, McQuillan, "Former Councilman Gets 5 Years for Slush Fund Fraud." *NBC New York.* NBC New York, 15 Dec. 2009. Web. 07 June 2017. <http://www.

nbcnewyork.com/news/local/Councilman-Martinez-Sentenced-79330047.
html>

18 "Warren Buffett looks for these 3 traits in people when he
hires them," *Business Insider*, January 4, 2017. Retrieved from
http://www.businessinsider.com/what-warren-buffett-looks-
for-in-candidates-2017-1.

19 Personal communication from retired city manager and ICMA Western Division
head, Kevin Duggan.

20 Not everyone went along, including police officer James Corcoran, Councilman
Victor Bello who feuded with Rizzo and wrote the district attorney, and Lorenzo
Valez, the councilmember who didn't get the $100,000 salary.

21 See The Center for Advancement of Public Integrity, "Rebuilding Bell, CA:
Review and Recommendations for the continued improvement of Accountability,
Oversight and Transparency. "Columbia University Law School Paper by Jenni-
fer Rodgers. at The City of Bell Scandal Revisited. February 19, 2015. Chapman
University.

22 Joe Pinsker, "Would a Hippocratic Oath for Bankers Lead to
Better Behavior?" *The Atlantic*, December 18, 2014. Retrieved
from https://www.theatlantic.com/business/archive/2014/12/
would-a-hippocratic-oath-for-bankers-lead-to-better-behavior/383867/.

23 The Athenian Oath is featured prominently on National League of Cities' web-
page: Retrieved fromhttps://www.nlc.org/the-athenian-oath.

24 Lewis Mainzer, "Vulgar Ethics for Public Administration," Administration and
Society, Vol 23, May 1991 3-28. Retrieved from: http://academic.udayton.edu/
RichardGhere/MPA%20524/2011%20course/Mainzer_Lewis_C.pdf. P. 1.

25 See The Center for Advancement of Public Integrity, "Rebuilding Bell, CA:
Review and Recommendations for the continued improvement of Accountability,
Oversight and Transparency. "Columbia University Law School Paper by Jenni-
fer Rodgers. at The City of Bell Scandal Revisited. February 19, 2015. Chapman
University.

26 See, Barbara Kogerman, "Orange County, California, City Managers Compensa-
tion Report The Cost of Local Government: A Comparative Analysis of Orange
County Municipalities' Expenditures for City Managers By Barbara D. Kogerman
Candidate, Laguna Hills City Council 2010 ."

27 David Eaves, "Hamburg's new transparency law: Lessons for Activists," *Tech President*, June 29, 2012. Retrieved from http://techpresident.com/news/wegov/22495/
hamburg%E2%80%99s-new-transparency-law-%E2%80%93-lessons-activists.

And Christian Humborg, "Hamburg's Transparency Law To Open Government More Than Ever." Transparency International. Blog. June 25, 2013. Retrieved from http://blog.transparency.org/2012/06/25/hamburgs-transparency-law-to-open-government-more-than-ever/.

28   Louis D. Brandeis Legacy Fund for Social Justice. Brandeis University. Retrieved from: https://www.brandeis.edu/legacyfund/bio.html

29   Judge Kennedy admonished the prosecution for not charging Adams. Jeff Gottlieb, "Judge questions why Bell's former police chief isn't facing corruption charges." *L.A. Times.* December 19, 2011, Retrieved from: http://articles.latimes.com/2011/dec/19/local/la-me-bell-adams-20111220 Steve Cooley said says his office could not build a case against Randy Adams, whose pay is an issue in the case against Rizzo and others.

30   MHM had worked as Bell's independent auditor since 2006 when it bought the city's previous audit firm, Conrad and Associates LLP. Conrad and Associates had performed audits for the city since 1994. "Controller's Review Finds Problems in Bell Audits." December 21, 2010. Press Release. State Controller's Office. Retrieved from: https://www.sco.ca.gov/eo_pressrel_controller_review_of_bell_audits.html

31   Jeff Gottlieb, "California seeks discipline for Bell's auditing firm," *L.A. Times,* May 25, 2012. Retrieved from http://articles.latimes.com/2012/may/25/local/la-me-bell-20120525.

32   Jeff Gottlieb, "Bell auditor fined, placed on two years' probation, L.A. Times blog. June 12, 2012. Retrieved from http://latimesblogs.latimes.com/lanow/2012/06/bell-auditors-fined-placed-on-two-years-of-probation.html.

33   Jeff Gottlieb, "Corruption-scarred Bell finds itself on better financial footing." *L.A. Times,* December 22, 2011. Retrieved from http://articles.latimes.com/2013/dec/22/local/la-me-bell-settlements-20131223.

34   Evan Halper and Marc Lifsher, "Bell Salaries Raise More Concerns about CalPERS." *L.A. Times,* August 6, 2010. Retrieved from http://articles.latimes.com/2010/aug/06/local/la-me-bell-pensions-20100806.

35   Evan Halper and Marc Lifsher, "Bell Salaries Raise More Concerns about CalPERS," *L.A. Times,* August 6, 2010. Retrieved from http://articles.latimes.com/2010/aug/06/local/la-me-bell-pensions-20100806. CalPERS said it would develop internal mechanisms and guidelines to spot excessive salaries. See, Cathy Bussewitz, "State lawmakers ponder bills prompted by Bell salaries," *The Associated Press,* August 17, 2010 .

Retrieved from http://www.whittierdailynews.com/general-news/20100817/ state-lawmakers-ponder-bills-prompted-by-bell-salaries.

36 Unfortunately, there have been numerous reports of cover ups of serious financial problems. See, Teri Sforza, "OC Watchdog: Weak audits endanger public purse," *Orange County Register*, May 3, 2016, and Jessica Garrison and Jeff Gottlieb, "Audits of city finances often cover up serious problems," *L.A. Times*, November 11, 2010. Retrieved from https://docs.google.com/ document/d/1m1nYtZhUkPAsZy9b6h8wIj187NIvFo4MaGs7eK1Gfoo/edit#.

37 Jessica Garrison and Jeff Gottlieb, "Audits of city finances often cover up serious problems," *L.A. Times*, November 11, 2010. Retrieved from https://docs.google.com/document/d/ 1m1nYtZhUkPAsZy9b6h8wIj187NIvFo4MaGs7eK1Gfoo/edit#.

38 Retrieved from https://en.wikipedia.org/wiki/Chart_of_accounts.

39 Unfortunately, since the legislators themselves are often the target of corruption probes, it is unlikely that they would approve such a proposal, Cooley said. Personal interview.

40 Former Los Angeles District Attorney, Steve Cooley, personal communication.

41 See, Office of Governor Edmund G. Brown, F.A.Q. Retrieved from: https://www. gov.ca.gov/s_faq.php.

42 Email from Jennifer Hanson in the State Controller's office.

43 The report is called a Comprehensive Annual Financial Report, or CAFR. As a former city manager who wishes to remain anonymous emailed me, "There are certain reporting requirements by the various municipalities, special district, counties, etc. where they send data to state offices such as the State Controller and Department of Finance etc. After they send these volumes of data, that doesn't mean the state offices that are receiving this data are actually looking at it in any close scrutiny. As an example the State Controller receives financial data, but they may only perform audits when something big hits the news and they are then forced to respond to the public outrage. Cities do issue an annual Comprehensive Annual Financial Report (CAFR). The report is filed with the state controller's office, but there is little concern of a state audit."

44 Personal interview with John Sibley, former city manager of the city of Orange, CA.

45 Attorney General Jerry Brown was running for governor, John Chiang was running for reelection as state controller, and Steve Cooley was running for attorney general.

46   States With Most Government Employees: Totals and Per Capita Rates http://www.governing.com/gov-data/public-workforce-salaries/states-most-government-workers-public-employees-by-job-type.html

47   Evan Halper and Marc Lifsher, "Bell Salaries raise more concerns about CalPERS." August 6, 2010. Retrieved from: http://articles.latimes.com/2010/aug/06/local/la-me-bell-pensions-20100806.

48   Michael J. Mishak, "California Gov. Jerry Brown defends cutting redevelopment agencies," *L.A. Times*, January 27, 2011. Retrieved from http://articles.latimes.com/2011/jan/27/local/la-me-jerry-brown-20110127.

49   An unfunded mandate occurs when one level of government requires an inferior level of government to do things (e.g., recycling) without funding.

50   See, State Controller's website. Retrieved from https://www.sco.ca.gov/eo_about_func.html.

51   Joe Mathews and Mark Paul, *California Crackup: How Reform Broke the Golden State and How we can fix it,* The University of California Press, 2010 , p. 44.

52   See, Robert McChesney, *Digital Disconnect: How Capitalism is Turning the Internet Against Democracy*, London: The New Press, 2013.

53   Ruben Vives, personal communication.

54   At the same time, it was an engaged public that swept Rizzo and the council from power and restored democracy (Chapter 6).

55   "A crisis in Civic Education" a report by the American Council of Trustees and Alumni, January 2016. Retrieved from https://www.goacta.org/images/download/A_Crisis_in_Civic_Education.pdf. See also, Richard D. Kahlenberg and Clifford Janey, "Putting Democracy Back into Public Education ," The New Century Foundation. Retrieved from : https://tcf.org/content/report/putting-democracy-back-public-education/. See also, Campaign for the Civic Mission of Schools and Alliance for Representative Democracy, From Classroom to Citizen: American Attitudes on Civic Education, Washington, DC: Campaign for the Civic Mission of School, 2004. Retrieved from http://www.ncsl.org/documents/public/trust/ClassroomToCitizen04.pdf. Supporting parties were the U.S. Department of Education, the Carnegie Corporation, and the Knight Foundation.

56   Eric Garcetti and William A. Covino, "Tackling a civic engagement crisis in Los Angeles," *Los Angeles Daily News*, May 12, 2014. Retrieved from http://www.dailynews.com/2014/05/12/tackling-a-civic-engagement-crisis-in-los-angeles-eric-garcetti-and-william-a-covino/.

57 "A Crisis in Civic Education." a report by the American Council of Trustees and Alumni, January 2016. Retrieved from https://www.goacta.org/images/download/A_Crisis_in_Civic_Education.pdf.

58 Richard D. Kahlenberg And Clifford Janey, "Is Trump's Victory The Jump-start Civics Education Needed?" *The Atlantic*, November 10, 2016. etrieved from https://www.theatlantic.com/education/archive/2016/11/is-trumps-victory-the-jump-start-civics-education-needed/507293/.

59 Mike Maciag, "Voter Turnout Plummeting in Local Elections," *Governing Magazine*, October, 2014. Retrieved from http://www.governing.com/topics/politics/gov-voter-turnout-municipal-elections.html#graph.

60 Alexis De Tocqueville, *Democracy in America*, Translated by George Lawrence and edited by J. P. Mayer, New York, Anchor Books, 1969, pp. 69–70. See also, Valerie Straus, "Many Americans know nothing about their government. Here's a bold way schools can fix that," *Washington Post* , September 27, 2016. Retrieved from https://www.washingtonpost.com/news/answer-sheet/wp/2016/09/27/many-americans-know-nothing-about-their-government-heres-a-bold-way-schools-can-fix-that/?utm_term=.2f1b1b-0de0ea. See also, Matthew Shaw, "Civic Illiteracy in America," *Harvard Political Review*. Retrieved from http://harvardpolitics.com/culture/civic-illiteracy-in-america/. And, Richard D. Kahlenberg and Clifford Janey," Is Trump's Victory The Jump-start Civics Education Needed? *The Atlantic*, November 10, 2016. Retrieved from https://www.theatlantic.com/education/archive/2016/11/is-trumps-victory-the-jump-start-civics-education-needed/507293/.

61 Richard D. Kahlenberg and Clifford Janey, Is Trump's Victory The Jump-start Civics Education Needed? *The Atlantic*, November 10, 2016. Retrieved from https://www.theatlantic.com/education/archive/2016/11/is-trumps-victory-the-jump-start-civics-education-needed/507293/.

62 Dahlia Lithwick, "They were trained for this moment, *Slate*, February 28, 2018. Retrieved from https://slate.com/news-and-politics/2018/02/the-student-activists-of-marjory-stoneman-douglas-high-demonstrate-the-power-of-a-full-education.html.

63 Maywood, population 27,000. Its city hall is .8 miles from Bell's city hall . The comparable figures for the other cities are: Commerce, 12,973, 3.4; Bell Gardens, 42,000, 3.2; Cudahy, 24,000, 2.2.

64 Adolfo Lores , "Agency takes a look at southeast cities' governance," *L.A. Times*, April 8, 2013. Retrieved from http://articles.latimes.com/2013/apr/08/local/

la-me-southeast-cities-20130408. Also see, Consolidated-City County. Retrieved from https://en.wikipedia.org/wiki/Consolidated_city-county.

65   "Bright Spots In Community Engagement," Case Studies of U.S. Communities Creating Greater Civic Participation from the Bottom Up. Retrieved from https://www.knightfoundation.org/media/uploads/publication_pdfs/BrightSpots-final.pdf.

66   San Antonio Area Foundation. "Engaging the Public at the Local Level to Strengthen Civic Engagement." Retrieved from: http://www.saafdn.org/Portals/0/Uploads/Documents/research/Engaging_the_Public_at_the_Local_Level_to_Strengthen_Civic_Engagement.pdf

67   Citizens' Rights, Participation and Transparency. Retrieved from http://ajuntament.barcelona.cat/ciutadania/en/, and Fernardo Pindado Sanchez "By Engaging our Emotions." Retrieved from http://www.zocalopublicsquare.org/2017/06/22/engaging-emotions-art-can-strengthen-democracies/ideas/nexus/.

68   Awards to innovative projects for the quality of democracy given out by the city council of Barcelona. Retrieved from: http://punttic.gencat.cat/en/article/awards-innovative-projects-quality-democracy-2017

69   International Observatory on Participatory Democracy. Retrieved from: https://oidp.net/distinction/en.

70   See, Tony Anderson, "The Path to Improving Civic Engagement," *Governing Magazine*, February 27, 2015 . Retrieved from http://www.governing.com/gov-institute/voices/col-path-improving-civic-engagement.html.

71   See the Participatory Governance Initiative at the University of Arizona. https://spa.asu.edu/content/about-pgi.

72   Ken Adelman, "It's Not a Big Deal if You Elect Not to Vote," *Orange County Register*, November 2, 1992.

73   "The lesson of Bell: A watchful citizenry is still crucial." Editorial. *L.A. Times.* December 11, 2013. Retrieved from: http://www.latimes.com/opinion/editorials/la-ed-bell-trial-20131211-story.html

74   Judge Kennedy's remarks at Oscar Hernandez's sentencing hearing.

75   Hildy Gottlieb, "Consumer or Citizen?" posted on May 20, 2012. Retrieved from http://hildygottlieb.com/2012/05/20/consumer-or-citizen/.

76   Jill Blair and Malka Kopell." 21st Century Civic Infrastructure: Under Construction." Prepared for the Forum for Community Solutions, The Aspen Institute Spring 2015. Retrieved from: http://informingchange.com/blog/21st-century-civic-infrastructure-2

77 Matthew D. Moore and Nicholas L. Recker, "Social Capital, Type of Crime, and Social Control," *Crime & Delinquency*, 2016, Vol. 62(6), pp. 728-747. Retrieved from http://journals.sagepub.com/doi/pdf/10.1177/0011128713510082; Justin David Barker, (2012), "Social capital, homeless young people and the family," *Journal of Youth Studies*, 2012, 15:6, pp. 730-743, DOI: 10.1080/13676261.2012.677812. Martin K.S., Rogers B.L., Cook J.T., Joseph H. M., "Social capital is associated with decreased risk of hunger," Soc Sci Med, 2004 Jun, 58(12):2645-54; Glenn D. Israel, Lionel J. Beaulieu, Glen Hartless, "The Influence of Social Capital on Test Scores: How Much Do Families, Schools & Communities Matter?" *Rural Sociology*, 66(1), 2001, pp. 43-68. Retrieved from https://pdfs. semanticscholar.org/3577/20514273d5187ae9dfea74233f9226ac7ff6.pdf. And, Milner H. (2001) "Social Capital, Civic Literacy and Political Participation: Explaining Differences in Voter Turnout" In, Dowding K., Hughes J., Margetts H. (eds), *Challenges to Democracy. Political Studies Association Yearbook*, (Palgrave Macmillan, London, 2001). Retrieved from https://link.springer.com/ chapter/10.1057/9780230502185_6.

78 "Community Heart and South," Blog. Retrieved January 1, 2018, from http:// www.communitymatters.org/about-civic-infrastructure.

79 Mathew Desmond, Evicted. (Crown Publishers), 2016, p. 70.

80 Sociologist Robert Putnam defines social capital as the "connections among individuals—social networks and the norms of reciprocity and trustworthiness that arise from them ." Similarly, in her classic, *The Death and Life of Great American Cities*, Jane Jacobs explains how civic infrastructure functions: "The first thing to understand is that the public peace—the sidewalk and street peace—of cities is not kept primarily by the police, necessary as the police are. It is kept primarily by an intricate, almost unconscious, network of voluntary controls and standards among the people themselves, and enforced by the people themselves." See, *The Death and Life of Great American Cities*, (Random House, 1961), p.

81 Tom Hogen-Esch "Failed State: Political Corruption and the Collapse of Democracy in Bell, California." California Journal of Politics and Policy, 3 (1), pp. 1-28. 2011.

82 Tom Hogen-Esch, personal communications.

83 The United States Election Project. Retrieved from: http://www.electproject. org/2016g.

84 This section enumerating disengagement by young people first appeared a paper I authored: Promoting Civic Engagement With a Course on Local Politics. Paper presented on the panel on Local Politics and Civic Engagement;

Conference within a Conference: Teaching and Learning Political Science; Western Political Science Association, Las Vegas, Nevada April 4, 2015 Retrieved from: https://wpsa.research.pdx.edu/papers/docs/Promoting%20 Civic%20Engagement%20with%20a%20Course%20on%20Local%20Politics.pdf. This paper relied on data first reported in Young People and the News: A Report from the Joan Shorenstein Center on the Press, Politics, and Public Policy," JFK School of Government, Harvard University, July 2007. p. 3. Retrieved from http://shorensteincenter.org/wp-content/uploads/2012/03/ young_people_and_news_2007.pdf. "Millennials in Adulthood: Detached from Institutions, Networked with Friends," March 7, 2014. See, http://www. pewsocialtrends.org/2014/03/07/millennials-in-adulthood/. And "Low voter turnout likely, conservatives more enthusiastic, Harvard youth poll finds." Retrieved from http://www.iop.harvard.edu/sites/default/files_new/Harvard_PressReleaseSpring2014.pdf. And, The California Civic Engagement Project Policy Brief Issue 9, January 2015. Retrieved from http://explore. regionalchange.ucdavis.edu/ourwork/projects/copy2_of_UCDavisCCEPPolicyBrief92014YouthVote.pdf

85 Institute of Politics, *Harvard University: Survey of Young Americans' Attitudes toward Politics and Public Service: 25th Edition*, 2014. See, http://www.iop.harvard. edu/sites/default/files_new/Harvard_ExecSummarySpring2014.pdf.

86 Katie Reilly, "A generational gap in American patriotism," Pew Research Center, July 3, 2013. Retrieved from http://www.pewresearch.org/ fact-tank/2013/07/03/a-generational-gap-in-american-patriotism.

87 University of California at Davis Center for Regional Change. Retrieved from: http://169.237.124.55:8080/CRC/ourwork/projects/copy_of_UCDavisCCEPPolicyBrief92014YouthVote.pdf/view

88 Webinar March 24, 2015. Civic Engagement Project. University of California, Davis. Retrieved from: http://ccep.ucdavis.edu/

Appendix 1:
List of Names

LAST	FIRST	TITLE
Adams	Randy	Bell Police Chief
Aleshire	David	Attorney, City of Bell
Alvarez	Violeta	BASTA, councilmember
Artiga	Luis	Defendant, Councilmember
Aryan	Alfred	Bell resident
Bass	George	Bell council that hired Rizzo
Bass	Janice	George Bass' widow.
Belcher	Steve	Bell staff
Bello	Victor	Defendant, Councilmember
	Best, Best, and Krieger	Law firm for city under Rizzo
Bramble	John	Rizzo's predecessor
Braun	Harland	Attorney for Spaccia
Briones	Leo	BASTA consultant
Brown	Jerry	Attorney General, Governor, signed Bell legislation
Brown	Howard	City Manager, current
Brown	Tom	Attorney and Rizzo consultant
Burnside	Susan	BASTA, ran recall
Bustamante	Angela	Clerk
Carrillo	Pedro	Rizzo friend and interim city manager

Gutglueck	Mark	*San Bernardino Sentinel*, reporter and editor
Hall	Henry	Judge, Preliminary Hearing
Hampian	Ken	City Manager, interim (one-month)
Harber	Danny	City Councilmember elected in recall
Harris	Kamala	Attorney General, follows Jerry Brown. U.S. Senator
Hassett	Sean	Deputy District Attorney, Spaccia trial
Henson	Tye	Bell Staff
Hernandez	Oscar	Defendant, Mayor
Holguin	Mike	PID Investigator
Hubler	Shawn	*L.A. Times* columnist and reporter who helped Vives
Hudson	Jeff	Public Integrity Division
Huntsman	Max	Deputy District Attorney, Spaccia trial
Jacobo	Teresa	Defendant, Councilmember
Jensen	Rolf	City Council that hired Rizzo
Johnson	Ray	City Council that hired Rizzo
Kaye	Ron	Attorney, George Cole
Kennedy	Kathleen	Judge, all Bell trials
Kessel	Alex	Attorney, George Mirabal
Knoll	Corina	Reporter, *L.A. Times*
Kopp	Shepard	Attorney, Teresa Jacobo
Lam	Jack	City Manager, Rancho Cucamonga
Purmalis	Pete	Public Integrity Division
Quiroz	Gerardo	Car wash owner shaken down by Rizzo
Quintana	Anna Maria	Councilmember
Quintana	Maximino	Anna Maria Quintana's father

Vives	Ruben	Reporter, *L.A. Times*, who broke Bell story with Jeff Gottlieb
Walker	Dale	BASTA leader
Wasserman	Lauren	Worked with Rizzo in Rancho Cucamonga
Werrlein	Pete	Councilmember and political wheeler dealer who owned Western Auto and was friends with Mickey Cohen; card club scandal
Wilmore	Doug	Bell's first permanent city manager following Rizzo
Woosley	Bryon	City Manager following Pitts
Yoshimo	Kimi	Editor, *L.A. Times*
Zuel	Bob	Worked under Rizzo in Hesperia

Index

CPSIA information can be obtained
at www.ICGtesting.com
Printed in the USA
LVHW080447191220
674548LV00004B/23